SEAGULL ESSAYS

Series Editor: ALBERTO TOSCANO

A trial, an attempt, a test. But also a weighing up, an assaying of unknown quantities and imponderable qualities. The essay has been called 'the strictest form attainable in an area where one cannot work precisely' (Robert Musil) and the essayist depicted as one who composes in the very act of experimenting, who attacks their object from multiple angles and 'puts into words what the object allows one to see under the conditions created in the course of writing' (György Lukács).

An art of transitions, thresholds, mediation and impurity, the essay evades the posture of the objective expert just as it refrains from the subjective cult of creativity. Exacting without a pretence to exactness, its subject matter, Adorno once suggested, 'is always conflict brought to a standstill'.

Seagull Essays is a wager that, in times pervaded by formulaic writing and automated script, the essay is a living form, open to further trials and tests, insubordinate to rigid demarcations between the arts, the sciences and the humanities.

SEAGULL
BOOKS
•
CELEBRATING
40 YEARS

Praise for *Terms of Disorder*

'Toscano casts a discerning eye over selected key concepts—terms of disorder—that have, in their dynamic development, lent shape to the troubled present of western marxism. Homage to both Raymond Williams and Cedric Robinson, the book toggles between historical analysis and profound polemic. Toscano's wise and lucid prose clears ground to re-articulate this corner of marxism with an internationally urgent whole.'
—Ruth Wilson Gilmore, author of *Abolition Geography*.

'*Terms of Disorder* is a welcome guide to finding a political vocabulary for a global order in dissolution and mutation, full of profound insights and unexpected connections. Toscano's erudition and encyclopedic knowledge are dazzling. A book to study carefully from one of the most important and agile Marxist voices writing today.'
—Avery F. Gordon, author of *The Hawthorn Archive: Letters from the Utopian Margins*.

'Testing the meaning of familiar words, unmooring the names of politics to open up new continents and possibilities for theory and practice: this is the wager of Alberto Toscano's *Terms of Disorder*. At stake here is the invention of a communist politics up to the challenges of our time of turbulence and transition. Playing with the calendar of the 1917 Russian revolution, Toscano writes that we are after October but before February, which means that the Bolshevik explosion remains with us for better or worse, but we lack the experience of a rupture in state domination that compels and enables thinking anew the riddle of liberation. The keywords in this book provide readers with an excellent compass to navigate this uncertain time.'
—Sandro Mezzadra, professor at the Department of the Arts, University of Bologna.

'Astonishing erudition graces a fair number of books. Far fewer combine that with bold generation of new ideas and connections. Still less often do both of those qualities coexist with fierce attention to grounding big, transformative ideas to make them broadly understandable. Toscano here hits the trifecta of those virtues in a worthy extension of the tradition of popular education through the study of keywords.'
—David Roediger, Foundation Professor of American Studies at University of Kansas and author of *Class, Race, and Marxism*.

TERMS OF DISORDER

Keywords for an Interregnum

ALBERTO TOSCANO

LONDON NEW YORK CALCUTTA

Seagull Books, 2023

© Alberto Toscano, 2023

First published in volume form by Seagull Books, 2023

ISBN 978 1 80309 177 8

British Library Cataloguing-in-Publication Data

A catalogue record for this book is available from the British Library

Typeset by Seagull Books, Calcutta, India

Printed and bound in the USA by Integrated Books International

CONTENTS

In memory of Mike Davis (1946–2022).

Las luchas continúan.

Prologue

> The cities therefore being now in sedition and those that
> fell into it later having heard what had been done in the
> former, they far exceeded the same in newness of conceit,
> both for the art of assailing and for the strangeness of their
> revenges. The received value of names imposed for sig-
> nification of things was changed into arbitrary.

So wrote the Ancient Greek historian Thucydides in his account of
the civil war or *stásis* that plagued the city of Corcyra in 427 BCE—
as rendered by Thomas Hobbes in his 1628 translation of *The
History of the Peloponnesian War* (3.82). Whether a crisis be
punctual or protracted, the unsettling of a civic order is reliably
accompanied by an unmooring of the names of politics, by their
slackening, voiding, reversal or corruption.

The entries gathered in this book were composed in the last
decade and a half, a period in which multiple large-scale crises and
incomplete transitions—from the long downturn of the global
economy to the decline of US hegemony, from the prolonged
implosion of the socialist bloc to the aftermaths of decolonization,
now encompassed and exceeded by the unfathomed prospects of
planetary environmental collapse—intermingled in all kinds of
weird and frightening formations, though never fusing into that
'ruptural unity' longed for by revolutionary spirits. In the register
of praxis, the 'age of riots' has not spawned an epic 'rebirth of
history', though it has certainly proliferated no shortage of revenants
and returns, as well as some rehearsals for living otherwise.

As I have chosen to do in my subtitle, many have recently turned to Antonio Gramsci's naming of his moment, almost a century ago, as an *interregnum*, a time crowded with *morbid symptoms* and defined by the fact, and the feeling, that *the old is dying and the new cannot be born.* The ingredients of this pathological and often paralyzing betweenness are legion—economic, ecological, cultural, psychological—but my concern in the pages that follow is with the signification and charge of political names and concepts, and especially with those terms that radical and revolutionary traditions have forged, repaired or reinvented to guide their efforts to make the world anew.[1] A test of the powers lost or retained by such keywords seems germane now that we have

---

1 Though I've gathered my own thoughts about today's recombinant Right in a companion volume of sorts (*Late Fascism: Race, Capitalism and the Politics of Crisis* [London: Verso, 2023]), it is worth noting the hold that the idea of an interregnum holds for the traditions of twentieth-century reaction and their epigoni. For an instructive survey, see Roger Griffin, 'Between metapolitics and *apoliteia*: The Nouvelle Droite's strategy for conserving the fascist vision in the "interregnum"', *Modern & Contemporary France* 8(1) (2000): 35–53. On the eve of the Nazi *Machtergreifung*, Oswald Spengler had evocatively encapsulated the conservative-revolutionary worldview, writing of the 'anarchic intermezzo known today as democracy, which leads from the destruction of monarchical State supremacy by way of political, plebeian Rationalism to the Caesarism of the future. There are already signs, in the dictatorial tendencies of our time, of this Caesarism, which is destined to assume the unlimited mastery over the ruins of historical tradition.' See *The Hour of Decision, Part One: Germany and World-Historical Revolution* (Charles Francis Atkinson trans.) (London: George Allen and Unwin Ltd, 1934), p. 40. Spengler exemplifies two interlinked features of the right-wing vision of the interregnum: on the one hand, a penchant for cyclical or epochal conceptions of historical time (ages, rebirths, turnings, declines), on the other, a centring of the *rex* (sovereign, leader, Caesar) in the *interregnum* to the detriment of any socio-economic understanding of transition. See also Zygmunt Bauman, 'Times of Interregnum', *Ethics & Global Politics* 5(1) (2012): 49–56; and, for a survey of recent uses, Philippe Theophanidis, 'Interregnum as a Legal and Political Concept: A Brief Contextual Survey', *Synthesis: An Anglophone Journal of Comparative Literary Studies* 9 (2016): 109–24.

firmly entered that 'age of transition', that 'period of bifurcation and chaos', whose acknowledgment—as the late Immanuel Wallerstein suggested at the start of our century—is a precondition for any lucid strategic and discursive struggle.[2] As Wallerstein further observed in the wake of the Global Financial Crisis of 2007–2008, the 'question is no longer "how will the capitalist system mend itself, and renew its forward thrust?," but rather, "what will replace this system? What order will emerge from this chaos?" ' Whether we wish to or not, we have entered 'an arena of struggle for the successor system', and this struggle, whose complex inception can be dated to the world revolutions of 1968 and the economic crises of the 1970s 'may not be resolved before circa 2050'.[3] That struggle, and its temporalities, are being profoundly, irrevocably transformed by our warming condition, in which '[h]istory has sprung alive, through a nature that has done likewise'.[4] Ours is accordingly 'a world in the long interregnum between the accumulating certainty of the devastated and the uncertainty of the new',[5] meaning that 'the transformation of our political ideas must be of a magnitude at least equal to that of the geo-ecological transformation that climate change constitutes.'[6]

---

2 Immanuel Wallerstein, 'New Revolts Against the System', *New Left Review* 18 (2002): 37. For a compelling counter to this image of transition, which she takes to task as a fetter on our thinking and practice of freedom, see Avery F. Gordon, *The Hawthorn Archive: Letters from the Utopian Margins* (New York: Fordham University Press, 2018), pp. 54–65.

3 Immanuel Wallerstein, 'Structural Crisis', *New Left Review* 62 (2010): 140–41.

4 Andreas Malm, *The Progress of This Storm: Nature and Society in a Warming World* (London: Verso, 2017), p. 11.

5 Ian Baucom, *History 4° Celsius: Search for a Method in the Age of the Anthropocene* (Durham, NC: Duke University Press, 2020), p. 21.

6 Pierre Charbonnier, *Affluence and Freedom: An Environmental History of Political Ideas* (Andrew Brown trans.) (Cambridge: Polity, 2021), p. 246. See also Olúfẹ́mi O. Táíwò's discussion of the Afro-Guyanese scholar-activist Andaiye's thoughts on climate and the interregnum: 'The Point Is to Change It' in *Elite Capture: How the Powerful Took Over Identity Politics (And Everything Else)* (Chicago: Haymarket Books, 2022).

This book intends to make a modest contribution to a collective and conflicted endeavour to put to the test some of those political names whose value has become profoundly uncertain, if not necessarily arbitrary. As the bulk of its first entry[7] intimates, the inheritance, afterlives and prospects of communism loom large in this reckoning, and partly condition the constellation of entries I've assembled—whether in terms of strategic perspectives (dual power, transition) or in the pondering of those political names which throughout the nineteenth and twentieth centuries encompassed, qualified or rivalled the communist hypothesis (resistance, reform, Prometheanism, the people, radicalism, the left). That the penultimate entry concerns leadership, from the vantage of Black radical and revolutionary traditions, is intended to question and depose the *regnum* and the *rex* in that *interregnum*.

As Mike Davis acidly observed in response to the Russian invasion of Ukraine and 'Western' reactions thereto: 'We are living through the nightmare edition of "Great Men Make History". Unlike the high Cold War when politburos, parliaments, presidential cabinets and general staffs to some extent countervailed megalomania at the top, there are few safety switches between today's maximum leaders and Armageddon.'[8] It was in his

---

7 That entry was my own contribution to *The SAGE Handbook of Marxism* (2022), co-edited with my friends and comrades Beverley Skeggs, Sara Farris and Svenja Bromberg. For readers desiring more keywords for our interregnum, the *Handbook*'s three volumes should provide ample nourishment.

8 Mike Davis, 'Thanatos Triumphant', *Sidecar*, 7 March 2022 (available online: https://bit.ly/3QARzde; last accessed: 12 January 2023). I can't resist reproducing Davis' own grimly insightful reflection on the Gramscian legacy for our present:

Everyone is quoting Gramsci on the interregnum, but that assumes that something new will be or could be born. I doubt it. I think what we must diagnose instead is a ruling class brain tumour: a growing inability to achieve any coherent understanding of global change as a basis for defining common interests and formulating large-scale strategies . . . It also may be the case that our rulers are blind because

first book, *The Terms of Order*, that Cedric J. Robinson sought 'to abuse the political consciousness' structured by the myth of leadership.[9] While my own orientation has more affinities to that 'reconciliation of the political and the antipolitical' that Robinson ascribes to Marx than to his own project 'to subvert [the political] as a way or realizing ourselves', I am in no doubt that a pitiless critique of leadership as the fatal synthesis of authority and order is among the first items on our critical agenda—one intimately bound to the rediscovery and redefinition of the meaning of liberation, with which this collection ends.[10]

At a time when military brutality masquerades as denazification, when freedom is a corpse in the mouth of myriad reactionaries, when capitalist futures hang on the designs of a Communist party, and when the tattered spectre of 'the West' continues to haunt the world, assaying the sedimented contents and latent charge of some salient entries in the political lexicon of anti-systemic thought may not be the most futile employ for the time of the mind.

Vancouver
November 2022

---

they lack the penetrating eyesight of revolution, bourgeois or proletarian. A revolutionary era may dress itself in costumes of the past (as Marx articulates in *The Eighteenth Brumaire*), but it defines itself by recognizing the possibilities for societal reorganization arising from new forces of technology and economics. In the absence of external revolutionary consciousness and the threat of insurrection, old orders do not produce their own (counter-)visionaries.

9 Cedric J. Robinson, *The Terms of Order: Political Science and the Myth of Leadership* (Erica R. Edwards fore.) (Chapel Hill: University of North Carolina Press, 2016[1980]), p. 6.

10 Robinson, *Terms of Order*, pp. 3, 215.

ONE
Communism

I was a communist throughout.
Despite their certainties, despite my doubts
I always wanted this world ended.

—Franco Fortini, 'Communism' (1958)

The Many Voices of Communism

Stripped of a reference to communism, of a communist standpoint or perspective, Marxism loses its singular (and for many chimerical) status as a revolutionary science, to take its disciplinary place as another sociology, political economy or methodology. This subtraction of communism from Marxism is the chief premise for the periodic mainstream plaudits to Marx as an analyst of capitalism and crisis, now finally freed of the burdensome legacy of 'historical communism'. Contrariwise, the first two decades of the twenty-first century have also witnessed a wide-ranging theoretical effort to reassert the vitality of communism as the idea of a thoroughgoing alternative to capitalism, to what Marx once called our 'religion of everyday life'.

In what may appear a curious inversion of the 11th thesis on Feuerbach—'Philosophers have hitherto only interpreted the world in various ways; the point is to change it'—this assertion of the necessity of a communist perspective in the wake of the collapse, defeat, suicide or capitalist transfiguration of historical communisms, has often been accompanied by an emphasis on the need for a *philosophical* affirmation of communism as a prelude to a recovery or reinvention of a communist *politics*. Among its most prominent advocates, the return of communism as an idea or 'hypothesis' has been justified in terms of a historical context that bears far more analogies to the 1840s (as a time of revolutionary setbacks and unbridled capitalism) than it does to the titanic struggles against capitalism and imperialism that marked the 'short twentieth century'.[1] Sympathetic critics of this philosophical return of communism have stressed the strategic deficit that marks this debate, the loss of the perspective of *transition*, of the determinate and politically-oriented negation of the capitalist social order that distinguished Marx's proposal from the other communisms of his age.[2] Others have underscored the need to supplement and displace Marxian and philosophical conceptions of communism by fore-grounding the *common*, understood not as an objective product of capital, to be expropriated and appropriated by the proletariat, but as the substance and outcome of anti-capitalist practices of associationism—in a qualified return to Proudhon, as well as to a whole history of workers' self-management and self-organization.[3] From this latter standpoint, it is the common understood as materially embedded relationality and collective praxis, and not the common merely as a shared set of resources, which looms large.

These efforts partially overlap with an attention to practices and discourses of the *commons* that glimpse a living post-capitalist potential across a wide variety of collective practices that oppose the frameworks of possessive individualism and private property—whether in terms of the continued vitality of indigenous and sub-altern lifeways or in view of the production of the commons at the

---

1 Alain Badiou, *The Communist Hypothesis* (David Macey and Steve Corcoran trans) (London: Verso, 2010), pp. 66–67.
2 See Isabelle Garo, *Communisme et stratégie* (Paris: Éditions Amsterdam, 2019). Unless otherwise noted, all translations are my own.
3 Pierre Dardot and Christian Laval, *Common: On Revolution in the 21st Century* (London: Bloomsbury Academic, 2019).

cooperative cutting-edge of 'cognitive capitalism'.[4] Some of this literature has found succour in the increasing recognition of the late Marx's concern with communal forms, namely the Russian peasant community, or *obshchina*, but also the political institutions of the Haudenosaunee (Iroquois Confederacy), viewed as potential vehicles for an abolition of capitalist relations that could circumvent the need to replicate the ideal-typical stages of Western bourgeois development.[5]

The more classically political counterpart to this emphasis on practices of *commoning*, understood as instances of a communist praxis alternative to the historical horizon of state communism, has been a renewed interest in the *commune* as a political form, as well as in the possibility of experiences of dual power,[6] which would see islands of communism coexist, temporarily, with capitalist social and political relations. Efforts to draw on practices and ideas of the *common(s)* and the *commune*—with their attendant need to confront Marx and Marxism's complex relations to the very idea of *community* as both a brake upon and a horizon of revolution—aim, among other things, at shaking off the fetters on political praxis and

---

4 According to Vercellone, cognitive capitalism 'begins with the social crisis of Fordism and of the Smithian division of labour. The relation of capital to labour is marked by the hegemony of knowledges, by a diffuse intellectuality, and by the driving role of the production of knowledges by means of knowledges connected to the increasingly immaterial and cognitive character of labour. This new phase of the division of labour is accompanied by the crisis of the law of value-labour and by the strong return of mercantile and financial mechanisms of accumulation. The principal elements of this new configuration of capitalism and of the conflicts that derive from it are, in large measure, anticipated by Marx's notion of the general intellect.' See Carlo Vercellone, 'From Formal Subsumption to General Intellect: Elements for a Marxist Reading of the Thesis of Cognitive Capitalism', *Historical Materialism* 15(1) (2007): 16.

5 See Franklin Rosemont, 'Karl Marx and the Iroquois', *Arsenal/Surrealist Subversion* 4 (1989): 201–13; Teodor Shanin (ed.), *Late Marx and the Russian Road* (New York: Monthly Review Press, 1983).

6 See 'Dual Power' in this volume, pp, 170–95.

imagination imposed by the historical record of state (and party) communisms. They also endeavour to draw precious sustenance for contemporary communisms from subterranean or heretical traditions.

An analogous remark can be made regarding the contemporary prominence of the notion of *communization*. Updating a whole arsenal of insurrectionary Marxisms and ultra-left theories historically marginalized by Stalinist and Eurocommunist perspectives (from Amadeo Bordiga to strands of 1970s autonomism, passing through groups like Socialisme ou Barbarie or the Situationist International), theorists of communization generally display a steadfast fidelity to Marxian value theory in their drive to jettison the very notion of *transition* as defining the strategic horizon of communism.[7] This repudiation of transition, and especially of any notion of a transitional *programme* (and of programmes *tout court*), is often grounded in the passage from an antagonism to capital based on the collective identification of (industrial) workers waging *strikes* to contemporary struggles of increasingly wageless populations in the realm of circulation that coalesce in *riots*, as explored in the work of Joshua Clover.[8] As outlined by the group most responsible for honing the notion of communization:

> In the course of revolutionary struggle, the abolition of the state, of exchange, of the division of labour, of all forms of property, the extension of the situation where everything is freely available as the unification of human activity—in a word, the abolition of classes—are 'measures' that abolish capital, imposed by the very necessities of struggle against the capitalist class. The revolution is communization; it

---

7 See 'Transition' in this volume, pp. 143–69.
8 For further reflections on Clover's *Riot. Strike. Riot*, see Alberto Toscano, 'Limits to Periodization', *Viewpoint*, 6 September 2016 (available online: https://bit.ly/3X6V3Ha; last accessed: 13 January 2023).

does not have communism as a project and result, but as its very content.[9]

This chapter seeks to articulate an understanding of communism that maintains an emphasis on the strategic and political problem of transition, which—as my concluding section proposes—requires reflection on the very meaning of *abolition* in Marx and Marxism, as well as on the latter's relation to broader traditions of abolition*ism* (including but not exhausted by the abolition of feudal and patriarchal privileges, of racial slavery, of the death penalty, of police and prisons). To delineate communism in terms of the contemporary question of the transition from and abolition of capitalism, I will begin by providing a brief sketch of communism's pre-Marxian history. I will then explore some of the different articulations of communism in Marx's own work, reflect on the transvaluation of transition that took place in the 'long '68', and finally address the thorny issue of abolition itself.

Before undertaking this investigation, however, it might be both pertinent and useful to acknowledge the polyvalence and equivocity of communism, the fact that it is rarely if ever spoken of with 'one voice'.[10] It is not simply a matter of differences in political practice or orientation; what is at stake is the very location of communism in the conceptual networks of Marxism and affine discourses. Communism may define a *form of government* (the Commune, the dictatorship of the proletariat, the post-revolutionary state); a *mode of production* (in the divergent senses of primitive communism and post-capitalist communism); a *social formation*; a distinct type of *social relation*; 'the end of the *economy* as a separate and privileged domain on which everything else depends';[11] or even 'a life plan for

---

9 Théorie Communiste, 'Communization in the Present Tense' in Benjamin Noys (ed.), *Communization and Its Discontents: Contestation, Critique, and Contemporary Struggles* (Wivenhoe: Minor Compositions, 2012), p. 41.
10 Étienne Balibar, 'Althusser et "le communisme"', *La Pensée* 382 (2015): 9–20; here, p. 12.

the species'[12]—as well as the *party* or *movement* oriented towards the achievement of the aforementioned objectives.

Movement can in turn take the more restricted, if potentially global, characteristics of the *workers' movement* or, in a more abstract dialectical vein, as in Marx's arguably most celebrated (but also profoundly under-determined) definition of communism, 'the real movement which abolishes the present state of things'. The scope of communism has also been considerably extended beyond the various levels at which Marx (and Marxists) outlined the abolition of capitalism. Communism has been defined from a radical anthropological standpoint as a 'principle immanent in everyday life'[13]; it has been delineated as an ontological and 'technical' condition in excess of politics, 'the imbrication of everything and everyone'[14]; it has been articulated as a 'communism of thought', a movement intrinsic to thinking and human needs over and above any determinate social or political formation[15]; it has even been captured as a 'community of the possible' in which human individuals can fully actualize an opening to sociality and collectivity grounded in their biological makeup, and especially their linguistic capacities.[16]

---

11 Gilles Dauvé and François Martin, *Eclipse and Re-Emergence of the Communist Movement* (Oakland, CA: PM Press, 2015), p. 52.

12 Pietro Basso, 'Introduction: Yesterday's Battles and Today's World' in Amadeo Bordiga, *The Science and Passion of Communism* (Giacomo Donis and Patrick Camiller trans, Pietro Basso ed.) (Leiden and Boston: Brill, 2020), p. 88.

13 David Graeber, 'On the moral grounds of economic relations: A Maussian approach', *Journal of Classical Sociology* 14(1) (2014): 65–77; here, p. 68.

14 Jean-Luc Nancy, *Politique et au-delà: Entretien avec Philip Armstrong et Jason E. Smith* (Paris: Galilée, 2011), pp. 44–45.

15 Dionys Mascolo, *Le Communisme: Révolution et communication ou la dialectique des valeurs et des besoins* (Paris: Lignes, 2018[1953]).

16 Felice Cimatti, *Naturalmente comunisti: Politica, linguaggio ed economia* (Milan: Bruno Mondadori, 2011), pp. 139–69.

Moreover, there are a welter of communisms whose relation to the Marxian variant is historically, geographically or conceptually remote, from the aristocratic anti-property utopia of 'Platonic communism'[17]—itself an echo of 'Spartan communism'[18]—to the recovery of 'Incan communism' as an indigenous resource for revolutionary politics by the Peruvian thinker José Carlos Mariátegui; from the adoption by insurgent medieval peasants of the biblical dictum *omnia sunt communia* (everything in common) to the 1970s slogan of uprisings in the Italian 'social factory', *vogliamo tutto* (we want everything). The language of communism has also consistently posed a scandal in the face of the supposed sophistications of elite political discourse. As the Guyanese Marxist historian and revolutionary Walter Rodney observed in his lectures on the Russian Revolution in Dar es Salaam: 'Marxist writers have inevitably had to find new terms to describe society in the way it is seen by the members of oppressed classes. The language lacks the urbanity and refinement that the bourgeoisie developed as an expression of its own disassociation from sweat and cow dung.'[19]

Communism before Marx

Though a powerful claim can be advanced for the existence of 'communist invariants'[20] that long predated the consolidation of a world market, the modern acceptation of communism emerged around the time of the French Revolution. Jacques Grandjonc's lexicographic inquiries attest to an extended if lacunary history in Europe, beginning around the twelfth century, for several terms contiguous with communism, rooted in the realities of medieval communal life and punctuating the written record in the wake of the revolts of peasants and commoners. In the history of French usage, as detailed by eighteenth-century dictionaries, *communiste* would appear to emerge in the Middle Ages as an equivalent for *communalis* or *comunarius*—an officer of the *commune*. Alternatively, it could designate the members of a community of goods, more specifically a *communauté de main morte*—the kind of tacit community (*communauté taisible*) that villagers subjected to the rights of feudal lords over their property would establish to maintain possession of their lands and goods across generations.[21]

This understanding of 'communists' as members or partisans of a community of goods is also registered in Latin, Polish and Dutch in the sixteenth and seventeenth centuries, in terms like *communelli* and *communicantes* and with reference to the communal doctrines of radical Protestant sects like the Anabaptists, Hutterites and Waldensians, as well as to the peasant and communal insurgencies against feudal mastery that punctuate this phase of European history. It is in this context that the term *communista* appears in a Polish manuscript from 1569, alongside the neologism *oeconomista*.[22] In the eighteenth century, the term is used to refer to the inhabitants of rural communes or those with rights of communal usufruct over shared goods—a testament to the affinity between the *commons*, *community*, and *communism* that many contemporary authors continue to mine.

It is to the end of the eighteenth century that we must turn to see the tentative emergence of *communism* and *communist* as terms referring to political movements or ideologies oriented towards communal ownership and the abolition of private property. The libertine novelist, thinker and pornographer Restif de la Bretonne

---

21 Jacques Grandjonc, 'Quelques dates à propos des termes *communiste* et *communisme*', *Mots* 7 (1983): 143–48; here, p. 144.

22 Grandjonc, 'Quelques dates': 145.

(1734–1806) first uses the French term *communiste* in 1785, and in his book *Monsieur Nicolas* (1797) coins the modern term *communisme*, under the influence of Gracchus Babeuf's Conspiracy of Equals (Conjuration des Égaux) of 1796 against the Thermidorian Directory. Especially after Philippe Buonarroti's 1828 retelling of its defeated efforts to uphold the radical promise of the French Revolution against the Thermidorian revenge of the propertied classes, Babeuf's 'conspiracy' became a touchstone for the mid-nineteenth century crystallization of a communist workers' movement. The political and intellectual revolutions of the late eighteenth century appropriated the deep-seated languages of the *common*, the *commune* and the *community* and refunctioned them into wholesale challenges to class rule, state power, clerical authority and multiple forms of domination. A (disputed) fragment from the German poet Friedrich Hölderlin, penned in 1790, at the time of his close friendship with Hegel, is entitled 'the communism of spirits' (*Communismus der Geister*).[23] In 1794, the first attested use in German of *Kommunismus* is inscribed in the interrogation transcripts of an Austrian Jacobin.[24]

The repression of the radical, egalitarian wings of the French Revolution and its European avatars meant that the ruptural meaning of communism (as well as of some of its less successful French cognates: *communautiste, communismal, communionisme, communaliste*[25]), inaugurated in the 1780s and 1790s, was forced

---

23 Philippe Lacoue-Labarthe, introduction to Martin Heidegger, *La pauvreté* (*Die Armut*) (Philippe Lacoue-Labarthe and Ana Samardzija trans) (Strasbourg: Presses Universitaires de Strasbourg, 2004), p. 15; Jacques d'Hondt, 'Le meurtre de l'histoire' in *Hölderlin* (Jean-François Courtine ed.) (Paris: L'Herne, 1989), pp. 219–38.

24 Jacques Grandjonc, *Communisme/Kommunismus/Communism: Origine et développement international de la terminologie communautaire pré-marxiste des utopistes aux néo-babouvistes 1785–1842, Volume 1: Historique; Volume 2: Pièces justificatives* (Trier: Karl-Marx-Haus, 1989), p. 19.

25 Grandjonc, *Communisme/Kommunismus/Communism*, p. 21.

underground, only to re-emerge decades later as neo-Babouvist activists and intellectuals mixed with a surging workers' movement. Before the 'spectre' (or 'hobgoblin', in Helen Macfarlane's translation of the *Manifesto*) of communism would rear its head in the late 1830s and 1840s, utopian and egalitarian challenges to the status quo would be channelled by different discourses and terminologies, ones that Marx and Engels would later term 'critical-utopian socialisms'. In the writings of Charles Fourier, Saint-Simon, Robert Owen and others, neologisms like 'societal', 'industrialism', 'mutual', 'mutualism', 'cooperation' were coined. 'Socialism' itself is first recorded in the 1830s, and shortly thereafter will come to be juxtaposed to communism—in a terminological division within the 'anti-capitalist' camp that would repeat itself in the wake of the Russian Revolution.[26] Then, as Grandjonc recounts, we witness the appearance of '*communist*, recovered or recreated by the anonymous neo-Babouvists of the secret association of Egalitarian Workers in Paris or in Lyon at the end of 1830, and *communism*, which starts flowing after the public debates of July 1840 on the theory of these communists, which will only really gain momentum, and in an immediately international fashion, during the same year.'[27]

Both politically and discursively, 1840 is thus a watershed. On 1 July, in the Parisian neighbourhood of Belleville, a 'communist banquet' is held in the context of mass strikes supported by the expatriate workers and intellectuals of the Bund der Gerechten, the League of the Just, inheritor of the League of Outlaws (Bund der Geächteten), later to morph into the Communist League for which Marx and Engels will draft their famous *Manifesto*. Labour migration played a critical role in this communist fermentation; in particular, the 'small collectivity' of German emigré workers and

---

26 Raymond Williams, 'Communism' in *Keywords* (New York: Oxford University Press, 1985), pp. 73–75.
27 Grandjonc, 'Quelques dates': 143.

COMMUNISM

artisans 'radically redefined the concept of private property'.[28] 1840 was 'the key year for the distribution of the word *communisme* in the modern sense of common ownership of the means of production and the socialization of production; 1840 saw the foundation of the "communist party"; and 1840 saw the flourishing of the press of the various communist currents.'[29] In 1842, the neo-Babouvist activist Théodore Dézamy (1808–1850) would publish his *Code de la Communauté*, viewed by some as the most advanced theoretical document of the French communism of this period.

By 1842, *communisme* was a common term in French for 'all programs that espoused egalitarianism through the abolition of private property'.[30] In this same moment, the German labour leader Karl Schapper provided a limpid summary of this vision of communism, with its emphasis on the material presupposition for a radical democratic republicanism: 'Collective property is the first and most essential requirement of a free democratic republic, and, without it, this is neither thinkable nor possible. With an unequal division of property we remain completely and absolutely dependent on the wealthy.'[31] By June 1843, responding to the polemics of conservative Christian journalists against the 'artisan communism' of Wilhelm Weitling (whose authoritarian inclinations he nevertheless rejected), the young Mikhail Bakunin could write that 'communism has now become a global question and it is no longer possible for a statesman to *ignore* it, and even less can he *repress it through force alone*'. We are, he continued, 'on the eve of a great world-historical transmutation'.[32]

---

28 Jürgen Herres, 'Rhineland Radicals and the '48ers' in Terrell Carver and James Farr (eds), *The Cambridge Companion to The Communist Manifesto* (Cambridge: Cambridge University Press, 2015), p. 18.

29 Ahlrich Meyer, review of *Communisme/Kommunismus/Communism* by Jacques Grandjonc, *International Review of Social History* 38(1) (1993): 87–91; here, p. 89.

30 Herres, 'Rhineland Radicals', p. 17.

31 Herres, 'Rhineland Radicals', p. 18.

32 Mikhail Bakunin, 'Le communisme' (J.-C. Angaut trans.) in Jean-Christophe

Marx's Communism
The Critique and Overcoming of Other Communisms

In 1843, Marx—who that year had launched into a critical survey of literature on the theme, including Lorenz von Stein's *Der Sozialismus und Kommunismus des heutigen Frankreich* (Socialism and communism in France today) (1842)—still considered the communism espoused by the likes of Weitling or Étienne Cabet to be a 'dogmatic abstraction'. As he remarked to Arnold Ruge, in correspondence published in the *Deutsche-Französische Jahrbücher*:

> the advantage of the new movement [is] that we do not anticipate the world with our dogmas but instead attempt to discover the new world through the critique of the old. Hitherto philosophers have left the keys to all riddles lying in their desks, and the stupid, uninitiated world had only to wait around for the roasted pigeons of absolute science to fly into its open mouth.[33]

Some years later, Louis Auguste Blanqui would echo in his own pungent rhetoric this opposition to a static, apolitical image of communism as a confected utopian edifice, when he wrote that communism was ultimately 'a general result [*résultante*], and not an egg that can be laid and then hatched in a corner of the world by a two-legged bird without feathers or wings'.[34]

Marx's adoption (and transformation) of the language of communism was largely mediated by Friedrich Engels, whose conversion to communism came from conversations with Moses Hess, himself deeply impressed by the 'communist manifesto' of the Baron

Angaut, *Bakounine jeune hégélien: La philosophie et son dehors* (Lyon: ENS Éditions, 2007), pp. 151, 158.

33 Karl Marx, *Early Writings* (Rodney Livingstone and Gregor Benton trans, Lucio Colletti intro.) (London: Penguin, 1992), p. 207.

34 Louis Auguste Blanqui, 'Communism, the Future of Society' (1869) in Philippe Le Goff and Peter Hallward (eds), *The Blanqui Reader: Political Writings, 1830–1880* (London: Verso, 2018), p. 257.

de Colins, which spoke of a 'rational people's community (a commune as understood by committed communists)'.[35] Marx's communism, like the bulk of his concepts and arguments, was forged through *critique*. From 1844 to the end of his life, Marx, along with Engels, would repeatedly subject the communisms and socialisms of their day to exacting and often polemical evaluations. While his principal demarcation was from the wide gamut of socialisms—in the *Manifesto* subdivided into reactionary socialisms (feudal, petty-bourgeois and 'true' or 'German' socialisms), conservative/bourgeois, and critical-utopian—self-described communisms (those of the 'Icarian' utopian Étienne Cabet, or of the artisan-philosopher Weitling) would be repeatedly castigated by Marx for their penchant for asceticism and crude egalitarianism, or for a mere generalization of private property that failed to make the transition to *social* property, to a communism of productive abundance and the liberation of needs, rather than to a 'barracks' communism based on economic levelling and political regimentation.

Marx's 'insight' into the ways that capitalism bodied forth its own negation and overcoming in communism—critical to breaking with communism as an abstract dogma—would have to wait for his mature critique of political economy (especially the *Grundrisse*), but his philosophical 'vision' of communism, articulating a critique of political liberalism together with an anthropology of labour, would already find consummate expression in the *Economic-Philosophical Manuscripts* (or *Paris Manuscripts*) of 1844.[36] The notion that communism hinged on the passage from private to collective property was articulated with unprecedented depth by Marx in notes that drew on his critical readings of Hegel and Feuerbach, as well as, more distantly, his exposure to historical regimes of property in his earlier legal studies. The 'vision' of

---

35 Moses Hess quoted in Herres, 'Rhineland Radicals', p. 20.
36 R. N. Berki, *Insight and Vision: The Problem of Communism in Marx's Thought* (London and Melbourne: J. M. Dent & Sons, 1983).

communism elaborated in 1844 was capacious indeed, its overcoming of private property heralding a transmutation in consciousness, politics, and the very relationship of humanity to nature:

> [C]ommunism, as fully developed naturalism, equals humanism, and as fully developed humanism equals naturalism; it is the *genuine* resolution of the conflict between man and nature, and between man and man, the true resolution of the conflict between existence and being, between objectification and self-affirmation, between freedom and necessity, between individual and species. It is the solution of the riddle of history and knows itself to be the solution.[37]

Though yet to thoroughly rethink the juridical and economic category of private property as *capital*, with all of the profound repercussions of this shift on the very concept of communism (but also on the conception of man's relation to nature, which he would later address with the notion of *metabolism*), the notion that the 'resolution' of humanity's contradictory, alienated condition is to traverse history rather than dogmatically to negate it, already sets Marx apart from those competing communisms which he found guilty of peddling 'pocket editions of the new Jerusalem' or drafting recipe books for the cookshops of the future:

> The entire movement of history is therefore both the *actual* act of creation of communism—the birth of its empirical existence—and, for its thinking consciousness, the *comprehended* and *known* movement of its *becoming*; whereas the other communism, which is not yet fully developed, seeks in isolated historical forms opposed to private property a historical proof for itself, a proof drawn from what already exists, by wrenching isolated moments from their proper places in the process of development (a hobby horse Cabet,

---

37 Marx, *Early Writings*, p. 348.

[François] Villegardelle, etc., particularly like to ride) and advancing them as proofs of its historical pedigree.[38]

Here we can also see how the communist (workers') movement, but also the tendencies to communism inhering in capitalism, are first crystallized in the early Marx in terms of a movement in historical ontology itself. After the recovery and publication of the *Manuscripts* in the 1930s, their historical-philosophical and anthropological vision of communism became a crucial source for the renewal of Marxist thought. From Henri Lefebvre to Georg Lukács, Amadeo Bordiga to Raya Dunayevskaya, twentieth century revisionings of communism drew amply on Marx's economic and philosophical notebooks. As with so many aspects of the Marxist corpus, philology and militancy were never far apart—the first partial translation in English of the *Manuscripts*, for instance, was produced by the Johnson-Forest Tendency (led by Dunayevskaya and C. L. R. James) in a translation by Grace Lee Boggs (under the *nom de plume* Ria Stone).

Communist Individualism, Communist Freedom

I want to pause briefly on two interpretations of the legacy of the *Manuscripts*, by Herbert Marcuse and Galvano Della Volpe. Commenting on the passage that delineates the *positive* overcoming of private property, quoted above (p. 14), Marcuse—writing in the early 1940s from his American exile—saw this as warrant to draw from Marx's text the idea of a *communist individualism*. As he argued:

> It is, then, the free individuals, and not a new system of production, that exemplify the fact that the particular and the common interest have been merged. The individual is the goal. This 'individualistic' trend is fundamental as an interest of the Marxian theory [. . .] Communism, with

---

38 Marx, *Early Writings*, p. 348.

its 'positive abolition of private property', is thus of its very
nature a new form of individualism, and not only a new
and different economic system, but a different system
of life.[39]

This argument relied in turn on Marcuse's earlier investigations
(partially inflected by Heidegger's teaching) into the Marxian
anthropology of labour.[40]

Marx's conception of labour in the *Manuscripts* allowed one to
overcome liberal individualism as well as one-sided materialism,
by grasping the *social* and *sensuous* character of individuality. In
keeping with the Marx of the *1844 Manuscripts*, Marcuse depicts
labour as self-creation and man (*sic*) as an objectifying animal.
Production is appropriation, transformation, revelation and,
indeed, objectification. Marcuse's critical target is not objectification per se, but reification, understood as the obstacle to the
sensuous assumption of humanity's capacity for free and social
production. Note that the link between sensuousness, production
and objectification in the early Marx, as identified by Marcuse, also
involves an element of *passivity*—such that it is not merely a matter
of possessing objects but also of *being an object* (this too is part of
the definition of man as a social individual), of seeing man as an
'affixed, passive and suffering being'—even a being that finds a
certain enjoyment in such suffering.[41]

The effort to find in the early Marx a resource to critique and
surpass liberal (or social liberal) individualism would be given a
political steer in the Italian philosopher Galvano Della Volpe's

---

39 Herbert Marcuse, *Reason and Revolution: Hegel and the Rise of Social Theory*, 2nd EDN (London: Routledge, 2000[1941/1970]), pp. 283–86.

40 See Alberto Toscano, 'Liberation Technology: Marcuse's Communist Individualism', *Situations* 3(1) (2009): 5–22.

41 Marx, *Early Writings*, p. 390. For a further discussion of the question of sensuous suffering in Marx, see 'Excursus: Communism and the Senses' in this volume, pp. 34–52.

work. In 1946, Della Volpe drew from Marx's early writings a 'critique of the person' that would provide the prelude and groundwork for a conception of 'communist freedom'. Della Volpe also stressed how the idea of a *positive* suppression of private property required moving beyond the mere negation of the bourgeois order and towards a *socialization of nature*,[42] grounded in a conception of labour as inherently collective and mediated by technics. For Della Volpe, the '*total* man, in the communist sense, is at the same time extremely *individual*, differentiated.' But he (*sic*) cannot be *substantialized*: 'The person-substance, the *hypostatic individual* [. . .] which is the self-conscious man, this metaphysical receptacle of all moral inertia, privileges and abstract egoisms, is the dogma that hinders the understanding of how the individuality of man springs from that *spiritual concentration* that is *technicity*, synonym of sociality, *free* or *communist* technics.'[43]

Drawing on the *German Ideology*, Della Volpe argues that hitherto personal freedom has been a mere 'enjoyment of contingency' (*Genuss der Züfalligkeit*). *Classist* freedom, or traditional bourgeois freedom, is the freedom of contingency (*libertà del caso*)—by contrast with communist freedom, which is the individual ethical moment in the warp and woof of a normative community grounded in socialized labour. Notwithstanding its suggestiveness, this juxtaposition of a communist *libertas maior* with a liberal *libertas minor*—this 'direct contact and contrast between the problem of freedom and the perspective of communism'[44] polemically oriented against post-war social liberalism and social democracies—also bears the stamp of its time, not least in Della Volpe's use of the Soviet Hero of Socialist Labour Alexey Stakhanov as a paragon of this new freedom.

---

42 Della Volpe, *La libertà comunista*, p. 54.
43 Della Volpe, *La libertà comunista*, pp. 111–12.
44 Mario Tronti, 'Rileggendo "La libertà comunista" ' in Guido Liguori (ed.), *Galvano Della Volpe: Un altro marxismo* (Rome: Fahrenheit 451, 2000), p. 53.

Here, by way of correction, we could turn to an impressive recent effort to recover the centrality of *associational freedom* (rather than *communal equality*) in a reading of *Capital* from which Marx emerges as 'a radical republican and an (admittedly heterodox) Owenite communist'.[45] Rather than seeking communist freedom in a socio-technical anthropology of labour, we have here 'republicanism in the realm of production', the anticipation of 'a communist economy managed by deliberation and debate',[46] in 'a global system of interdependent cooperatives managing all production by nested communal deliberation'.[47]

Beyond Equality and Value

After the *Manuscripts*, the more speculative or philosophical dimensions of communism would lose salience in Marx's work, first as urgent political struggles took precedence, then as the critique of political economy both absorbed and transformed the earlier formulation of the 'riddle of history'. The discursive setting in which Marx and Engels wrote the *Manifesto* was one where communism had 'already come to indicate not only a scheme of social reform more ambitious than socialism [. . .]—in that its institutional aims included some public control of productive resources (and consequently the transformation of private, or "bourgeois" property)—but also a political orientation towards the working class'.[48] The articulation of this proletarian standpoint was already evident in the December 1847 programme of the Communist League: 'the overthrow of the bourgeoisie, the rule of the proletariat, the abolition of the old bourgeois society based on

---

45 William Clare Roberts, *Marx's Inferno: The Political Theory of Capital* (Princeton, NJ: Princeton University Press, 2017), p. 231.

46 Roberts, *Marx's Inferno*, p. 251.

47 Roberts, *Marx's Inferno*, p. 255.

48 David Leopold, 'Marx, Engels and Other Socialisms' in *Cambridge Companion to The Communist Manifesto*, p. 35.

class distinction and the establishment of a new society without class and without private property',[49] as well as in Engels' 1847 pre-*Manifesto* sketches, the 'Draft of a Communist Confession of Faith' and 'Principles of Communism'.

Marx's political re-articulations of communism cleaved closely to the struggles of his time—no more so than in the moment of the Paris Commune, as recorded in his *The Civil Wars in France*, where the reality of workers' self-emancipation and self-government, and the challenge of breaking the bourgeois state machine, made themselves intensely and tragically present.[50] Yet it was perhaps in the more prosaic ideological struggles within the social-democratic political wing of the German workers' movement that Marx made arguably his most enduring contribution to posing the problem of communism. For it was in the 1870s that Marx most clearly posed the problem of communism not just as a critique of the person, but as a *critique of equality*, one closely linked to the economic, juridical and political problematic of the *transition* from capitalism.

The parliamentary-capitalist or liberal saturation of the concept of equality is so powerful as to pose an enormous danger of capture and neutralization to any emancipatory politics. This risk is perhaps the central theme in Marx's critique of the social-democratic followers of Ferdinand Lassalle. It is also a critical concern for Engels who, in the same year as the 'Critique of the Gotha Programme' (1875), and after having himself proposed the substitution of the fallacious idea of a 'free people's state' with *Gemeinwesen* or *commune*, tells his correspondent August Bebel:

> The concept of a socialist society as a realm of *equality* is a one-sided French concept deriving from the old 'liberty, equality, fraternity', a concept which was justified in that,

49 Quoted in Herres, 'Rhineland Radicals', p. 22.
50 Henri Lefebvre, 'L'Avis du sociologue: état ou non-état' in *Colloque universitaire pour la commémoration du centenaire de la Commune de 1871* (Paris: Editions Ouvrières, 1972), pp. 173–90.

in its own time and place, it signified a *phase of development*, but which, like all the one-sided ideas of earlier socialist schools, ought now to be superseded, since they produce nothing but mental confusion, and more accurate ways of presenting the matter have been discovered.[51]

The fundamental thesis that can be gleaned from the 'Critique of the Gotha Programme' is that the equality waved like a banner by the social democrats subsumes the image of communism to a conception of work which is in the final analysis immanent not just to the ideology of bourgeois society, but to the functioning and material reproduction of capital and its relations of production, a reproduction itself sustained by a juridical ideology. In this perspective, every 'equality'—including the one imagined in the social democrats' programme as the equitable distribution of the product of labour—remains prisoner *both* to a neglect of the difference between labour and labour-power *and* to an image of justice that ignores how the inegalitarian laws of capitalist exploitation shape and limit the egalitarian ideology of rights. The equality of 'equal rights' to which social democracy refers is an equality in *measurement*. As Marx notes in the 1875 'Critique', 'equality consists in the fact that measurement is made with an *equal standard*, labour'. Consequently, 'this *equal* right is an unequal right for unequal labour'; *'It is, therefore, a right of inequality, in its content, like every right'*, since right 'by its nature can exist only as the application of an equal standard'.[52] Therefore,

> if the concept of equality is based on the same principle as the exchange of commodities, and if the commodity is the fundamental cell-form of capitalism, then the abolition of capitalism necessarily entails an end to the ideal of equality,

51 Karl Marx and Friedrich Engels, *Collected Works*, VOL. 45 (London: Lawrence & Wishart, 1991), p. 64.
52 Karl Marx and Friedrich Engels, *Collected Works*, VOL. 24 (London: Lawrence & Wishart, 1989), p. 86.

as a right that is always at odds with reality. But if that is
the case, then the concept of a socialist society that emerges
in Marx's critique of the law (which is embedded in his
critical theory of capitalism) is a paradoxical one; it is that
of a classless society without equal rights, a classless society
in which the law of equality is not realized, but, rather, is
no longer applied. Like [Walter] Benjamin, therefore, Marx
identifies the end of class society not with the establishment of a more just legal order, but rather with a liberation
from law, together with its insuperable legal antinomies.[53]

Every hope that one could ground a non-capitalist measurement
directly in right, equality *or* labour is revealed in its falsity, fatally
haunted by its immanence to the capitalist mode of production.
That is why Marx, and Lenin after him (in his 1917 book *State and
Revolution*), were compelled to mark their difference from the
social-democratic mainstream and to think communism not as the
liberation of a fundamental equality but as the invention of a non-
dominating way of experiencing and composing inequalities.[54]
Beyond measurement, outside of the homogeneous standard of an
'equal right', these inequalities will perhaps turn out to be no more,
and no less, than *differences*—thereby giving a political inflection
to the idea of a 'differentiated' individual already glimpsed by Della
Volpe in the *Manuscripts*.

If every equality is an equality of measurement, a measurement
originating in labour, money, the juridical status of the person or
right and law in general, perhaps we will need to cease imagining communism as a politics of equality. This was the view of
Louis Althusser, for instance, who, in his posthumously published

---

53 Duy Lap Nguyen, 'On the suspension of law and the total transformation
of labour', *Thesis Eleven* 13(1) (2015): 96–116; here, p. 114.
54 For further elaboration of this point, see my 'The Politics of Abstraction:
Communism and Philosophy' in Slavoj Žižek and Costas Douzinas (eds), *The
Idea of Communism* (London: Verso, 2010).

self-interview, *Les Vaches noires* (The black cows), warns that the 'demand for egalitarianism is historically an impasse and a trap', and who observes, with reference both to Marx's marginal notes (*Randglossen*) on the Gotha programme and Lenin's gloss on the same, that 'for unequal rights to cease, right itself must cease, and the real inequality of individuals among themselves must emerge'[55]—a real inequality, or difference, we might add, which we struggle to think or practice enmeshed as we are in the ideological and material apparatuses that secure capital's reproduction, and which will only surface in that singular process that Althusser himself calls *the formal subsumption of capitalism by communism*.

Transition after '68

To gauge the vitality of the problem of communism for contemporary theory it is worth thinking of the resurgent interest in the communist idea as itself inheriting the political and intellectual transformations crystallized by what shorthand dictates we call '1968', but which could go under the Italian monikers of *decennio rosso* (red decade) or *creeping May* (*Maggio strisciante*), the French *les années rouges* (the red years) or the 'world sixties'. This tumultuous context made possible the widespread recovery of that strand of Marx that identified 'the anti-capitalist revolutionary process both with a democratization (where necessary, a democratization of democracy itself, in the restricted forms it has hitherto assumed) and with a destruction of the class structure and its juridical, political and economic conditions of existence.'[56]

---

55 Louis Althusser, *Les Vaches noires: Interview imaginaire* (*le malaise du XXIIe Congrès*); *Ce qui ne va pas, camarades!* (G. M. Goshgarian ed.) (Paris: Presses universitaires de France, 2016), pp. 306, 308.

56 Étienne Balibar, 'The End of Politics or Politics without End? Marx and the Aporia of "Communist Politics" ' in *The Philosophy of Marx*, new and updated EDN (Chris Turner and Gregory Elliott trans) (London: Verso, 2017), p. 159.

Contributing in 1970 to the programme *Per il comunismo* (For communism) of the independent group il manifesto, Lucio Magri declared the *maturity* of communism, in light of the social development of *needs* that could be immediately realized but were blocked by capitalist social relations. '1968' had revealed the new forms of the classical Marxian logic of contradiction, making communism in its radical sense—a communism of the multidimensional development of social individuals through the collective appropriation of wealth in a transmuted relation to nature—a possible political programme 'for the first time in history'.[57] Prolonging the Marxian 'insight' into the immanence of communism in capitalism first truly crystallized in the *Grundrisse*, Magri and his comrades in il manifesto argued that capitalism had rendered possible a reversal or upturning of history. Accordingly, communism

is not a new political economy but the end of political economy, not a just state but the end of the state; not a hierarchy reflecting different natural worths, but the end of hierarchy and the full development of all; it is not the reduction of work but the end of work as an activity which is extrinsic to man, a pure instrument.

This did not mean that attaining the realm of freedom was in any sense a foregone necessity: 'The maturity of communism is only one face, the positive one, of a gigantic historical contradiction, whose other face is catastrophe.'[58]

Seven years later, in the wake of a sequence of ebbs and defeats, Magri would dissent from 'autonomist' claims about the presence of communism in contemporary social relations, and suggest that the very changes in class composition that from the sixties onwards

57 Lucio Magri, *Alla ricerca di un altro comunismo: Saggi sulla sinistra italiana* (Luciana Castellina, Famiano Crucianelli and Aldo Garzia eds) (Milan: Il Saggiatore, 2012), p. 172.
58 Magri, *un altro comunismo*, p. 176.

had made possible the growth in wealth and needs had also undermined the very idea of a capital spawning its own negation in the guise of a united, combative proletariat; capital, Magri declared, has broken 'the relation between the maturity of the revolution and the maturity of the subject supposed to carry it out. It produces its own putrefaction and that of the social body, but not its own gravedigger or the material required for the burial.'[59]

By contrast with Magri's realist reckoning with the paradoxical nature of this communist 'maturity', objectively rich but subjectively disoriented, Negri would instead stress the autonomy and 'self-valorisation' of the motley proletariat of the metropolis and social factory,[60] developing the tendency to communism in its own midst against an increasingly despotic and parasitic capitalist state. Retrieving Marx's own vision of communism embodied in the forms-of-life and association of workers themselves, rather than in any abstract political programme[61]—and, perhaps inadvertently, Georges Sorel's conception of the autonomy of proletarian morality—Negri would declare that 'Communism is normativity; it is the normalisation of a creative subjectivity.'[62] This kind of normativity must be defined from below as 'command over what one is.'[63] Accordingly: 'One may speak of a revolutionary communist norm only when the latter is grounded in the immediacy of use value and involves a reorganisation of social cooperation, over the arc of the social working day, tending—with a strong degree of acceleration—towards the abolition of the relation between surplus value and necessary labour.'[64]

---

59 Magri, *un altro comunismo*, p. 236.
60 Antonio Negri, *Il comunismo e la guerra* (Milan: Feltrinelli, 1980).
61 See Antonia Birnbaum, 'Between Sharing and Antagonism: The Invention of Communism in the Early Marx', *Radical Philosophy* 166 (2011): 21–28.
62 Antonio Negri, *Macchina tempo: Rompicapi liberazione costituzione* (Milan: Feltrinelli, 1982), p. 125.
63 Negri, *Macchina tempo*, p. 135.
64 Negri, *Macchina tempo*, p. 144.

The sense of maturity or imminence felt in the wake of '68 among ample sectors of the Marxist and communist counter-public sphere meant emphasizing communism as an immanent tendency within capitalism. It also involved challenging a Third Internationalist (or Stalinist) orthodoxy wedded to a mechanical stageism while reviving the polemics against 'socialism' (or social democracy) of the 1840s, 1870s or 1920s. This was most forthright perhaps in Althusser's contention that there is no such thing as a socialist mode of production.[65] In keeping with Althusser's asseverations against 'expressive totalities', his thinking about the virtuality of communism in capitalism is not grounded in a global tendency (of the kind limned by Negri), as in attention to the *traces* of communism in the present, and to their contingent recombination into a full-blown challenge or alternative to capitalist domination. As Althusser remarked:

> The forms of appearance of communist elements in capitalist society itself are innumerable. Marx himself listed an entire series of them, from the forms of education-work of children, up to the new relations at stake in proletarian organisations, the proletarian family, the proletarian community of life and struggle, stock companies, workers' cooperatives, etc. without mentioning the 'socialisation of production', which poses all sorts of problems, but needs to be retained.[66]

Althusser also mentioned 'proletarian inventions in the class struggle',[67] including the 1973 occupation at the LIP watch factory in Besançon (France), concluding that 'they are not all communist. They are elements for communism. Communism will take them

---

65 Louis Althusser, 'Livre sur l'impérialisme (1973) (extraits)' in *Écrits sur l'histoire (1963–1983)* (G. M. Goshgarian ed.) (Paris: Presses universitaires de France, 2018), p. 217.

66 Althusser, 'Livre sur l'impérialisme', pp. 130–31.

67 Althusser, 'Livre sur l'impérialisme', p. 131.

up, will unite them, complete them, develop their virtualities, by integrating them in the revolution of the relations of production which commands everything, and which is still absent from our world'.[68] But this tendency is not 'in things themselves', it requires both the Leninist capture of the *kairos* and the long march of transition to reassemble these 'elements of communism'. This is a communism not of totality, as much as of 'assemblage'.[69]

Althusser suggestively analogizes the contemporary detection and political coordination of traces, interstices or islands of communism to Marx's Epicurean metaphor, whereby capitalism was not born at the core of the feudal world, but in its *intermundia*, its in-between-worlds. Building on his rejection of the idea of a socialist mode of production and the chimeric idea of socialized (state) property, Althusser suggests that what matters for the prospect of communism is not relations of property as much as relations of production, where what is at stake is 'possession' (*Besitz*, *détention*) (of the means of production) not property (*Eigentum*, *propriété*). A communist mode of production will be defined by relations of production (and social forms) marked by the *possession* of productive forces by workers themselves and 'this communal [*communautaire*] possession [*détention*] *will have to do without every market relation*'.[70]

Distinguishing between a mode of production and a multiplicity of social formations, Althusser does acknowledge that this communism-to-come will not necessarily be homogeneous; there will be 'different forms of organisation of the *communal* or *communist relation* of production in social formations without classes'. Attention to the conditions of existence *and* inexistence of a communist mode of production, demands reflecting on the possibility that certain *forms* taken by particular social formations

---

68 Althusser, 'Livre sur l'impérialisme', pp. 131–32.
69 Berki, *Insight and Vision*, p. 5.
70 Althusser, 'Livre sur l'impérialisme', p. 161.

hinder the existence of a mode of production, leading to the theoretical and political question:

> *in which forms* (and not only in the nation-form) must a
> *socialist* social formation exist so that the communist mode
> of production, which exists in an antagonistic fashion
> within that social formation (Lenin) with the capitalist
> mode of production (Lenin), has real chances of *existing*,
> that is to say of triumphing over the elements of the
> capitalist mode of production that subsist, all the while pre-
> paring in advance the forms of existence of this communist
> mode of production?[71]

If Marxism is not to morph into a philosophy of history and disavow political contingency—if it is to be what Althusser called a 'finite' theory, open to the aleatory rather than closed into a system—little can be theoretically anticipated about the forms of transition and the nature of a non-bourgeois practice of politics (and even less about the social forms and relations of communism 'itself'). Even more reason why a critique of our images of communism, including Marx's own, remains vital, since, as Althusser noted:

> experience shows that even the vague representation of
> communism that men [*sic*] make for themselves,
> communists especially, is not extrinsic to their way of con-
> ceiving contemporary society and their immediate and
> imminent struggles. The image of communism is not
> innocent: it can nurture messianic illusions that guarantee
> the forms and future of present action, deviate them from
> the practical materialism of the 'concrete analysis of con-
> crete situations', nourish the empty idea of 'universality'
> which we find in some ambiguous ersatz variants.[72]

---

71 Althusser, 'Livre sur l'impérialisme', pp. 240–41.
72 Louis Althusser, 'Il marxismo come teoria "finita" ' in Louis Althusser et al., *Discutere lo stato: Posizioni a confronto su una tesi di Louis Althusser* (Bari: De Donato, 1978), p. 18.

Abolition Communism

How is capitalism to be undone? And what is the character of this undoing? Following a leitmotif in Marx's writings, itself echoing a broader communist discourse he did not create ex nihilo, the major name for this undoing is arguably *abolition* (this could also be thought of as the *content* of that form, or forms, that we call *transition*). Trying to define what he would elsewhere call the 'immutable tables' of the communism forged by Marx and Engels, Amadeo Bordiga, for instance, would assert—by contrast with the communist individualism mentioned above—that 'the original content of the Communist programme is the abolition of the individual as economic subject, holder of rights and actor of human history.' He did this while also warning that abolition should not be conceived as an act of will, something that would fly in the face of his demand for a 'reduction to zero of the individual factor in history'.[73] Against any 'Carlylean spectre' of historical heroism, what Bordiga calls for is an impersonal party for an anonymous revolution.

This trenchant fidelity to Marxian abolition is of course predicated on demarcating it from any Hegelian 'sublation' or 'overcoming'—terms that translate in English one of Marx's words for abolition, *Aufhebung*. It is in the latter that some, like the late French philosopher Lucien Sève,[74] have seen fit to identify a communist dynamic that carries a large quotient of conservation and is not reducible to a wholesale destruction. Building on his rejection of Sève's arguments—which he deems improbably reformist and philologically ungrounded—Patrick Theuret has provided an imposing audit of the Marxian language of abolition, helpfully itemizing abolition's targets.[75] Among those which are the

---

73 Bordiga quoted in Jacques Camatte (ed.), *Bordiga et la passion du communisme* (Paris: Spartacus, 1974), p. 98.

74 See Lucien Sève, 'Traduire *Aufhebung* chez Marx: Fausse querelle et vrais enjeux', *Actuel Marx* 64 (2018): 112–27.

object of *Aufhebung* we find, in the *Manifesto* alone: class antagonism; the scattering of means of production; bourgeois individuality, independence and freedom; the family and the exploitation of children by parents; the role of women as mere instruments of production; prostitution; exploitation (of man by man, of one nation by another); the town–country distinction, etc. Objects of *Abschaffung* (the term most commonly used for the abolition of slavery in German) are, inter alia: feudal property, personal property, nationality, eternal truths, religion, inheritance and bourgeois relations of production. These negations are summed up and crystallized by the abolition of private property— or, in Marx's mature lexicon, of the capital relation.

Against Sève's insistence that *Aufhebung* is far more of a super-session, a conserving negation or even extension, a *dépassement*, than a destructive movement, Theuret points out that in French translations approved by Marx, *Aufhebung* was rendered most frequently as *suppression, abrogation* or *abolition*, while in the English ones checked by Engels as *abolish, do away, destroy*. And there is of course an ampler galaxy of terms that Marx (and Marxists) drew upon, including *dissolution, Auflösung*—with its prosaic resonances with *Lösung*, solution, and its 'messianic' ones with *Erlösung*, redemption.[76]

The language of abolition was of course deeply entangled with that of slavery. Though the use of the slave analogy in Marxism has been the object of Black radical critique,[77] it is also worth noting

75 Patrick Theuret, *L'ésprit de la revolution: Aufhebung; Marx, Hegel et l'abolition* (Montreuil: Le Temps des Cerises, 2016); See also ' "Aufhebung", Karl Marx et la revolution', *Faire Vivre le PCF!*, 8 May 2019 (available online: https://bit.ly/3Hinaha; last accessed 19 January 2023).

76 See Étienne Balibar, 'The Messianic Moment in Marx', *Citizen Subject: Foundations for a Philosophical Anthropology* (Steven Miller trans.) (New York: Fordham University Press, 2017).

77 See Robbie Shilliam, 'Decolonizing the Manifesto: Communism and the

not just Marx's passionate investment in American abolitionist politics, but also how an unorthodox Marxist politics was interwoven, already in the nineteenth century, with the 'slave's cause':

> After the [American Civil] war, an abolitionist–labor alliance found organizational expression briefly under Marxist auspices. Former abolitionists, Chartists, Owenites, utopian socialists, followers of Proudhon, labor, and 'free love' advocates like [Stephen Pearl] Andrews and Victoria Woodhull joined the First International, begun with Marx's formation of the IWA in 1864 in London. Despite Marx's criticism of utopian socialism in contrast to his own brand of allegedly scientific socialism, many of these reformers were the first converts to Marxism. Abolitionists such as Richard Hinton, a follower of John Brown who led a black regiment during the Civil War, and William West, who had brought up the plight of wage slaves in the pages of the *Liberator* before the war, were prominent in the First International, which earned the support of [Charles] Sumner and [Wendell] Phillips. Andrews translated and Woodhull published Marx's *Communist Manifesto* (1848) in the United States for the first time in her newspaper, *Woodhull and Claflin's Weekly* [. . .] After the suppression of the [Paris] commune, the IWA, now headquartered in New York, held a huge demonstration in sympathy that included an all-black Skidmore guard named after Thomas Skidmore.[78]

The nexus of anti-slavery abolitionism and the international workers' movement, of the abolition of racial domination and the

Slave Analogy' in *The Cambridge Companion to The Communist Manifesto*, pp. 195–213.

78 Manisha Sinha, *The Slave's Cause: A History of Abolition* (New Haven: Yale University Press, 2016), p. 370.

abolition of capital, has made itself felt at various junctures, often involving a creative appropriation of mainstream communist discourse and dogma for Black peoples' liberation projects.[79] In 1930s Alabama, African American sharecroppers could mobilize the Communist Party as a vehicle for self-organization. This even included a militant translation of its otherwise worst phase, that of Third Period sectarianism, appropriating the Stalinist rhetoric of a 'new world' through Black traditions that 'emphasized both a struggle for survival and the transcendent hope of deliverance'.[80] In the domain of culture, the spiritual 'Give Me That Old Time Religion', was adapted, with the new ending 'It was good enough for Lenin, and it's good enough for me.'[81] As Aimé Césaire wrote in his 1956 letter to Maurice Thorez, bidding farewell to the French Communist Party: 'what I want is that Marxism and communism be placed in the service of black peoples, and not black peoples in the service of Marxism and communism'[82]—a sentiment that could well be echoed by other subjects, in other domains.

79 See W. E. B. Du Bois, 'Abolition and Communism, ca. 1951', MS 312, W. E. B. Du Bois Papers, Special Collections and University Archives, University of Massachusetts Amherst Libraries (available online: https://bit.ly/3D0yVGm; last accessed: 19 January 2023); Jesse Olsavsky, 'The Abolitionist Tradition in the Making of W. E. B. Du Bois' Marxism and Anti-Imperialism', *Socialism and Democracy* 32(3) (2018): 14–35; Kate A. Baldwin, *Beyond the Color Line and the Iron Curtain: Reading Encounters between Black and Red, 1922–1963* (Durham, NC: Duke University Press, 2002); Carole Boyce Davies, *Left of Karl Marx: The Political Life of Black Communist Claudia Jones* (Durham, NC: Duke University Press, 2007).

80 David Roediger, 'Where Communism was Black' in *Towards the Abolition of Whiteness* (London: Verso, 1994), p. 57. Roediger's text is a review of Robin D. G. Kelley, *Hammer and Hoe: Alabama Communists During the Great Depression* (Chapel Hill, NC: University of North Carolina Press, 1990).

81 Roediger, 'Where Communism was Black', p. 58.

82 Aimé Césaire, 'Letter to Maurice Thorez' (Chike Jeffers trans.), *Social Text* 103 (2010[1956]): 150.

As anti-racist protests against police murders and mass incarceration have taken hold in our own day, abolitionist imaginaries have come to the fore, articulated especially around the thematic of prison abolition, and more recently the abolition of the very institution of the police. There is no straight line or mutual reduction between these contiguous but distinct senses of abolition—a certain abolition of capital may see the persistence of the prison, a certain kind of decarceration could be perfectly compatible with the reproduction of the capital relation. And yet there is much to be gained from creating, or better recovering, lines of communication between contemporary theories of abolitionism and the 'many-headed' communist lineage I've sought to track here—not least in terms of thinking the relation between the negation of the contemporary forms of domination and the conjunction of the 'traces' or 'elements' of liberated collective life.[83] As Ruth Wilson Gilmore enjoined in an interview in the wake of the mass insurgencies in response to the murders of George Floyd, Breonna Taylor and far too many others:

> abolition has to be 'green'. It has to take seriously the problem of environmental harm, environmental racism, and environmental degradation. To be 'green' it has to be 'red'. It has to figure out ways to generalize the resources needed for well-being for the most vulnerable people in our community, which then will extend to all people. And to do that, to be 'green' and 'red', it has to be international. It has to stretch across borders so that we can consolidate our strength, our experience, and our vision for a better world.[84]

Such a red and green abolitionist internationalism, which is also to say a communism for an age of disaster capitalism, will perforce

---

83 See 'Freedom' in this volume, pp. 214–34.
84 'Ruth Wilson Gilmore Makes the Case for Abolition', *The Intercept*, 10 June 2020 (available online: https://bit.ly/3ZLgxuG; last accessed: 19 January 2023).

also have to confront the vexed issue of what is to be done with the vast socio-technical and energetic ensembles that have long made capital into a climactic, ecological and geological agent. If communism may also be understood, in Jacques Camatte's evocative formulation, as 'the resurrection of dead labour',[85] how much of that dead labour will need to be 'left in the ground' or disactivated, along with all the supervisory and political functions that permit its reproduction and amortization? How can we prise apart the communist use values of the machinery integral to and form-determined by capital from the place of that machinery in the valorization process? And what does this mean now that the meaning of machinery must be stretched to include algorithms, logistical and communication systems, and the whole material framework of our social relations? Whether we are evaluating the potentials for reconfiguring or refunctioning capitalist infrastructures in a communist horizon,[86] or delineating the urgency of an 'ecological war communism' in a warming, pandemic world,[87] these are practical and theoretical questions that any real move to abolish the present state of things cannot avoid.

---

85 Jacques Camatte, *Capital and Community: The Results of the Immediate Process of Production and the Economic Work of Marx* (David Brown trans.) (London: Unpopular Books, 1988), p. 126.

86 Jasper Bernes, 'Logistics, Counterlogistics and the Communist Prospect', *Endnotes* 3 (2013) (available online: https://bit.ly/3wgfup4; last accessed: 19 January 2023); Alberto Toscano, 'Lineaments of the Logistical State', *Viewpoint Magazine*, 28 September 2014 (available online: https://bit.ly/3ZOB3dQ; last accessed: 19 January 2023); Nick Dyer-Witheford, Atle Mikkola Kjøsen and James Steinhoff, *Inhuman Power: Artificial Intelligence and the Future of Capitalism* (London: Pluto, 2019).

87 Andreas Malm, *Corona, Climate, Chronic Emergency: War Communism in the Twenty-First Century* (London: Verso, 2020).

Communism and the Senses

> All who love their art seek the essence of technique to show
> that which the eye does not see—to show truth, the micro-
> scope and telescope of time, the negative of time, the
> possibility of seeing without frontiers or distances; the tele-
> eye, sight in spontaneity, a kind of *Communist decoding of*
> *reality.*
>
> —Dziga Vertov

> How does one *paint an ideology*? [...] It does not suffice
> simply to reproduce an image: an image charged with
> ideology never makes itself seen as the image of ideology.
> It must be worked over in order to produce this minuscule
> interior distance, which unbalances it, identifies it, and
> condemns it.
>
> —Louis Althusser, 'Sur Lucio Fanti'

The divisions and variations internal to the very concept of
communism can serve as a privileged point of entry into the
political vicissitudes of contemporary art and current critical inter-
rogations about the entanglement of politics and aesthetics. Vice
versa, some light may be shed on the communist hypothesis in
politics by how it has been articulated, problematized and
represented in the arts. To evaluate the contemporary meaning of
communism in and for art, one would need to navigate through
four more or less doctrinal definitions of communism: as the
emancipation of human (and inhuman) *sensation*, as *ideology* (or
proletarian worldview), as a practice of *destruction* (of the status
quo), and as a new type of *social relation*. It is in the force field of
tensions and contradictions, historical and theoretical, generated

by these four definitions that we may begin to glimpse how communism could be artistically (and politically) reactivated or, to use a term from Deleuze, counter-effectuated.

Though attention inevitably and immediately gravitates towards the vicissitudes of the avant-gardes as companions, promoters or victims of the communist enterprise in its statist Soviet guise—to propagandists and fellow travellers, to the militant and the ostracized—communism and the aesthetic have been clinched tight from day one. In the more anthropological among Marx's own writings, the aesthetic problem of communism is that of man's capacity both to produce and to sense, as this capacity is variously stifled, transformed and alienated in the divided conditions of labour under capital's dominion. When the communist future isn't subject to a proto-Taylorist geometry of discipline (as in Engels' *On Authority*), the few 'images' of a liberated communist humanity provided by (the early) Marx and Engels—scornful as they nevertheless were of those writing 'recipes for the cookshops of the future'—are bound to an aesthetic utopia. As Marx wrote in *The German Ideology*:

> The exclusive concentration of artistic talent in particular individuals, and its suppression in the broad mass which is bound up with this, is a consequence of division of labour. Even if in certain social conditions, everyone were an excellent painter, that would by no means exclude the possibility of each of them being also an original painter, so that here too the difference between 'human' and 'unique' labour amounts to sheer nonsense. In any case, with a communist organisation of society there disappears the subordination of the artist to local and national narrowness, which arises entirely from division of labour, and also the subordination of the individual to some definite art, making him exclusively a painter, sculptor, etc.; the very name amply expresses the narrowness of his

professional development and his dependence on division of labour. In a communist society there are no painters but only people who engage in painting among other activities.[88]

The 'communist organisation of society' is thus to be understood, aesthetically, as a domain of generalized (or generic) *singularity*, in which there is no contradiction (indeed no difference), between the *human* and the *unique*. This regime of singularity is explicitly formulated in terms of universalization (the detachment from any 'local and national' narrowness, as well as from any geographically specialized role within the world market) and of the obliteration of genre, as well as of professional distinction. Generic communist humanity is here a humanity without genre, and communist organization is a mechanism for the elimination of distinction, of all sociological indicators of power and hierarchy. To get to the root of the matter, the *expropriation* of capitalism—the obliteration of the division of labour and of its foundations in exploitation and property—is the opportunity for the reappropriation of man.

As Marx has it in his Paris manuscripts of 1844: 'Communism is the *positive* supersession of *private property* as *human self-estrangement*, and hence the true *appropriation* of the *human* essence through and for man'.[89] Leaving the term 'aesthetic' to oscillate between its doctrinal, historical, philosophical and 'physiological' (*aisthesis* = sensation) acceptations, we might want to ask what is the aesthetic dimension in and of this essence? What does Marx intend when he speaks in the same notebooks of communism as a 'fully developed naturalism' which 'equals humanism'? What 'metabolic' function might art be accorded if communism is to be grasped as 'the realised naturalism of man and the realized humanism of nature'? And can we still operate with a

---

88 Karl Marx and Friedrich Engels, *The German Ideology* (Amherst: Prometheus Books, 1998), pp. 417–18.
89 Marx, *Early Writings*, p. 348.

humanist communism of sensation in light of the machinic communism that is so forcefully proposed in Lenin's famous slogan about electricity and Soviets, and which was in turn so inventively and subversively instantiated in Dziga Vertov's cinematic practice? To disentangle some of these questions it is worth delving a little more into Marx's often neglected 'aesthetic' thinking—his own political logic of sensation.

The very domain whose 'real abstractions' Marx will employ his later years in hunting down and dissecting, the economy, is itself defined in 'aesthetic' terms. Before developing his social dialectic of the commodity form in the theory of fetishism (which has its own 'aesthetic' references, the 'original' fetish being a ritual artefact, and commodities themselves being displayed in an intricate play of veiling and unveiling), Marx will approach the realm of the economic on the basis of that kind of sensual materialism he had learnt from Feuerbach: 'This *material*, immediately *sensuous* private property is the material, sensuous expression of *estranged human life*.' Economic alienation is thus both an *anaesthesia* of man's most intimate creative (or better, objectifying) capacities *and* something which is *felt*, in an almost tactile manner. The economy does not merely have a formal structure of appearance (as Marx will later painstakingly 'reveal'), it has an (alienating) material expression.

Private property is 'sensuous'. The distribution of the sensible, to speak with Jacques Rancière, is here extremely complex, since the senses are *both* on the side of estranged human life *and* of the estranging economy. Or, capitalist distribution (as founded on the exploitation of that productive commodity, living labour power) is for Marx the key abstract machine in the distribution of the sensible, in the expropriation of man's senses, now in the service of his own estrangement and of the absorption of sensuousness by property itself: 'In *everyday, material industry* [. . .] we find ourselves confronted with the *objectified powers of the human essence*, in the form of *sensuous, alien, useful objects*, in the form of estrangement.[90] Both at the level of labour (power) and that of the product (the sensuous commodity, the object of estrangement) what is called for in the early Marx is a psychology of industry which is at one and the same time an aesthetics of the economy.[91]

As many have noted, Marx's ontology is indeed a relational one,[92] and the sensuousness that the economy leeches off the worker is paralleled by a transfer of relationality from humans to things (or, more precisely, to commodities other than labour power). Far from merely pitting humans against things—in what would inevitably be a losing, or rather a self-defeating, battle—Marx recognizes the necessity of objects, as indispensable materializations of human activity. The 'object, which is the direct activity of his individuality, is at the time his existence for other men, their existence and their existence for him'.[93] Anachronistically speaking, the object is a sort of 'interface' between man's individual creativity and his collective sociality. Sensuousness—whether creative or estranged—is always a shared, partitioned sensuousness. Productively and aesthetically, man is a 'social individual'. But an object—the concretion of human effort and ingenuity—is not (necessarily) a commodity, and the 'aesthetic' (and revolutionary) question thus concerns the possibility of a use of objects that would not be subordinated to the impersonal and inhuman sensorium of capitalism itself.

Private property, like the capitalism of which it is an intimate component, is of course not a simple evil for Marx, to be banished unthinkingly. It is through private property—with its bloody and barbarous history—that man can treat himself (which is to say his relations) as an object, and thus be transformed: 'Private property

---

90 Marx, *Early Writings*, p. 354.

91 See Alberto Toscano and Jeff Kinkle, 'Seeing Socialism' in *Cartographies of the Absolute* (Winchester: Zero, 2015), pp. 78–100.

92 See, for instance, Étienne Balibar, *The Philosophy of Marx* (London: Verso, 1995), pp. 32–33.

93 Marx, *Early Writings*, p. 349.

is the sensuous expression of the fact that man becomes objective for himself'. So, what kind of objectivity and sensuality is heralded by communism? First and foremost, appropriation should not be seen as a kind of humanist and metaphysical hypostasis of property: 'the positive supersession of private property, i.e. the *sensuous* appropriation of the human essence and human life, of objective man and of human *works* by and for man, should not be understood only in the sense of *direct*, one-sided *consumption*, of *possession*, of *having*.' Rather, the organized onset of communism is to be understood as a radical upheaval in the very structure of relationality, and, in a 'naturalistic' vein, this transformation is to be physiological, organic:

> All his *human* relations to the world—seeing, hearing, smelling, tasting, feeling, thinking, contemplating, sensing, wanting, acting, loving—in short all the organs of his individuality, like the organs which are directly communal in form, are in their *objective* approach or in their *approach to the object* the appropriation of that object. This appropriation of *human* reality, their approach to the object, is the *confirmation of human reality*. It is human *effectiveness* and human *suffering*, for suffering, humanly conceived, is an enjoyment of the self for man.

No longer mediated by the sensuousness of property, man is capable of developing 'directly communal' organs, with this community being understood in terms of a certain relation to the *object*. In the '*life* of *private property*' on the contrary, the social character of individuality cannot be experienced, and man remains estranged, alienated from the community of sensation. Note how, contrary to those anaesthetic utopias whereby emancipated man would drift along in somatic bliss, Marx has a profound (some might say proto-psychoanalytic) anthropological sense for the complex nature of sensation, whose logic implies than man may take 'enjoyment' not only in 'effectiveness', but also in *suffering*.

Communism is also, for Marx, the social appropriation of pain, no longer stifled by the sovereignty of the 'sense of having'.[94]

> To be *sensuous*, i.e. to be real, is to be an object of sense, a *sensuous* object, and thus to have sensuous objects outside oneself, objects of one's sense-perception. To be sensuous is to *suffer* (to be subjected to the actions of another). Man as an object of sensuous being is therefore a *suffering* being, and because he feels his suffering [*Leiden*], he is a *passionate* [*leidenschaftliches*] being. Passion is man's essential power vigorously striving to attain its object.[95]

Marx's aesthetics of pain has nothing decadent or morbid about it, precisely because the experience of suffering is not to be imagined as a lonely pursuit, a mark of refinement and distinction, but as a corollary of a social (or *transindividual*)[96] mode of perceiving. One cannot emphasize enough the uniqueness of Marx's concept of a social organ (and social organization) of perception, whereby, within communism, sociality is an intimate aspect of the individual: 'the senses and enjoyment of other men have become my *own* appropriation. Apart from these direct organs, *social* organs are therefore created in the *form* of society; for example, activity in direct association with others, etc., has become an organ of my *life expression* and a mode of appropriation of *human* life.' And further: 'immediate *sensuous nature* for man is, immediately, human sense perception (an identical expression) in the form of the *other* man who is present in his sensuous immediacy for him'.[97]

From a critical standpoint, however, we could say that Marx here belongs to the 'subjectivist' history of aesthetics, from Homer to Nietzsche, laid out by Heidegger in the first volume of his

---

94 Marx, *Early Writings*, p. 352.
95 Marx, *Early Writings*, p. 390.
96 Balibar, *Philosophy of Marx*, p. 30.
97 Marx, *Early Writings*, p. 355.

Nietzsche, to the extent that for Marx 'my object can only be the confirmation of one of my essential powers'. His social aesthetics can be read in terms of an expression, externalization or self-objectification of an *essential human capacity,* whose sociality sometimes appears more innate than constructed. And yet the structure of Marx's inexorably *political* project is that it is only with the 'communist organisation of society', which is to say, only in the wake of a thorough revolution and destruction of the status quo, that what was in a sense always already there—the transcendentally social structure of human sensing—can emerge and unfold. Only through an organized and deliberate process can human 'essence' (qua ensemble of social relations) structure society—this is, after all, the temporal structure of emancipation. This is also felt in the theorization of the link between communism and nature. It is through the existence of a *humanized* nature, and the specific objects of the senses that all the senses including the '*human* sense, the humanity of the senses' can be brought forth. And emancipation can only be concrete once it organizes a means to liberate the aesthetic from the domination of need, of the realm of necessity: '*Sense* which is a prisoner of crude practical need has only a *restricted* sense'. This 'restricted' sense remains an 'abstract' sense of 'abstract' objects (as 'food' is for a starving man).

Capitalism, as a system of exploitation built, if not on the bare life, at least on the abstract labour and concrete domination of workers, is also viewed by Marx as a kind of anaesthetic machine.[98] Taking as its standard—its '*universal* standard, in the sense that it applies to the mass of men—the *worst possible state of privation* which life (existence) can know', the capitalist 'turns the worker into a being with neither needs nor senses and turns the worker's

---

98 It would be worth exploring the forms of anaesthesia, some by way of hedonic hyper-stimulation, that have marked different moments in the history of capitalism. For a rich investigation of this theme, see Susan Buck-Morss, 'Aesthetics and Anaesthetics: Walter Benjamin's Artwork Essay Reconsidered', *October* 62 (1992): 3–41.

activity into a pure abstraction from all activity',[99] whence the ideal of 'the *ascetic* but *productive* slave'. The less you are, the more we have . . . Anticipating the grim apercus of Horkheimer and Adorno, Marx thus writes of life under capitalism that 'its true manner of enjoyment is therefore *self-stupefaction*, this *apparent* satisfaction of need, this civilisation *within* the crude barbarism of need'.[100] Communism, as the politics of human emancipation, and as the 'real movement which abolishes the present state of things', cannot therefore but be a radically sensory question: 'The supersession of private property is therefore the complete *emancipation* of all human sense and attributes.'

But what happens to the concept of emancipation when it passes through the filters of anti-humanism, whether artistic or philosophical? What is an emancipation that would take a formal, subtractive or machinic guise? In the end, is emancipation irreducibly 'aesthetic'? In the twentieth century, the sombre realities of political action have often obliged one to answer 'no' to that last question. And yet some thinkers have tried to cleave as closely as possible to the research programme laid out by Marx in those early writings. Chief among them is probably Herbert Marcuse. Much, if not all, of Marcuse's work rests on these pages of Marx on the emancipation of the senses. Indeed, it lies behind the position advocated in his last work, *The Aesthetic Dimension*. There, Marcuse writes:

> In contrast to orthodox Marxist aesthetics I see the political potential of art in art itself, in the aesthetic form as such. Furthermore, I argue that by virtue of its aesthetic form, art is largely autonomous vis-à-vis the given social relations. In its autonomy art both protests these relations, and at the same time transcends them. Thereby art subverts the dominant consciousness, the ordinary experience.[101]

---

99 Marx, *Early Writings*, p. 360.
100 Marx, *Early Writings*, p. 363.
101 Herbert Marcuse, *The Aesthetic Dimension: Toward a Critique of Marxist Aesthetics* (Boston: Beacon Press, 1978), p. ix.

The link to the *1844 Manuscripts* is worth stressing because, unlike Adorno, Marcuse's conviction regarding the emancipatory impetus or political potential of art is not based primarily on it being a vehicle of negativity and an exposition of the administered world— it is also the immediately sensuous dimension, indeed the *biological* dimension of artistic experience, and of its connection with political liberation, which preoccupies Marcuse (thus returning us to Marx's singular discussion of social organs of perception). Having said that, the themes of autonomy and transcendence indicate a crucial element that Marcuse shares with a 'classical' tradition in Marxist aesthetics, which sought to be both didactic and critical. This is the idea that art works as a force of anti-ideological disruption by its articulation not just of negativity, but also of a kind of *distance*, a *gap* vis-à-vis the status quo.[102] How such

---

102 This position is given a potent anti-humanist inflection in Louis Althusser's writings on art. Commenting on Brecht, Althusser sees the brilliance of his theatre and its alienation effect in being able to inscribe the distance between staged representation and reality within the stage itself. Equally, meditating on the paintings of Leonardo Cremonini and Lucio Fanti, Althusser stresses this theme of the exposure of gaps and the production of displacements as key to the anti-ideological function of art. In Cremonini, Althusser glimpses the possibility of moving from ideological 'abstract painting' to the anti-ideological function of 'painting the abstract', which is to say, the capacity to paint, or to expose, relationality itself. For Althusser, Cremonini is able to inscribe his own 'abstract relations' to the painting within the painting itself, turning these relations into its very 'matter'. He does not paint faces (the faces, inevitably, of subjects of interpellation), or deformity, but *processes* of deformation. Thus, both in its form and in its content this art moves against the ideology of the creator and the consumer, the ideology of full, social and aesthetic relationality under capitalism. Real works of art let us 'perceive' (and not know) in some sense *from within*, by an *interior distance*, the very ideology in which they are caught. The freedom of man passes through the knowledge of real, abstract relations—this is why, in aesthetics as well as politics, Althusser can hold that theoretical anti-humanism is the necessary prelude to practical humanism. See Louis Althusser, 'Écrits sur l'art' in *Écrits philosophiques et politiques*, VOL. 2 (Paris: Librairie générale française, 2001), pp. 553–620. For further reflections on Althusser's engagement with Cremonini, abstraction and ideology, see Alberto Toscano, 'Materialism

43

an aesthetics of distance, which is also an aesthetics of dissent, is rendered compatible with a kind of 'naturalism' regarding sensation is one of the interesting questions raised by a reading of Marcuse—and indeed by trying to articulate Marx's early politics of sensation with his mature critique of political economy.

In his investigation of the aesthetic dimension then, Marcuse wishes to remain with the centrality of the emancipation of the senses, as an antidote to *the reification of Marxist theory itself*. The antidote is not just provided by an attention to the senses but also by the theme of aesthetic *transcendence*. How do these two dimensions, seemingly prohibited by the original Marxian framework, come together? Marcuse's answer involves the dialectic of sublimation and desublimation within aesthetic form:

> Under the law of the aesthetic form, the given reality is necessarily *sublimated*: the immediate content is stylized, the 'data' are reshaped and reordered in accordance with the demands of the art form, which requires that even the representation of death and destruction invoke the need of hope—a need rooted in the new consciousness embodied in the work of art. Aesthetic sublimation makes for the affirmative, reconciling component of art, though it is at the same time a vehicle for the critical, negating function of art. The transcendence of immediate reality shatters the reified objectivity of established social relations and opens a new dimension of experience: rebirth of the rebellious subjectivity. Thus, on the basis of aesthetic sublimation, a *desublimation* takes place in the perception of individuals—in their feelings, judgments, thoughts; an invalidation of dominant norms, needs, and values. With all of its affirm-ative-ideological features, art remains a dissenting force.[103]

Without Matter: Abstraction, Absence and Social Form', *Textual Practice* 28(7) (2014): 1221–40.

103 Marcuse, *Aesthetic Dimension*, pp. 7–8.

This dissensus is simultaneously a matter of desublimating the senses and of sublimating form. And yet, even if we maintain an inextricable link between the being of communism and the being of sensation, even going to the extent of positing something like a communism of sensations—must this remain within the bounds of *human* sensation, within the parameters of emancipation set out by Marx in 1844?

We can turn here to that moment in Soviet cinema—perhaps the consummate crystal of communist art—when an aesthetically revolutionary cell, around the director Dziga Vertov, sought to mutate the eye from theatrical spectator to a revolutionary 'agent of critical production'.[104] Born of an explosive merger of political aesthetics and aesthetic politics, the documents issued by Vertov's Council of Three (in which he was flanked by Mikhail Kaufman, his brother and the eponymous 'man with a movie camera', and Elizaveta Svilova, his wife and editor) identify a *subject* (the *kinoks* or 'cinema-eye men'), an *enemy* ('Cinematography' as theatre of memory and representation of man: ' "Cinematography" must die so that the art of cinema may live. WE *call for its death to be hastened'*), a name for *being* (movement), and the basic *element* of aesthetic construction and articulation (the interval). Moreover, however restricted and familial Vertov's cell, it indicates one of the key aspects of the avant-garde's response to the problem of communism and art: the need to anticipate communist social relations (of production, distribution, and consumption—as well as collaboration) within artmaking itself, to make the fashioning of new *aesthetic* relations simultaneously into the eliciting of new *social and political* relations.

---

104 Annette Michelson, introduction to Dziga Vertov, *Kino-Eye: The Writings of Dziga Vertov* (Kevin O'Brien trans., Annette Michelson ed.) (Berkeley, CA: University of California Press, 1984), p. *xix*. All quotes from Vertov and the Council of Three are from this collection.

Throughout the texts produced by this group we can identify three crucial demands, related respectively to the question of genre, the struggle with the aesthetic of humanism, and the relation to politics: (1) 'The cinema must die so that the art of cinema may live.' (2) 'The eye must be emancipated from man.' (3) 'We still need a cinematic October.' The first demand is strikingly encapsulated in a poem contained within an 'appeal' from 1922. Confrontationally adopting the second person, addressed among others to 'You—exhausted by memories', this text seeks to drama-tize the death of a cinema of representations (or even of Eisensteinian 'attractions', still too 'thematic' for the *kinoks*) as the necessary prelude to the emergence of a cinema that would develop the autonomous life of sensation in the montage of movement. The sheer violence of the image is striking, a violence done directly to the cinema *as organism*.

> A friendly warning:
> Don't hide your heads like ostriches.
> Raise your eyes.
> Look around you—
> There!
> It's obvious to me
> as to any child
> The innards,
> the guts of strong sensations
> are tumbling out
> of cinema's belly,
> ripped open on the reef of revolution.
> See them dragging along,
> leaving a bloody trail on the earth
> that quivers with horror and disgust.
> It's all over.[105]

---

105 Vertov, 'Kinoks: A Revolution (From an Appeal at the Beginning of 1922)' in *Kino-Eye*, pp. 11–12.

Are we still in the ambit of the Marxian problematic of social organs? Sensation (or movement), revealed by the incision of the Vertovian image of cinema, bears an arresting affinity with Adorno's demand apropos of the New Music from Darmstadt: 'it would be necessary to eliminate unsentimentally every vestige of the organic that does not originate in its principle of artifice, its thoroughgoing organisation.'[106] Vertov does not oppose the *mechanism* of montage to the *organic body* of cinema. He dissolves this opposition to demonstrate how the new cinema transfigures the physiological and theatrical eye of the habituated spectator into a kino-eye, a sort of transhuman conduit for a life of sensation that can only be experienced in its vital truth to the degree that it is machinically constructed and composed. In other words, the emancipation of the senses demands an emancipation (of the camera-eye) *from* the senses, and, in a sense, an emancipation from the human. Here the relationship between technological and aesthetic innovation, on the one hand, and the political logic of sensation, on the other, means that the communist imperative to destroy the present state of things turns into an attempt to abolish (or at least radically transform) the very organs of social perception. Without an anthropology of sensation—except for a condemnatory anti-humanist one—Vertov's art, in its deep polemical urge, often hovers around the point of convergence between communist emancipation and nihilist obliteration.

In this respect it is congruent with one of the key traits discerned by T. J. Clark in the 'war modernism' of Kazimir Malevich and his colleagues, which he explains as follows: 'It is because War Communism was both chaos and rationality, both apocalypse and utopia—because it presented itself as such, in a flurry of apocalypse and utopia—that it gave rise to the modernism we are looking at.'[107]

106 Theodor W. Adorno, 'Vers une musique informelle' in *Quasi una Fantasia: Essays on Modern Music* (London: Verso, 1998), p. 306.
107 T. J. Clark, *Farewell to an Idea: Episodes in a History of Modernism* (New Haven: Yale University Press, 2001), p. 242.

Clark writes of 'the extraordinary being-together in 1920 of the grossest struggle with the realm of necessity and the grandest (or at least, most overweening) attempt to imagine necessity otherwise. Imagining otherwise was for a while actually instituted as part of the state apparatus.'[108] In his study on Stalinism as Gesamtkunstwerk, Boris Groys will go even farther arguing that, far from the Soviet avant-garde being simply betrayed by the socialist-realist reaction and the nationalist productivism that followed the second revolution of 1929, 'the Stalin era satisfied the fundamental avant-garde demand that art cease representing life and begin transforming it by means of a total aesthetic-political project'.[109] The UNINOVIS (an acronym for 'Affirmers of New Forms in Art') group to which Malevich belonged, along with El Lissitzky, had indeed anticipated the all-powerful plan as a political and aesthetic object, positing the Economy as the subject and object of art (Marx's critiques having been forgotten or crushed underfoot by the productivist drive). Interestingly, this hypostasis of the Economy went hand in hand not with a social individual as discussed in Marx's manuscripts (texts which incidentally went undiscovered until 1932), but with a kind of aesthetic and mystical fusion of individual and collective, an artistic image of communist nihilism: 'if we want to attain perfection, the self must be annihilated—just as religious fanatics annihilate themselves in the face of the divine, so the modern saint must annihilate himself in the face of the "collective", in the face of that "image" which perfects itself in the name of unity, in the name of coming-together'.[110]

---

108 Clark, *Farewell to an Idea*, p. 245.

109 Boris Groys, *The Total Art of Stalinism: Avant-Garde, Aesthetic Dictatorship, and Beyond* (Charles Rougle trans.) (Princeton, NJ: Princeton University Press, 1992), p. 36.

110 Kasimir Malevich, *UNOVIS Almanac I* (June 1920), quoted in Clark, *Farewell to an Idea*, p. 226.

This dovetails with the second demand contained in the declarations of Vertov's Council of Three. The 'emancipation of the camera' from the habituated eye is the very condition for the 'inhuman' experience of the life of sensation. Together with many of his contemporaries, Vertov will thus come, in this cinema which could be termed a 'communism of sensations' or a 'communism of movements', to equate the promise of revolution with a liberation from the human depicted as a *habitus* of representation. In Vertov's cinema the revolution is in principle the harbinger of an unfettered, inhuman sensation. In the transvaluation of the eye into the 'kino-eye', we glimpse the promise—at the intersection of political and aesthetic militancy—that the emancipation of human subjects will entail the emancipation of the inhuman from the representational habitus of humanity. Yes, this is a break from reality into the real but into a real that will never be sundered from its construction:

> The mechanical eye, the camera, rejecting the human eye as crib sheet, gropes its way through the chaos of visual events, letting itself be drawn or repelled by movement, probing, as it goes, the path of its own movement. It experiments, distending time, dissecting movement, or, in contrary fashion, absorbing time within itself, swallowing years, thus schematising processes of long duration inaccessible to the normal eye.[111]

Vertov's cinema is thus marked by a systematic *anachronism*, a capacity to 'denature' time and envelop it, along with movement as an element, material, or rather, as a *medium* of construction. But both the time and character of Vertov's cinematic emancipation in a way invert Marx, for whom the emancipation of the senses was inseparable from a thoroughgoing socialization and humanization:

111 Vertov, 'The Council of Three' in *Kino-Eye*, p. 19.

The eye has become a *human* eye, just as its object has become a social, *human* object, made by man for man. The *senses* have therefore become *theoreticians* in their immediate praxis. They relate to the *thing* for its own sake, but the thing itself is an *objective human* relation to itself and to man, and vice-versa. Need or enjoyment have therefore lost their *egoistic* nature, and nature has lost its mere *utility* in the sense that its use has become *human* use.[112]

Vertov's own project of anti-humanist emancipation will instead come up against the humanist inhumanity of Stalinism, wrecked by the hardening of the revolution, by a socialist state that could endure only insofar as it was itself endlessly and expediently *represented*, albeit at times through the formidable talents of the surviving constructivists (see, for instance, the remarkable propaganda publication, for foreign use, 'USSR in Construction', in which Lissitzky himself took part). Whether or not we concur with Clark's diagnosis of the 'horrors of modernity', the political and aesthetic catastrophe suffered by the likes of Vertov was indeed horrific. In the notes and journals that track the disintegration of the *kinoks* and Vertov's increasing desperation at his marginality we can read the following, grimly physical description from 1934:

We went about covered from head to foot with naphtaline, our irritated skins unable to breathe, smeared with stinking caustic liquids, fighting off attacks of lice. Our nerves were always on edge, and we controlled them by willpower. We did not want to give up. We had decided to fight to the finish.[113]

The third demand, that of an 'October in cinema', does not go away. What does this demand entail? *That the art of the revolution must not represent the revolution.* A generalized parallelism must be

---

112 Marx, *Early Writings*, p. 352.
113 Vertov, 'On My Illness' in *Kino-Eye*, p. 188.

invented between political and artistic militancy, the services rendered by the latter taking the form of an *enactment* of the revolution, a *transposition* of revolutionary injunctions into its own domain, specified to its own categories (not the people, but movement; not the party member, but the *kinok*; not labour, but the interval ...).

In the end, Vertov's tragically enthusiastic machinic communism may be linked to the aesthetic dimension promoted by Marcuse, when the latter writes that the 'truth of art lies in its power to break the monopoly of established reality (i.e. of those who established it) to define what is real. In this rupture, which is the achievement of the aesthetic form, the fictitious world of art appears as true reality.'[114] But, as the most faithful and inventive epigones of Vertov knew (especially Chris Marker and his comrades in collective and worker-led cinema groups, like the Groupes Medvedkine and the production unit SLON)[115] the destructive creation of new forms and the shattering of the 'monopoly of constituted reality' (or, as the filmmaker Peter Watkins would have it, the Monoform)[116] is inseparable from the generation of new, communist social relations. This requirement cannot be satisfied by 'the re-presentation as aesthetics of what was once social interaction, political discourse, and even ordinary human relations'.[117]

---

114 Marcuse, *Aesthetic Dimension*, p. 9.

115 See Catherine Lupton, *Chris Marker: Memories of the Future* (London: Reaktion, 2005), especially the chapter 'A Grin without a Cat' on the period of Marker's militant collaborations between 1967 and 1977. For a detailed account of the new social, productive, and distributive relations established in this cinematic practice, through the prism of one of Marker's collective projects, see Laurent Véray, *Loin du Vietnam* (Paris: Editions Paris expérimental, 2004). The militant films jointly made by Marker, his comrades, and factory workers from Besançon and Sochaux have been collected in 2 DVDs published by Editions Montparnasse, *Les Groupes Medvedkine* (2006).

116 Peter Watkins, 'Notes on the Media Crisis', *Comparative Cinema* (available online: https://bit.ly/40whl6v; last accessed: 23 March 2023).

And that is indeed because, following the political aesthetics immanent to Marx's notion of emancipation, the production of new sensory relations is inextricable from the real movement of abolishing the old ones.

---

117 Julian Stallabrass, writing apropos of 'relational aesthetics' in *Art Incorporated* (Oxford: Oxford University Press, 2004), p. 182. Nicolas Bourriaud does indeed speak of a 'formal communism' in his book *Postproduction* to identify the new artistic tendency to the production of novel 'modes of sociality' and the development of seemingly non-commoditized forms of cultural reappropriation. Without sounding too maximalist, we could say that without the real and creative movement of abolishing (rather than escaping) the present state of things, communism will precisely only ever remain . . . formal. In other words, I suspect that the 'communism of forms' is perfectly compatible with the communism . . . of capital.

· TWO

Radicalism

There are probably few entries in our political lexicon more unstable or ambivalent than 'radicalism'. Frequently associated with extremism, and with the supposed affinities between the opposite poles of the political spectrum, it emerged in the wake of the modern revolutions and was often used to qualify a now faded or corrupted term, 'reform'.[1] In recent memory, it was even enlisted to sublate the deflation of political ideologies under neoliberalism, in the guise of Anthony Giddens' 'radical centre'. Throughout, its relationship to the idea of 'revolution', especially with the recoding of the latter by Marx and his epigones, has been uncertain. Is radicalism a premise, a prelude, or a diversion from a totalizing transformation of human affairs? Or is it a sign of debility and defeat, as the objective possibilities of change either vanish or are fundamentally curtailed? Immature premonition or impotent passion, the disabused realist might regard radicalism pejoratively as a 'philosophical' (i.e. ideological) supplement or surrogate for the political. Radical philosophy would thus come onto the scene when, for whatever reason, revolutionary politics has been shunted into the background. Vice versa, radical philosophy would be made obsolescent by the upsurge of real politics. Something of this relationship is invoked, with a characteristic blend of melancholy and intransigence, in Adorno's well-known dictum: 'Philosophy, which once seemed outmoded, remains alive because the moment of its realisation was missed. The summary judgement that it had

---

1 See 'Reform' in this volume, pp. 75–83.

53

merely interpreted the world is itself crippled by resignation before reality, and becomes a defeatism of reason after the transformation of the world failed.'[2]

The Advantages of Backwardness?

The inaugural and decisive inquiry into the volatile link between philosophy, revolution (as philosophy's simultaneous realization and termination) and the 'radical' is arguably Marx's 'A Contribution to the Critique of Hegel's *Philosophy of Right*: An Introduction', written in 1843 and published in 1844 in the *Deutsch-Französische Jahrbücher*. It is there that we encounter—as the answer to the riddle of German backwardness—the proletariat, not as a given reality, but as a tendency and project ('the formation of a class with radical chains').[3] It also in that famous—and thus often hastily read—text that, in a much-quoted passage, the crucial link between philosophical radicalism and revolutionary political 'humanism' makes itself manifest:

> The weapon of criticism certainly cannot replace the criticism of weapons; material force must be overthrown by material force; but theory, too, becomes a material force

2 Theodor W. Adorno, *Negative Dialectics* (E. B. Ashton trans.) (London: Routledge, 1990), p. 3. See also the stimulating reflections on the syntagm 'radical philosophy' in Peter Osborne, 'Radicalism and Philosophy', *Radical Philosophy* 103 (2000): 6–11. Though Osborne's attempt, after Rancière, to discern the dialectic of (re)politicization and depoliticization (or realization) within radicalism is instructive, his contention that radicalism 'is the political correlate of the temporal logic of modernity, the logic of the new' (p. 8) is under-determined, and does not do justice to the specific temporality of Marxian radicalism, which cannot be reduced in this respect to 'romantic naturalism' (p. 7).

3 Karl Marx, 'A Contribution to the Critique of Hegel's *Philosophy of Right*: An Introduction' in *Critique of Hegel's 'Philosophy of Right'* (Annete Jolin and Joseph O'Malley trans, Joseph O'Malley ed.) (Cambridge: Cambridge University Press, 1970), p. 141.

once it seizes the masses. Theory is capable of seizing the masses once it demonstrates *ad hominem*, and it demonstrates *ad hominem* once it becomes radical. To be radical is to grasp matters at the root. But for man the root is man himself.[4]

As countless of Marx's writings attest to, from *The Holy Family* to *Herr Vogt*, from *The German Ideology* to *Capital* itself (whose footnotes are gems of the genre), the *ad hominem* in the guise of blistering polemic, satire and 'character assassination' was part and parcel of Marx's mode of thought. Inverting Althusser's formulation, one might even say that it was the *practical* anti-humanism required by his theoretical humanism.[5] But though the 1843 Introduction is not devoid of dark wit and invective, the stakes lie elsewhere. It is temporality, in the multiple and interacting dimensions of religious secularization, socio-economic development and revolutionary timing, which illuminates the articulation between philosophy and radicality, and which might provide us with some orientation as to the current fortunes of 'radical philosophy'.

Marx's plea for radicalization is insistently contextualized in terms of German *backwardness*. What is perhaps most arresting about this text is precisely how the most generic of programmes, universal social emancipation ('the total redemption of humanity'), is meticulously and strategically situated within a very singular political predicament. Having lyrically encapsulated the results of the critique of religion ('the prerequisite of every critique'), which he regards as having been 'essentially completed' for Germany,

---

4 Marx, 'A Contribution', p. 137.

5 Perhaps only Guy Debord, with a brilliance that was often wasted on desultory targets, tried to follow Marx in marrying these two senses of the *ad hominem*. See especially *"Cette mauvaise réputation . . . "* (Paris: Gallimard, 1993), and the texts in Situationist International, *The Real Split in the International* (John McHale trans.) (London: Pluto, 2003), where he and Gianfranco Sanguinetti write: 'We want to bring a radical critique to bear—a critique *ad hominem*' (p. 171).

Marx is faced with the obstacle that prevents the prolongation of the unmasking of religious abstraction into the unmasking of social abstraction, of 'the critique of heaven [. . .] into the critique of earth, the critique of religion into the critique of law, the critique of theology into the critique of politics'. The retrograde character of the German states and the underdevelopment of their civil society obviate the role of critique as a productive, immanent negativity. In Marx's biting words: 'For even the negation of our political present is already a dusty fact in the historical junkroom of modern nations. If I negate powdered wigs, I still have unpowdered wigs'.[6] Only the *ad hominem* in its most violent and undialectical guise is called for, criticism as the 'brain of passion', organizing the destruction of an enemy which it is not even worth refuting, because 'the spirit of these conditions is already refuted'. When faced with an anachronistic regime that 'only imagines that it believes in itself', a laughable 'German ghost', criticism can only play the role of a particularly brutal and unflattering mirror: 'Every sphere of German society must be described as the *partie honteuse* of German society, and these petrified conditions must be made to dance by singing to them their own melody'.[7]

But the German anachronism is double: on the one hand, the farce of restoration without revolution in practice ('the *oeuvres incomplètes* of our actual history'); on the other, the anticipation of the future in theory ('the *oeuvres posthumes* of our ideal history, philosophy').[8] It is the latter which alone is worthy of the kind of immanent critique that would be capable of extracting, from the productive negation of the purely speculative image of 'future history', the weapons for a genuine overturning of the status quo. In other words, the radicalism of (the critique of) philosophy is dictated by the paradoxical coexistence of practical backwardness and theoretical advance. The German 'thought-version [*Gedankenbild*]' of the

---

6 Marx, 'A Contribution', p. 132.
7 Marx, 'A Contribution', p. 133.
8 Marx, 'A Contribution', p. 135.

modern state is an abstraction that is adequate to its real correlate outside of Germany ('just across the Rhine'). This makes the 'criticism of the speculative philosophy of right' into one which, though enunciated from a position of backward specificity, of arrested development, is capable of attaining a real universality, and thus opening onto a practical horizon of transformation. To be properly radicalized, the situation surveyed by Marx is thus compelled to pass through philosophy. Neither a practical repudiation of philosophy nor a philosophical overcoming of practice are possible: 'you cannot transcend philosophy without actualising it', nor can you 'actualise philosophy without transcending it'.[9]

Again, it is important to stress that though these may appear as universally binding statements—and they certainly are concerned with the universal, with humanity as 'the world of man, the state, society'—they are strictly singularized by Germany's temporal anomaly, its disjunctive synthesis of political retardation and philosophical anticipation. This anomaly even permits Marx to hint at Germany's comparative revolutionary advantage, when he asks: 'can Germany attain a praxis *à la hauteur des principes*, that is to say, a revolution that will raise it not only to the official level of the modern nations, but to the human level which will be the immediate future of these nations?'[10]

---

9 Marx, 'A Contribution', p. 136. See also the important interpretation of Marx's radicalism, as crystallized in the 1843 Introduction, in Kouvelakis, *Philosophy and Revolution*. Kouvelakis makes the following germane comment about the link between criticism, radicalism and politics: 'How to make criticism radical and how to make it practical are henceforth inseparably linked questions, each of which presupposes the other. Solving them requires going beyond the philosophical form of criticism, which also means going beyond the unreflected character of practice' (p. 325). I am indebted to Kouvelakis' book for its elucidations and suggestions regarding the link between radicalism and time.

10 Marx, 'A Contribution', p. 138.

Notwithstanding Marx's faith in theoretical emancipation and his conviction that theory is not a mere collection of ideas but 'an *active* principle, a set of *practices*',[11] its practical conversion appears thwarted by the absence of the 'passive element' or 'material basis' for revolutionary praxis. This basis would ordinarily be found in the domain of civil society, in the sphere of needs: 'A radical revolution can only be a revolution of radical needs, whose preconditions and birthplaces appear to be lacking.' In other words, the 'theoretical needs' that emerge from the immanent critique of philosophy do not translate into 'practical needs'. Furthermore, whilst in other (economically and politically advanced) societies, political revolutions take place where a class of civil society lays claim to 'universal dominance [. . .] in the name of the universal rights of society', the slackness and amorphousness of German civil society means that it possesses neither a distinct class of liberation—a momentary 'soul of the people'—nor a class of oppression, a 'negative representative of society'.[12] This further symptom of backwardness, though initially appearing to quash the latter's 'advantages', reveals itself as the supreme, if in many respects supremely aleatory or even desperate, opportunity for revolutionary change. The sheer disaggregation of the German polity means that the 'classical' model of partial and political revolution is inoperative: 'In France it is the actuality, in Germany the impossibility, of gradual emancipation which must give birth to full freedom'.[13] Despite his allegedly enduring Feuerbachianism,[14] Marx could not countenance a praxis simply determined at the level of essence or of philosophy. As he unequivocally put it: 'It is not enough that thought strive to actualise itself;

11 Kouvelakis, *Philosophy and Revolution*, p. 324.

12 Marx, 'A Contribution', p. 140.

13 Marx, 'A Contribution', 141. The concluding paragraph puts this both boldly and ironically: 'Germany, enamoured of fundamentals, can have nothing less than a fundamental revolution' (p. 142).

14 Louis Althusser, 'Marxism and Humanism' in *For Marx* (Ben Brewster trans.) (London: Verso, 1996), pp. 225–27.

actuality must itself strive toward thought'.[15] This embryonic version of Marx's later 'method of the tendency'[16] dictates that radical emancipation find its objective or 'positive possibility' in 'the formation of a class with radical chains', the proletariat. And it is here that the radicality of philosophy is matched by the radicality of a social and political subject: 'Just as philosophy finds its material weapons in the proletariat, so the proletariat finds its spiritual weapons in philosophy'.[17]

The Theology of Revolution from the Standpoint of the Proletariat

The singular constellation of concepts that emerges in the young Marx's confrontation with the predicament of Germany in the early 1840s—binding together the results of the critique of religion, the analysis of economic backwardness, the function of philosophy and the dislocated and dislocating character of historical time—has arguably beset radical philosophy ever since. And it is the themes of the 1843 Introduction that we can still find at work 80 years later in an emblematic and instructive confrontation between two intimately related but conflicting ways of thinking philosophy's radicalism, a confrontation that might even allow us to delineate some of the antinomies of radical philosophy that endure into the present. Toward the conclusion of his seminal 1923 essay 'Reification and the Consciousness of the Proletariat', the theoretical core of *History and Class Consciousness*, Georg Lukács directly addresses the 'theology of revolution' that Ernst Bloch had examined and dramatized in his 1921 book on the sixteenth-century radical

---

15 Marx, 'A Contribution', p. 138.
16 'Freedom and subordination, whether in theory or in practice, are only given within the tendency, within the movement, within the specificity of the class struggle that materially prepares the destruction of the existing order.' Antonio Negri, 'Crisis of the Planner-State' in *Books for Burning: Between Civil War and Democracy in 1970s Italy* (Timothy S. Murphy ed., Arianna Bove, Ed Emery and Francesca Novello trans) (London: Verso, 2005), p. 15.
17 Marx, 'A Contribution', p. 142.

reformer and leader of the German Peasants' War, Thomas Müntzer.[18]

From around 1910 through World War I, but especially in the years 1912–14, Bloch and Lukács—both of whom were associated with Georg Simmel and took part in Max Weber's Sunday seminars in Heidelberg—had entered into an intense theoretical dialogue, even a symbiosis. As Bloch put it, reminiscing in his final years on his relationship with Lukács: 'We were like communicating vessels; the water was always at the same level in both [. . .] I was as much Lukács's disciple as he was mine. There were no differences between us.'[19] But while Bloch, even once he 'reconciled' himself with Stalinism,[20] maintained alive his 'anarcho-Bolshevik' leanings,[21] Lukács—first with his properly Leninist 'turn' in 1922 and far more intensely in his later repudiation of *History of Class Consciousness* and turn to a realist, 'neo-classical' Marxism[22]—broke drastically with his tragic, utopian and messianic inclinations of the 1910s.

---

18 Ernst Bloch, *Thomas Münzer als Theologe der Revolution*, 2nd EDN (Leipzig: Reclam, 1989[1962]).

19 Michael Löwy, 'Interview with Ernst Bloch', *New German Critique* 9 (1976): 37, 40. The entire interview is devoted to this matter. On the relationship between Bloch and Lukács, see also Michael Löwy, *Georg Lukács: From Romanticism to Bolshevism* (Patrick Camiller trans.) (London: New Left Books, 1979), pp. 52–56.

20 See his remarkable 1937 attack on those who broke with the USSR over the Moscow trials, which is entirely organized around the comparison between the divergent reactions to the French revolutionary Terror by German writers (Klopstock, Schiller, Goethe) and philosophers (Kant, Hegel), with the latter striking the proper attitude of comprehension, rather than facile moralism. See Ernst Bloch, 'A Jubilee for Renegades', *New German Critique* 4 (1975): 17–25, and the article by Oskar Negt in the same issue.

21 I borrow the term from Michael Löwy, *Redemption and Utopia: Jewish Libertarian Thought in Central Europe: A Study in Elective Affinity* (Hope Heaney trans.) (London: Athlone Press, 1992). This excellent and captivating work deals at length with Bloch and Lukács under this rubric.

22 For a compelling periodization of Lukács's political and theoretical trajectory, see Löwy's *Georg Lukács*.

The 'Reification' essay is a remarkable document in this respect. Not only does its theory of the proletariat as subject-object of history effectively expunge Lukács's tragic dualism of an ethical subject with no worldly effect; the dialectical and epistemological claims made on behalf of the proletariat[23] are also intended to serve as a critique of any (pseudo-)revolutionary or radical thought that abides within the 'antinomies of bourgeois thought'—that is, any theorizing that cannot critically grasp and practically terminate the pernicious effects of reification and the contemplative attitude the latter induces.

In keeping with our discussion of Marx in the first section, it should be noted that the entirety of Lukács's essay can be regarded as an excavation of Marx's dictum from the 1843 Introduction, which also serves as its epigraph: 'To be radical is to go to the root of the matter. For man, however, the root is man himself'. One angle into Lukács's 1923 essay involves considering how the thesis of reification, which critically combines the Marxian analysis of commodity fetishism with the insights on rationalization and calculation of his erstwhile mentors Simmel and Weber, permits Lukács to separate true, Marxist radicalism from those political philosophies which—incapable of identifying the sole subject that can break the spell of contemplative capitalism—only simulate radicalism while remaining trapped within the confines of bourgeois thought. Such philosophies ignore at their own peril the lapidary injunction that governs 'Reification and the Consciousness of the Proletariat': 'there is no solution that [cannot] be found in the solution to the riddle of commodity-structure'.[24] In this regard, Bloch's *Thomas Müntzer* seems a natural target, inasmuch as, despite its fervent allegiance to the Bolshevik revolution, it strives

23 'The self-understanding of the proletariat is therefore simultaneously the objective understanding of the nature of society'. Georg Lukács, 'Reification and the Consciousness of the Proletariat' in *History and Class Consciousness* (Rodney Livingstone trans.) (Cambridge, MA: The MIT Press, 1971), p. 149.
24 Lukács, 'Reification and the Consciousness of the Proletariat', p. 83.

to identify a supra-historical, meta-political and meta-religious *Ubique* (an everywhere), a utopian omni-directionality that cannot be exhausted or contained by socio-economic dialectic or political strategy. I will consider Lukács's attack and then assess the extent to which it captures the thrust of Bloch's theology of revolution.

The critique of Bloch sits squarely within Lukács's treatment of the fate of humanism in Marxism, which is to say in the revolutionary theory that adopts and intensifies the political-epistemological 'standpoint of the proletariat'. It is almost as if Lukács were correcting what might have appeared to the reader as the presence within the analysis of reification of his own earlier romantic anti-capitalism—the protest against capitalism as an engine of dehumanization. Lukács tries to purge humanism of myth, which is to say of its debilitating compromise with reified bourgeois conceptuality. In keeping with his Hegelian fidelities (the antidote to his earlier Kantian leanings), if humanism is really to dislocate the structures of reification, its immediacy must be overcome. Accordingly: 'If the attempt is made to attribute an immediate form of existence to class consciousness, it is not possible to avoid lapsing into mythology: the result will be a mysterious species-consciousness [. . .] whose relation to and impact upon the individual consciousness is wholly incomprehensible'.[25]

The picture that emerges is that of a battle between two humanisms: the first, which founds itself on the results of what Lukács calls 'classical philosophy' (up to and including Hegel), identifies a transcendental and trans-historical kernel of humanity to be ethically and cognitively rescued from its capitalist dehumanization (this is also the most general matrix for romantic anti-capitalism); the second, a proletarian, revolutionary humanism, reinvents Protagoras' adage to argue that 'man has become the measure of all (societal) things', insofar as 'fetishistic objects' have been dissolved into 'processes that take place among men and are

---

25 Lukács, 'Reification and the Consciousness of the Proletariat', p. 173.

objectified in concrete relations between them.[26] The articulation
of this revolutionary humanism possibly constitutes Lukács's most
unequivocal act of separation from his ethically rigorist and dualist
past, and from any trans-historical opposition to the bourgeoisie.
Capitalism can only be exploded from the inside, by an agent
formed in the process of reification itself. Conversely, a revolutionary humanism can only arise when social life is thoroughly
subsumed under capitalist relations, when 'in this objectification,
in this rationalisation and reification of all social forms [. . .] we
see clearly for the first time how society is constructed from the
relations of men [sic] with each other'.[27]

Lukács is accordingly opposed to any theory of 'communist
invariants'[28] that would posit a trans-historical revolutionary drive.
This is explicit where he opposes slave revolts to proletarian revolutions while adding a further dialectical and epistemological twist
to the traditional Marxist differentiation. Unmediated by the
objectivity of social form (the commodity), slave consciousness can
never, for Lukács, attain to 'self-knowledge': 'Between a "thinking"
slave and an "unconscious" slave there is no real distinction to be
drawn in an objective social sense.' While it might be politically
mobilizing, the slave's awareness of his oppression has no true and
lasting effect because it is not rooted in social objectivity.[29]

26 Lukács, 'Reification and the Consciousness of the Proletariat', p. 185.
27 Lukács, 'Reification and the Consciousness of the Proletariat', p. 176.
28 On this concept, formulated by Alain Badiou, see Badiou and Balmès, *De
l'idéologie* and Alberto Toscano, 'Communism as Separation' in *Think Again:
Alain Badiou and the Future of Philosophy* (Peter Hallward ed.) (London:
Continuum, 2004). Badiou returned to this notion in *The Communist
Hypothesis*.
29 The reader can turn to the last chapter of this book, 'Freedom', for a radical
refutation by another communist philosopher of this differentiation of worker
and slave at the intersection of consciousness and the commodity. Angela
Davis' reading of Frederick Douglass' autobiographical writings upends the
very terms of Lukács's account. It is interesting to recall in this regard that
shortly before his death, Lukács played a prominent role in efforts to organize

In other words, it is only because the worker is the 'self-consciousness of the commodity', and thus a subject-object (rather than a powerless alternation between these two poles), that 'his knowledge is practical. *That is to say, this knowledge brings about an objective structural change in the object of knowledge*.'[30] Moreover, it is only this 'privileged' position within the logic of the social totality that permits the worker—if and when he is able to politicize his consciousness—not to struggle against seemingly inert 'facts', but rather to grasp the *tendency* inscribed in his very exploitation. The epistemological *and* political specificity of Marxism is to be located in this relation to tendency, in its being a 'theory of reality which allots higher place to the prevailing trends of the total development than to the facts of the empirical world'.[31]

It is on the grounds of this dialectical and political epistemology, which radically distinguishes the proletariat's self-knowledge from that of any 'pre-historical' class, that Lukács examines Marx's humanism. Lukács rejects the contention that Marx ever hypostasized an abstract general man, arguing instead that the 'standpoint' of man is such only when, qua subject-object of the historical dialectic, he is 'integrated in the concrete totality' (i.e.

---

the international campaign of solidarity to free Angela Davis, corresponding with the Italian Communist Party leader Enrico Berlinguer, as well as Bloch and Günther Anders, and the novelist Elsa Morante. See Georg Lukács, Ernst Bloch and Enrico Berlinguer, 'Carteggio su Angela Davis' in Lelio La Porta (ed.), *Critica marxista* 5 (1988): 105–21. The collection of Davis' writings which Lukács had proposed, via Berlinguer, to Editori Riuniti, *La rivolta nera* (The Black rebellion), was published in 1972—Lukács's death prevented him for writing the preface for this volume, but it was printed with an international appeal for her liberation which he had published in *L'Unità* in early 1971. On Lukács, reification and race, see also Gregory R. Smulewicz-Zucker, 'Linking Racism and Reification in the Thought of Georg Lukács' in Gregory R. Smulewicz-Zucker (ed.), *Confronting Reification: Revitalizing Georg Lukács's Thought in Late Capitalism* (Leiden: Brill, 2020), pp. 252–70.

30 Lukács, 'Reification and the Consciousness of the Proletariat', p. 169.
31 Lukács, 'Reification and the Consciousness of the Proletariat', p. 183.

when he is singularized as proletarian . . .). The upshot of this is that man '*both is and at the same time is not*.'[32] It is the specificity lent by capitalism to this ontological uncertainty or intermittence of man which for Lukács—set on burning all of his bridges with utopianism, messianism and religiosity—separates Marxist humanism from all of those forms of anti-capitalism that begin with the human (essence) and treat in unmediated, non-dialectical terms the impossibility of attaining humanity under capitalism. By contrast, the very concept of reification is aimed at surpassing 'the dilemmas of empiricism and utopianism, of voluntarism and fatalism' that beset any (romantic) anti-capitalism that has yet to discover the materialist philosopher's stone: the commodity form. The understanding of reification thereby allows Lukács to grasp the antinomies of anti-capitalist radicalism as derivative forms of the overall antinomies of bourgeois thought, stemming from the latter's incapacity to think tendency and to identify the subject-object capable of revolutionizing the totality from within.

The harshness of Lukács's judgement of Bloch's *Müntzer* arises from the foregoing specification of a revolutionary Marxian humanism. As the foremost communist exemplar of the utopian strand which he depicts as the historical counterpart of the Christian dualism that left the City of Man unscathed while deporting human wishes to the City of God, for Lukács Bloch is unable to extricate himself from a theology—however 'revolutionary'— which impotently juxtaposes a transcendent humanization to a dehumanized world, the empirical to the utopian. Within this 'utopian counterpart' to a quietist and servile Christian ontology, Lukács isolates two strands (which in turn compose a further antinomy, another blocked duality): on the one hand, a view of empirical reality for which the latter can only be transformed by an Apocalypse; on the other, a radical interiorization, whereby

---

32 Lukács, 'Reification and the Consciousness of the Proletariat', pp. 189–90.

humanity can only be attained in the figure of the saint. In either case, change is but a semblance.

Giving short thrift to the 'intrinsically praxeological' character of Müntzer's vision,[33] Lukács intensifies Engels' judgement on the role of theology in the German Peasants' War, not treating it merely as an anachronistic 'flag' and 'mask' for concrete social demands, but as an impediment and a diversion: 'Real actions then appear—precisely in their objective, revolutionary sense—wholly independent of the religious utopia: the latter can neither lead them in any real sense, nor can it offer concrete objectives or concrete proposals for their realisation.' What's more, the duality between man's inner being and his empirical conditions—joined but not mediated by a theology of history (predestination, chiliasm, etc.)—is viewed by Lukács, in a variation on Weber's thesis, as 'the basic ideological structure of capitalism', such that it was 'no accident that it was the revolutionary religiosity of the sects that supplied the ideology for capitalism in its purest forms (in England and America)'. Thus, whether we look at Bloch's attempt to supplement the 'merely economic' dimension of historical materialism with a utopian spark, or at 'the way in which the religious and utopian premises of the theory *concretely impinge* upon Müntzer's actions',[34] we encounter the same symptomatic incapacity to overcome bourgeois thought, the same *hiatus irrationalis* between principle and practice, the spirit and the letter, the spiritual and the economic. For Lukács, only the proletariat, 'as the Archimedean point from which the whole of

---

33 See the critical comments on Lukács's treatment of Bloch's *Thomas Münzer* in Tommaso La Rocca, *Es Ist Zeit: Apocalisse e Storia—studio su Thomas Müntzer (1490–1525)* (Bologna: Cappelli, 1988), pp. 191–95. This is to my knowledge the only text that specifically deals with these revealing passages in *History and Class Consciousness*. It would be interesting to consider how this 1920s differend is prolonged in the dispute over expressionism that pitted Bloch against Lukács in 1938. See *Aesthetics and Politics* (London: New Left Books, 1977), pp. 9–59.

34 Lukács, 'Reification and the Consciousness of the Proletariat', p. 192.

reality can be overthrown', can suture this hiatus and herald a 'real social revolution' capable of 'restructuring [. . .] the real and concrete life of man', thus abolishing the reified duality between the utopian and the economic.[35]

In many respects, Lukács's harsh if exceedingly brief critique of Bloch's utopianism remains emblematic of dialectical arguments against transcendent, religious or messianic radicalisms, and it is mainly for this reason that I have presented it here. I cannot do justice to Bloch's own proposal in these remarks, but I think it is worth identifying those points of contrast between these two communist philosophers that might shed some light on the persisting tensions, contradictions and antinomies within the contemporary understanding of philosophical radicalism. The clue lies perhaps in Bloch's 1924 review of *History and Class Consciousness*, 'Actuality and Utopia', which, while recognizing Lukács's towering achievement, chastises him for carrying out 'an almost exclusively sociological homogenisation' of the processes of revolution, transformation and humanization.[36]

Turning to Bloch's *Thomas Müntzer*, it is evident that Lukács's criticism, by aligning the theology of revolution on the antinomies of bourgeois thought—as a paroxystic transcendence of the world which is powerless to unhinge the latter's material constitution—papers over the specificity of Bloch's treatment of the religious and his conceptualization of a utopian excess which, though not simply transcendent, is both metapolitical and metahistorical. This much

35 Lukács, 'Reification and the Consciousness of the Proletariat', p. 193. 'Already the mechanical separation between economics and politics precludes any really effective action encompassing society in its totality' (p. 195).

36 Quoted in John Flores, 'Proletarian Meditations: Georg Lukács' Politics of Knowledge', *Diacritics* 2(3) (1972): 21. See also the reflections on Bloch's review in Andrew Arato and Paul Breines, *The Young Lukács and the Origins of Western Marxism* (London: Pluto Press, 1979), pp. 184–86, and Anson Rabinbach, 'Unclaimed Heritage: Bloch's *Heritage of Our Times* and the Theory of Fascism', *New German Critique* 11 (1977): 17–19.

transpires from Bloch's own reflections on Weber's sociology of religion. In a crucial passage of the book, which also relies on Marx's account of the historical masks of revolution in the *Eighteenth Brumaire of Louis Bonaparte*, Bloch argues for the relative autonomy of 'moral and psychological complexes' without which it is impossible to comprehend the appearance of phenomena such as the German Peasants' War, but also to capture 'the deepest *contents* of this tumultuous human history, this lucid dream of the anti-wolf, of a finally fraternal kingdom'—which constitutes an indispensable stimulus to collective revolutionary action. To quote Jameson's perspicacious commentary on Bloch:

> in Müntzer's theology, the very truth-coefficient of a theological doctrine is measured by collective need, by the belief and recognition of the multitudes themselves. Hence a theological idea, in contrast to a philosophical one, already implies in its very structure a church or group of believers around it, and exists therefore on a protopolitical, rather than a purely theoretical level.[37]

Recalling Marx's own treatment of Germany's potentially revolutionary anachronism in the 1840s, discussed above, Bloch—unlike Engels, Karl Kautsky and even more so Lukács himself—does not see the theological impetus of the 'revolution of the common man' of 1525 as the mere index of socio-economic immaturity. On the contrary, he views it as one of those situations that bears witness to the fact that 'the superstructure is often in advance of an [. . .] economy that will only later attain its maturity.'[38] Once again, we see how the configuration of the relationship between social transformation and historical time is among the foremost sources of

---

37 Fredric Jameson, *Marxism and Form* (Princeton, NJ: Princeton University Press, 1971), pp. 156–57.

38 Bloch, *Thomas Münzer*, p. 51. I have relied on the French translation by Maurice de Gandillac: *Thomas Münzer: Théologien de la revolution* (Paris: Julliard, 1964).

divergence in how the very project of a radical philosophy may be understood. The positive use of anachronism suggested by Marx, and given an extreme form by Bloch—as a recovery and repetition of Müntzer for a revolutionary present—is denied by Lukács, for whom the revolutionary utopianism of the German Peasants' War was simply a by-product of a situation wherein a real restructuring of life was 'objectively impossible'.[39] In effect, as the tone of his multiple references to the Russian Revolution suggests, Bloch saw a potential revolutionary advantage in the bond between, on the one hand, the theological-utopian impulse and, on the other, a 'backward' and peripheral place within the capitalist world order. Some of the comments on the social base of the Peasants' War likewise echo the critique of a linear and developmental philosophy of history that transpires from one of the drafts of Marx's famous letter on the Russian mir, where he approvingly quotes the following line from an American writer: 'the new system to which the modern society is tending will be a revival in superior form of an archaic social type.'[40]

The rejection of what Bloch perceives in Lukács and in aspects of the Marxist tradition as an excessive homogenization of the historical dialectic, as the purging of all non- or anti-social contents, carries over into his treatment of the dualities of inner and outer, heavenly and worldly, theological and political, utopian and empirical—the very dualities that Lukács perceived as the anti-nomies that ultimately reduced pre-proletarian politics to impotence. Rather than a historically determined contradiction or an irrational hiatus between theological semblance and political weakness, Bloch discerns in Müntzer—as the very emblem of the

---

39 Lukács, 'Reification and the Consciousness of the Proletariat', p. 193. For Bloch, on the contrary, Müntzer's tragic defeat should never be hypostasized into a historical inevitability, and he should never be treated as a mere 'Don Quixote'.

40 Karl Marx, 'The "First" Draft' in Shanin (ed.), *Late Marx and the Russian Road*, p. 107.

tensions and potentialities of the peasants' revolt—the short-circuit or disjunctive synthesis between the poles of these supposed polarities. Joining the 'absolute natural right' of a millenarian Christianity (theocracy qua equality) to a strategic grasp of social forces and political forms (the alliance with the miners and the formation of the League of the Just), Bloch's Müntzer combines '*the most efficacious at the real level and the most efficacious at the surreal level* and puts them both at the summit of the same revolution.'[41] Perhaps more than any other, this formulation captures Bloch's ideal of a revolutionary (and therefore realist) inscription of utopian content into the course of history. It also governs his reading of Marx.

Rather than the undertaker of utopian illusions, Marx is for Bloch the real heir to a subterranean lineage of chiliastic communism, whose pivotal contribution lies in soberly identifying the immanent means for the realization of a supra-historical drive to 'mystical democracy'. 'His aim,' writes Bloch, 'is to impose on the world through a hard-fought struggle, waged according to the wisdom of this very world, the edenic order required by rational socialism, which is profoundly millenarian, but which had been conceived hitherto in a far too arcadian manner, as a kind of beyond.'[42] Or, as Bloch puts it in a remarkable image in *Spirit of*

---

41 Bloch, *Thomas Münzer*, pp. 93–94. For a historical treatment of how 'millenarian revolutions' may synthesize political realism with theological surrealism, see Mike Davis, *Late Victorian Holocausts: El Niño Famines and the Making of the Third World* (London: Verso, 2001), pp. 177–209; see also Toscano, *Fanaticism*, chap. 2.

42 Bloch, *Thomas Münzer*, p. 89. See also Ernst Bloch, 'Karl Marx, Death, and the Apocalypse: Or, the Ways in This World by Which the Inward Can Become Outward and the Outward Like the Inward' in *Spirit of Utopia* (Anthony A. Nassar trans.) (Stanford, CA: Stanford University Press, 2000), where Bloch writes that 'Marx thoroughly purified Socialist planning of every simple, false, disengaged and abstract enthusiasm, of mere Jacobinism' (p. 236). For Bloch's provocative treatment of Marx's alleged 'secularisation' of Christian and utopian contents, see 'Karl Marx and Humanity: Stuff of Hope'

Utopia, Marx is only homogeneous with capitalism in the same sense that the detective must somehow mimic the criminal. Bloch's view of socialist revolution and planning, which Lukács dismisses in *History and Class Consciousness* as a misunderstanding of the economy which separates it from the political, also stems from this attempt to think through a kind of rational millenarianism. It also echoes Bloch's captivating treatment of the relationship between interiority and political action in Müntzer.

Sharing with Lukács an interest in the antinomic relationship between theological transcendence and political immanence, Bloch spends much of *Thomas Müntzer* dissecting and castigating Luther's capitulation to earthly authority and denial of mystical interiority. Luther's ultimate Manicheanism 'remains static, it does not entail any demand to suppress the tension, to re-establish, at least in the heavenly Kingdom, the very unity of this Kingdom.'[43] In a sense then, Bloch perceives in Müntzer not an overcoming of the antinomy of the empirical and utopian, which is perhaps ultimately irreducible, but another way of articulating it, which would simultaneously do justice to social needs and spiritual drives. More strikingly, Bloch's Müntzer approaches the stringent demands and risks of collective revolutionary action in order to free up the religious subject from the burden and the distraction of an exploitative order. In a remarkable twist, rather than a humanist effort to merely alleviate suffering, Müntzer's theologically driven revolt is aimed at freeing up subjects from vulgar economic suffering, *so that they may finally be free for Christian suffering* (and redemption). As Bloch writes, when Müntzer 'straightens up the bent backs, it is in order to allow them to bear a real burden. If the people has fallen low enough so that, having itself become creature, it has more to fear from the creature than from God, it is entirely

---

in *The Principle of Hope*, VOL. 3 (Neville Plaice, Stephen Plaice and Paul Knight trans) (Oxford: Basil Blackwell, 1986).

43 Bloch, *Thomas Münzer*, p. 136.

mistaken when it imagines that its masters are still established and commanded by God.'[44] This vision of communism as a freeing up of radical and economically irreducible utopian drives is also evident in Bloch's treatment of the state in the same period. In *Spirit of Utopia* he writes of the state as 'a great instrumental organisation for the control of the *inessential*', armed with a 'purely administrative Esperanto', and whose only 'justification [. . .] is the simplifying, frictionless functioning of its organizational method, placed in the middle of illogical life, its only, entirely instrumental logic, the logic of a state of emergency.'[45] Thus, correcting Lukács's negative estimation, it is not the demarcation of politics from the economy that is at stake in Bloch, but the excess (though not the outright separation) of the utopian over the empirical. Radical political struggle and violence—the 'categorical imperative with a revolver in hand', as Bloch has it—are necessary not for their own sake, but as the stepping stones towards an incommensurable and metapolitical aim. Or, to borrow Bloch's effective allegory, 'the Messiah can only come when all the guests have sat down at the table.'[46] Likewise, Bloch is not merely juxtaposing millenarian immediacy to economic mediation but thinking through the kind of immediacy that could be produced on the basis of a rigorous traversal of worldly determinations (class struggles, planning, material needs, etc.). Adorno captured this aspect of Bloch's thinking well: 'For just as, in the words of Bloch's master, there is nothing immediate between heaven and earth which is not mediated, so too there can be nothing mediated without the concept of mediation involving a moment of the immediate. Bloch's pathos is indefatigably directed to that moment.'[47]

---

44 Bloch, *Thomas Münzer*, p. 178.

45 Bloch, *Spirit of Utopia*, p. 240.

46 Bloch, *Spirit of Utopia*, p. 246.

47 Theodor W. Adorno, 'The Handle, the Pot and Early Experience' in *Notes to Literature*, VOL. 2 (R. Tiedemann ed., S. Weber Nicholsen trans.) (New York: Columbia University Press, 1992), p. 219.

Whither Radical Philosophy?

This brief exploration of Bloch's and Lukács's divergent responses to the injunctions of Marx's early radicalism has merely sought to make manifest some of the principal directions within the volatile force field of radical philosophy. In particular, I think that this communist differend from the early twenties reveals that, at least within a Marxist ambit, the relation between the concrete situation and its horizon of transformation can be seen to split according to two conceptually differentiated but intertwined axes.

First, in temporal terms: while Lukács's position stresses the articulation between capitalist tendency, the critical present and the revolutionary *kairos* which is to be seized by the organized proletariat, he appears to dismiss the benefits of anachronism mooted in Marx's 1843 Introduction. Inversely, it is by exacerbating this element of anachronism, by locating radicality in the super-structure's anticipation of the base, that Bloch can dismiss the canonical view of Müntzer's theology as hindrance or supplement, and instead give it pride of place as the bearer of revolutionary and utopian content.

Second, this divergent appreciation of the temporal coordinates of revolutionary change is bound up with two incompatible views of historical and political agency. Where Lukács presents the proletariat as the practical and epistemological 'Archimedean point' capable of unhinging the capitalist totality, Bloch revels in the subjective metahistory of a utopian kernel whose drive and directionality—despite all the mutations in instruments, organizations and motivating ideologies—remains invariant from the fifteenth-century Taborites to the Bolsheviks. To borrow Lukács's formulation, we are thus confronted with two potent, and alternative ways, to grasp politically and conceptually the statement that man '*both is and at the same time is not*', or, in Blochian terms, both is and is not-yet. Whether the antinomy signified by the names and texts of Lukács and Bloch is resolvable or not, or whether we should indeed treat it as a constitutive tension that maintains 'radical philosophy' in a perennial state of incompletion and unrest, is an open question. What is clear is that the insistence of contemporary radical thought on the enigmas of philosophical anthropology (in the writings of Paolo Virno and Giorgio Agamben on human nature and bare life),[48] the political repercussions of messianism (from Jacques Derrida's *Spectres of Marx* to the various strands of the Paul 'revival') and the possibility of a rational and partisan subjectivity (in Badiou, Žižek, and others)[49] suggests that there are still rich seams to be mined in the problematic of radicalism inaugurated by Marx and so compellingly, if incompatibly, recast by Lukács and Bloch.

---

48 The entire debate over the 'biopolitical' can be conceived in many respects as a way of folding the singularity of the capitalist present (conceived in post-workerist thought under the Marxian aegis of 'real subsumption') onto a metahistorical and metapolitical anthropological content. See Alberto Toscano, 'Always Already Only Now: Negri and the Biopolitical' in Timothy S. Murphy and Abdul-Karim Mustapha (eds), *The Philosophy of Antonio Negri, Volume 2: Lessons on Constitutive Power* (London: Pluto Press, 2007).

49 I've investigated the contemporary legacy of Lenin's 'political epistemology' of partisanship in 'Partisan Thought', *Historical Materialism* 17(3) (2009): 175–91, and 'With Lenin, Against Hegel? *Materialism and Empirio-Criticism* and the Mutations of Western Marxism', *Historical Materialism*, 28 April 2018 (available online: https://bit.ly/3RARMh9; last accessed: 4 February 2023).

THREE

Reform

For some years now, advocates of a pragmatic, sensible left have staked their entitlement to alternate in overseeing the administration of the status quo on the abandonment of any lingering attachment to the lost object of revolution. As everybody knows, with political maturity comes mourning, a reconciliation with reality, fallibility and finitude, the abandonment of a debilitating melancholy. This familiar refrain, echoing across post- and counterrevolutionary times, weaves together a rhetoric of gradual improvement with a nervous allergy to upheavals.

Yet the present moment is perhaps unique in the pervasiveness of what we could justifiably term a melancholy of reform. The economic crisis of 2007–8 predictably morphed into an opportunity for the reiteration, intensification and entrenchment of the selfsame dynamics that occasioned it in the first place. Residual regions of non-commodified social life were again primed for stripping and colonization. In this context, the post-war Euro-Atlantic compact between big labour, big capital and big government has become an imaginary focal point for those still wedded, however nebulously, to the notion of social emancipation, while also nourishing the toxic imaginaries of far Rights eager to present nationalist redemption in the guise of ethnically exclusive redistribution.

The pining for the post-war boom and the *trente glorieuses*— 'when we still used to make things', when working classes formed communities, when even ardent capitalists recognized the notion that some domains of social life are *a priori* unmarketable—can

75

readily be registered in popular culture and radical thought alike, as well as in incoherent ideological constructs like Red Toryism or Blue Labour. When the corrosive criticisms and energetic struggles to which Fordism and the welfare state were subject aren't simply neglected, they are depicted as culprits of an ebbing of progressivism, irresponsible pretexts for capitalist revenge. Works whose ideological compass is set by post-war social democracy are likely to chastise 'the sixties' for making excessive demands and thus spoiling a good thing through a petulant inflation in needs and demands—not to mention supplanting redistribution with liberation, and crowding out the solidity of class with a swarm of other subjects.

Whatever the historical judgement on the causalities and limits of really-existing social democracy, it is evident that current struggles against 'austerity' and its strategies of accumulation by dispossession draw their impetus from the immediate need to defend elements of that post-war compromise. These fights at the point of reproduction—in schools and universities, hospitals and public transport, around benefits and pensions—revive a deeply felt common sense regarding social rights, one that often relies on that virtuous dialectic between labour and citizenship that long informed a dominant strain of progressive opinion. Education as a public good, universal free health provision at the point of use, the right to a living wage—so many demands which, having germinated in the workers' movements of the nineteenth century, attained, in the wake of post-war reconstruction, an unprecedented actuality in certain privileged and conflicted loci of capital accumulation (the 'Global North').

Is a new reformism a possible outlet of the struggles which are accompanying our long recession? In its dominant twentieth-century form, reformism retained for a long time its connection to the regulative ideal of social revolution. Fundamental transformation was to mature gradually, even imperceptibly, out of the socializing tendencies inherent to modern capitalism, channelled and checked by organized labour and its parties. Such a philosophy of history and action fared much better in some economic conjunctures than others. Until ruling class strategies and organic crisis undermined it, the curve of capitalist accumulation could plausibly resemble a cumulative movement towards emancipation.

Ever since the last, thwarted burst of genuine reformism in the guise of the socialization measures proposed by Rudolf Meidner in Sweden, the very notion of reform has been fundamentally evacuated of meaning or irrevocably traduced.[1] With the mutation of social democracy into social liberalism, reform has come to mean either the rollback of the outcomes of social democracy, in ominous expressions such as 'pension reform', or the (much rarer) proposal of initiatives to alleviate inequality or offset the more parlous effects of the profit motive, without, needless to say, in any way questioning it. Whereas the reformism born of the Second International was comforted by a teleology at once economic and ethical, those who may present themselves as reformist today are advocates not so much of a *telos* as a *katechon*—the Biblical notion, revived by Carl Schmitt, of that brake which restrains the Antichrist's dominion over the Earth. Whether to prevent its degeneration into barbarism or the bursting apart of its integument, or both, capital is to be embedded, fettered, civilized, made 'socially responsible', 'ethically conscious', 'green'.

Though it could be argued that high, Keynesian reformism also didn't fundamentally intervene on the basic parameters of capital as a social relation,[2] the 'reformism' of today's social liberals is immeasurably more cosmetic. Indeed, as we are reminded of daily, it can only present itself as a benevolent political manager of

---

1 See Robin Blackburn, 'A Visionary Pragmatist', *Counterpunch*, 22 December 2005 (available online: https://bit.ly/3Hy8KZ4; last accessed: 4 February 2023).
2 See Geoff Mann's superb study, *In the Long Run We Are All Dead: Keynesianism, Political Economy and Revolution* (London: Verso, 2017).

accumulation on the upswing of the business cycle and descends into impotent pantomime as soon as it is faced with a crisis.

This reformism without reforms can be contrasted with the proliferation of prescriptions for reform shorn of reformism; measures, be they political or economic, that propose radical alterations of current relations of power and production, without heralding a fundamental upheaval in the social structure, or an overall strategy for transformation. These range from fiscal interventions into the superpower of transnational finance (the Tobin tax) to political measures against new patterns of exploitation and welfare retrenchment (the guaranteed basic income), from proposals for audits of odious debt and policies of sovereign default (in the cases of Ecuador and Greece) to the socialization of pension funds. We can speak of reforms without reformism here in the sense that, notwithstanding declarations that another world is possible, the connection between such measures and a broader horizon of emancipatory social change remains pretty opaque. For most observers, neither the laws of motion of capital nor the collective biography of labouring classes provide the sense of a 'progressive' movement that a reformism could assume and channel into egalitarian and liberatory ends.

Historically, the reproach against reformism was the one that could also be levied theologically against the *katechon*: in restraining the devil you also postpone redemption, indefinitely. Concretely, this took the form of polemics against the *embourgeoisement* of proletarian forces, the biopolitical regimentation of the population under welfare systems, and the division and decomposition of class solidarities by a racialized and gendered stratification of privilege, in labour aristocracies co-opted both nationally and internationally. Just as waves of paranoid securitization have made many nostalgic for visions of classic liberalism, so the current waning of reformism may lead one to hanker after a social-democratic purgatory poised between the hell of capitalism unbound and a heaven forever unstormed. Even worse than being co-opted is becoming simply 'surplus to requirements'.

But capital's relation to its own limits, revealed in crisis and employed by ruling classes to intensify their control over the social product, makes the project of imposing social and political limits to capital appear not just strategically counter-productive, but increasingly utopian, as capital continues to try to emancipate itself even further from the working class. The victories of socialist reformism were always, in the words of Shelley's *A Philosophical View of Reform*, 'trophies of our difficult and incomplete victory, planted on our enemies' land'. But they were also functional to the reproduction of the class relation in ways beneficial to capitalist expansion. Perhaps the ebb of class struggle on a mass scale, with its not insignificant geopolitical context, has considerably eroded the collective intelligence of the capitalist class, no longer schooled by its conflicts with labour to strategize over the long term.[3] The increasing despair of even the most moderate of our contemporary Keynesians testifies to this.

The reformist hypothesis has long been abandoned by the political class, which can at the very best imagine palliative measures directed at restraining the further degeneration of the status quo, but never at actually presenting a plausible path for public welfare. Crisis management and diminishing returns have replaced the promise of growth and affluence. From the 1990s debt-fuelled euphoria that things have never been better to the depressive nostrum that things will never again be as good, in a little over a

---

3 One is reminded here of Guy Debord's bitter aperçu in *Comments on the Society of the Spectacle* (Malcolm Imrie trans.) (London: Verso, 1990), p. 20:

> We believe we know that in Greece history and democracy entered the world at the same time. We can prove that their disappearances have also been simultaneous. To this list of the triumphs of power we should, however, add one result which has proved negative: once the running of a state involves a permanent and massive shortage of historical knowledge, that state can no longer be led strategically.

decade. But the possibilities of reviving, even in a considerably altered guise, a classical social-democratic reformism, with its reliance on waged work as the crucial mediator of political rights, seem far-fetched. Incapable of thinking the structural determinants of unemployment, together with the principled desirability of a radical diminution of work and the elimination of the compulsion to labour to produce noxious commodities under noxious conditions, the response to the 2007–8 crisis and its protracted aftermath, including on much of the left, appears to imagine that 'a society founded on work', to quote the Italian constitution, remains the irremovable horizon of our social and economic life. A Fordist nostalgia impedes the elaboration of forms of antagonism pertinent to a situation in which the relation between class and labour, the place of industry, the overall dynamic of accumulation and the international division of labour have mutated drastically from the *trente glorieuses*, not least because of the intimate bonds between dominant conceptions of economic abundance and unsustainable regimes of accumulation grounded in fossil capital and unchecked extractivism.

It would be both myopic and moralistic to denounce the spontaneous philosophy of reformism that arises out of today's struggles. Though in the final analysis there is no need to believe in the sacrosanct character of waged labour to struggle against redundancies, nor in the benevolence of state institutions to oppose privatizations, it is also true that the ideologies articulated in and by the institutions at the sharp end of 'austerity' cannot but serve as the initial material from which to fashion a consequent antagonism. In this respect, the struggles in public sectors that have already been intensely subjected to forms of managerialism and competitive discipline, when not extensively privatized, will of necessity be inhabited by a contradictory reformism—at once upholding the 'values' embodied in such institutions and subjecting them to critique, asserting the significance of the 'public' as a domain of relative non-commodification while experiencing the parlous effects of governmental control. Or, defending our trophies, while never forgetting we are on the enemies' land.

The classical prospect of a teleological reformism, and the strategic council of caution and gradualism that accompanied it, alongside now faded or collapsed visions of progress and affluence, no longer persuade. Luxemburg's objection to Bernstein's notion that capitalism could adapt its way out of crisis by means of credit, the unification of capitals, and the spread of communication seems rather incontrovertible in our age of personal banking and credit default swaps. But the seemingly more sober idea of a reformist *katechon* taming capitalist barbarism, so widespread today, is not any more persuasive for that. It is not simply the case that the balance of forces speak against it; it appears to rely on the prospect of something like a capitalism without capitalism: a durable manner of embedding accumulation, neutralizing its tendencies to crisis, and arresting its intensifying exploitation of labour and nature, as well as its expulsion of ever greater swathes of the world into various forms of superfluity.

Contrary to idealist narratives of a mere failure of political will, or an inability of new generations to rein in their disruptive demands and desires, the most progressive framework for channelling and containing the pathologies born of the imperative to accumulate, social democracy, fell victim to the difficulty of maintaining its social compact in a global capitalist environment. Though the specific modes of the restoration of class power were in no way predetermined, it is hard to gainsay the conclusion that in a capitalist system a reformist compromise can only be maintained, temporarily, through a fortunate conjunction of the balance of class forces, the cycle of accumulation, and the specific political strategies of workers' movements and capitalist states. The recognition that capitalism can never be fully domesticated is both painful and important. As Fredric Jameson has noted: 'We must support social democracy because its inevitable failure constitutes the basic lesson, the fundamental pedagogy, of a genuine left.'[4]

If capitalism in the end can neither be bridled nor tamed, what hope for reformism? In its classic guise, none. Though the spectre of social democracy haunts every statement and demonstration against current class-based assaults on public services and social welfare, the historical conditions for social democracy are absent. But this is no reason either to repudiate recent movements, in keeping with a sterile purism, or to hold unrelentingly to the discriminating mantra, either revolution or reform. At this juncture, it may be more opportune to identify whether, in the absence of a reformist project, any structural reforms, growing out of and extending defensive struggles, could be formulated.

Almost half a century ago, André Gorz proposed this notion of structural (or non-reformist, or revolutionary) reform, as way of thinking a non-insurrectionary politics outside of the purview of social-democratic reformism. In *Strategy for Labor*, he asked a question that is still on our agenda: 'Is it possible *from within*—that is to say, without having previously destroyed capitalism—to impose anti-capitalist solutions which will not immediately be incorporated into and subordinated to the system?' Whereas a 'reformist reform is one which subordinates its objectives to the criteria of rationality and practicability of a given system', a 'not necessarily reformist reform is one which is conceived not in terms of what is possible within the framework of a given system and administration, but in view of what should be made possible in terms of human needs and demands.'[5] Though Gorz's talk of 'limiting mechanisms which will

---

4 Fredric Jameson, 'Lenin as a Political Thinker' in *Valences of the Dialectic* (London: Verso, 2009), p. 299.

5 André Gorz, *Strategy for Labor: A Radical Proposal* (Boston: Beacon Press, 1967), p. 6. Gorz's distinction has proven to be a useful framing for the contemporary politics of abolitionism. See Ruth Wilson Gilmore, *Abolition Geography: Essays Towards Liberation* (Brenna Bhandar and Alberto Toscano eds) (London: Verso, 2022), pp. 19–20 and 265–66.

restrict or dislocate the power of capital' may recall a view of reform as *katechon*, it is the political meaning of structural or non-reformist reforms that should hold our attention.

To discipline capital is to empower labour; a structural reform is 'by definition a reform implemented or controlled by those who demand it'. In other words, what is at stake is the possibility of political re-composition, re-skilling and emancipation that is channelled by reforms whose aim is not merely to restrain a degenerative process or to benefit from a progressive one, but to, at one and the same time, make concrete gains *within* capitalism which permit further movement *against* capitalism. Reformism as *katechon* depends on the pessimistic principle of a piecemeal resistance against an otherwise inevitable catastrophe in permanence; reformism as *telos* relies on the optimistic principle of piecemeal victories that go with the grain of history. A politics of non-reformist reform, or of reforms without reformism, relies instead on a practice, devoid of guarantees, of bringing together the antagonistic needs that grow out of defensive tactics, with a broader strategy of federating those struggles that constitute themselves into limits to capital. Gorz's distinction, between reformist and non-reformist reforms, could thus serve as a heuristic tool for an inventory of current measures, born of struggle, that move beyond the utopia of managing capital towards the investigation of means to counter and undermine its power.

FOUR

The Left

with Matteo Mandarini

Four decades ago, the Italian political thinker Mario Tronti wrote an article in the journal *Laboratorio politico* with the title 'Sinistra' (left).[1] In it, he confronted the crisis of this political identity or position as a dimension of the organic crisis of the 1970s—a crisis we know took on a kaleidoscope of forms: economic crisis, ideological crisis, legitimation crisis, etc. Tronti begins by setting out a genealogy: from the left's birth in the French Assembly of 1789, to its encounter with the workers' movement, which pushes it away from progressive-liberal origins to a radical-democratic high point.[2] Tronti's intervention—and the debate it initiated[3]—is of particular interest, in retrospect, because it took place at a moment when the outlines of neoliberal ascendancy began to be drawn across multiple political, economic, institutional and ideological axes, coming together in a new planetary rationality, a *nouvelle raison du monde.*[4]

The intervening time since this Italian debate on the fate of the left is, broadly speaking, that in which most of the thinkers that

---

1 Mario Tronti, 'Sinistra', *Laboratorio politico* 3 (1981): 132–47.

2 Tronti, 'Sinistra', p. 133.

3 See Massimo Cacciari et al., *Il concetto di sinistra* (Bompiani: Milano 1982).

4 Pierre Dardot and Christian Laval, *La nouvelle raison du monde: Essai sur la société néolibérale* (Paris: La Découverte, 2009); translated into English as *The New Way of the World: On Neoliberal Society* (Gregory Elliott trans.) (London: Verso, 2014).

Giorgio Cesarale surveys in his recent volume *A Sinistra* (On the left) produced the bulk of their analyses and theoretical contributions.[5] We might see this as a forty-year period bookended by crises and transitions. Equally, we may regard it as an interregnum in which crisis became—in the words of Dario Gentili—a mode of government.[6] More precisely, we might understand conjunctures of crisis as those where the orienting right/left political *topos* is unsettled, leaving all parties in a state of disorientation, bereft of the 'cognitive maps'—the situational representations of one's place within the political totality—without which strategic action is blind and powerless.[7] It is at this juncture that the option of abandoning the cardinal cartography of conflict polarized by the right/left dichotomy makes itself powerfully felt. Responding to Tronti, Massimo Cacciari argued against any attempt to reterritorialize politics once again on the right/left axis, now deemed no longer able to organize thought or practice: 'The axial representation of the political system is constitutively unable to account for critical situations, for the production of discontinuities in processes, or to describe intrinsically *unstable* situations.'[8]

That Cesarale felt the need to undertake this work of theoretical reconnoitring today may be regarded as a symptom of such an instability. Ours is a time when once again the *topoi* of the political map are undermined by processes that exceed them: seemingly ungovernable technological and economic shifts; the pathological

5 Giorgio Cesarale, *A Sinistra: Il pensiero critico dopo il 1989* (Bari: Laterza, 2019). Among the thinkers whom Cesarale engages with are Giorgio Agamben, Alain Badiou, Étienne Balibar, Luc Boltanski, Wendy Brown, Judith Butler, David Harvey, Ernesto Laclau, Jacques Rancière, Wolfgang Streeck, and Slavoj Žižek.

6 Dario Gentili, *Crisi come arte di governo* (Bologna: Quodlibet 2018).

7 On Jameson's concept of cognitive mapping, see Cesarale, *A Sinistra*, p. 118. See also Alberto Toscano and Jeff Kinkle, *Cartographies of the Absolute* (Winchester: Zero Books, 2015).

8 Massimo Cacciari, 'Sinisteritas' in *Il concetto di sinistra*, p. 10.

erosion of the class and elite alliances that allowed parliamentary liberalism to appear as the untranscendable horizon of the political; a globalization no longer imaginable as a force for progress and homogenization; nature breaking into history as anthropogenic change triggers phenomena—from global warming to pandemic contagion—which test our very parameters for political action.

Perhaps this also explains why *A Sinistra* does not try to define the term 'left'. In some ways, it is less concerned with identifying what left *is*—a task that still seemed both possible and urgent to Tronti in the early 1980s—than with presenting, as the title suggests, thinking *on* or *from* the left. While many of the thinkers under review by Cesarale are preoccupied with both the necessity and the urgency of *orientation* in our present, with that work of strategic cartography that is the task of theory, they are less concerned with, or capable of, infusing new meaning into the idea of the left. Perhaps this is because once the axis along which the specular pairing found its image breaks down, neither left nor right can find in their Other the rationale for their existence. What is it to think on the left when the agonistic space that structured classical political modernity is dis-oriented, when it loses its bearings in a kind of cognitive disaster? Etymologically, disaster betokens an ill-starred event, but we may also view it as a loss of that starry map that guides action. Recall Georg Lukács's melancholy musings from the *Theory of the Novel*: 'Happy are those ages when the starry sky is the map of all possible paths—ages whose paths are illuminated by the light of the stars.'[9] The closest we come to a definition of what it is to think on the left in *A Sinistra* is probably when Cesarale tells us that what links the various thinkers discussed in the book is the '*non*-necessity of order, its *contingency*, which impacts all contemporary power relations'.[10] Interestingly, Tronti—in passing—had mentioned a similar characteristic: 'To

---

9 Georg Lukács, *The Theory of the Novel* (London: Merlin, 1978), p. 29.
10 Cesarale, *A Sinistra*, p. *xii*.

say that you're on the left means saying that you're open to the new,'[11] which he explains as being linked to the fact that the right constitutes itself as the bulwark against change—as the defender of the 'established order'.

How can we revisit the supposedly foundational nexus between the left and the new, or the contingent, today? In what follows, we want, first, to explore how a modernist affinity of the left with radical change has been unsettled by the disjunction of a certain right from its historical association with conservatism or reaction. In a second moment, we want to think not so much about the way in which left theory thinks contingency or novelty, but how the very emergence of a left can itself be thought of as a kind of event or encounter, and how our current moment might see both the dis-aggregation of a certain left and the incipient possibility of new left formations, ones that may finally break the mould of that revolutionary encounter between radical liberal ideologues and plebeian labouring forces identified by Tronti and others.

If the acceptance of contingency and opening to the new is characteristic of the left, it is hard, after the last four decades, to see the neoliberal right as defender of the constituted order in any straightforward way. Was Thatcherism not a revolution? Not only economic and institutional, transforming the nature and function of the state to its very roots, but a cultural revolution, a transformation of subjectivities themselves and a displacement of the very space of political confrontation that allowed left and right mutually to define one another.[12] Many neoliberals—and public choice

---

11 Tronti, 'Sinistra', p. 134.

12 Stuart Hall, *The Hard Road to Renewal: Thatcherism and the Crisis of the Left* (London: Verso, 1988), especially the essay 'Gramsci and Us': 'Thatcherism's project was to transform the state in order to restructure society: to decentre, to displace, the whole post-war formation; to reverse the political culture which had formed the basis of the political settlement—the historic compromise between labour and capital—which had been in place from 1945 onwards' (p. 163).

theorists who shared many of the former's assumptions and aims[13]—view themselves as working 'with the grain of human nature—with human self-interest'.[14] They argue that the prerogatives of this interested nature can be advanced not by proposing classical Rightist policies, but by replacing inefficient alternating political policy choices with a more 'rational', calculable and hence putatively fair (non-partisan) set of representations by which society, state and economy can be ordered. Those embarking upon the 'pursuit of the disenchantment of politics by economics [...] by management'[15]—or 'politics without romance'[16]—argued that politics becomes dangerous if it enables the formation of collective will or decision making. For typically, politics—they contend—is driven by ideologically organized interests looking out for their own, indifferent to any 'figment of social justice'.[17] Democratic politics allow revanchist majorities to crush beleaguered minorities (which here ultimately denote propertied elites rather than

13 Robert Chernomas and Ian Hudson, *The Profit Doctrine: Economists of the Neoliberal Era* (London: Pluto, 2017), especially pp. 78–105; Matthew Flinders and Jim Buller, 'Depolitisation: Principles, Tactics and Tools', *British Politics* 1 (2006): 293–318; Noel Thompson, 'Hollowing Out the State: Public Choice Theory and the Critique of Keynesian Social Democracy', *Contemporary British History* 22(3) (2008): 355–82; Wang Hui, 'Depoliticized Politics, from East to West' (Christopher Connery trans.), *New Left Review* 41 (2006): 29–45.

14 See Daniel Stedman Jones, *Masters of the Universe: Hayek, Friedman, and the Birth of Neoliberal Politics* (Princeton, NJ: Princeton University Press, 2012), p. 130. James M. Buchanan goes as far as to call this 'the wisdom of centuries'. See his 'From Private Preference to Public Philosophy' in *The Economics of Politics*, IEA Readings 18 (Lancing: The Institute of Economic Affairs, 1978), p. 17.

15 William Davies, *The Limits of Neoliberalism* (London: Sage, 2014), pp. 4 and 212.

16 James M. Buchanan, 'Politics Without Romance' in *The Logical Foundations of Constitutional Liberty* (Indianapolis: Liberty Fund, 1999), pp. 45–59.

17 Friedrich Hayek, 'Whither Democracy?' in *New Studies in Philosophy, Politics, Economics, and the History of Ideas* (London: Routledge, 1990), p. 157.

oppressed groups). The effect of all of this was to shift the state away from being the arena where political struggle could be contended between organized, antagonistic parties representing different or even rival interests.[18]

For neoliberals and public choice theorists, the state should be restructured in accordance with the 'economic theory of politics', using 'ordinary economic assumptions about the 'utility-maximising behaviour of individuals',[19] which the state regulates by the spread of markets or market-like mechanisms throughout the social body. Independent central banks or auditing bodies with 'key performance indicators'—the striving for which supposedly forces (or 'nudges') public bodies (schools, hospitals and care providers, universities, etc.) to 'up their game' by competing for 'customers'— are portrayed as impartial, 'neutral' arbiters because governed by 'objective' measures of efficiency to which all are subject and which measure success 'objectively' through the pervasive power of proliferating ratings, auditing and bench-marking agencies.[20] This process of disenchantment of politics by economics allows for an agreed language and standard of measure to act as a conduit—to 'channel the self-serving behaviour of participants'[21]—towards optimal goals for society. Representation here does not relate to different interests. Instead, a 'construction of a global language'—of business and public policy—operates as 'a measurement framework' enabling a 'blanket economic audit'.[22] Hence, conflict is not

---

18 That this strategy of depoliticization was itself articulated in antagonistic, authoritarian, and populist forms (as Thatcherism itself made plainly evident, from the jingoist boost of the Falklands War to the crushing of the Miners' Strike) is of course testament to the way in which actually-existing neoliberalism always required supplementation by the ideologies and practices of the 'old' right—family and flag above all.

19 Buchanan, 'From Private Preference to Public Philosophy', pp. 89 and 17.

20 See Davies, *Limits* and Michael Power, *The Audit Society: Rituals of Verification* (Oxford: Oxford University Press, 1997).

21 Buchanan, 'From Private Preference to Public Philosophy', p. 17.

organized by contending parties; it is simply not computed for. Under this paradigm there exists no rival scale of 'values', of languages, of standpoints that might enter into conflict. Neoliberal restructuring conjured away the postulated collective as imputed source of legitimacy by disaggregating it into units that are ultimately even more abstract than the symbolized people of the state or nation.[23] What is this if not revolutionary? Does it not return us to Giacomo Leopardi's critique—which in some ways echoes Hegel's—of the French Revolution's hypostasis of Reason as the ordering principle of the new times?

> They did not see that the dominion of pure reason is one of despotism on a thousand counts, but I will summarize just one. Pure reason dispels illusion and fosters egoism. Egoism, shorn of illusions, extinguishes the nation's spirit, virtue, etc., and divides nations by head count, that is, into as many parts as there are individuals. *Divide et impera.* Such division of the multitude, especially of this kind and resulting from this cause, is more the twin than the mother of servitude.[24]

In short, openness to the new, to 'contingency', to a revolution transmuting the social order is not—is no longer—that which distinguishes the left. Indeed, how often does the left find itself in a defensive posture, one often characterized in terms of resistance? Resist privatization, resist the degradation of rights, defend the autonomy of institutions of learning from subordination to 'social goals' (framed, typically, by business needs), and so on.[25] The claim

---

22 Davies, *Limits*, p. 109.

23 See 'The People' in this volume, pp. 104–32.

24 Giacomo Leopardi, *Zibaldone di pensieri* (Milan: Mondadori, 1983), p. 131.

25 Pierre Bourdieu proposed that the contemporary political field was polarized between neoliberals subverting social (and welfare) relations in order to conserve capitalist relations of domination, on the one hand, and emancipatory social forces obliged to invent and construct a new social order

that the right only celebrates the sort of change in which 'everything needs to change so everything can remain the same', risks giving the left false succour. Capitalism is quite happy with 'the new', for it has yet to find something it cannot commodify and is always on the lookout for a new 'fix' (to borrow from David Harvey) for its limits and contradictions.

Perhaps awareness of the contingency of order is also no longer a sufficient demarcation point between the poles of the political spectrum. And in any case, can the right really be said to be unaware of contingency? Does it not rather display a considerable sensitivity to it? A feeling for contingency, for turnings and events, is most certainly present in thinkers of the Conservative Revolution—as manifested in the (oft quoted by Heidegger) line from Friedrich Hölderlin's poem 'Patmos': 'But where danger is, grows / the saving power also'.[26] Hayek would surely not disagree—his attack on planning and endorsement of 'catallaxy' was as much against the conceit that the contingent should be captured and constrained, as it was about wanting to resist overbearing central government. So, if neither openness, novelty, contingency, or even just an orientation towards change demarcate the left from the right, perhaps we're on the wrong track? Maybe an opening can be found if instead of abandoning these terms, we problematize and rearticulate them—namely by thinking of novelty and contingency not in terms of the ideological desires, political aims, or theoretical objects of the left, but in terms of its origins (in a sense resonating with Walter Benjamin's thinking of *Ursprung* but also Marx's *Ursprüngliche Akkumulation*)?

---

in the guise of conserving post-war forms of solidarity and security, on the other. See his article 'Neo-liberalism, the Utopia (Becoming a Reality) of Unlimited Exploitation' in *Acts of Resistance: Against the New Myths of Our Time* (London: Polity, 1998), pp. 94–105.

26 Most famously perhaps in *The Question Concerning Technology and Other Essays* (New York: Harper and Row, 1977), p. 28.

A first step might be to interrogate and perhaps bracket the genealogy, the tale of origins that not only tethers the political, and thus the left, to a very precise—ultimately European—history. This is a remarkably narrow narrative, historically speaking, soldering the left, on the one hand, to the conflict with absolutism signalled by 1789, and, on the other, to the moment the state began to lose its 'monopoly over politics'[27] in a narrow geographical location, the European 'core'—specifically Franco-Germany.[28] This genealogy is not wrong, but, as Tronti himself notes, it ties politics and hence the left to its bourgeois filiation. No surprise then, that as its plebeian energies come to be sapped or repressed (be it in the psychoanalytic or carceral sense), the left drifts back into the purview of a now rudderless bourgeois subjectivity—witness the dead ends of sundry Third Ways.

What is perhaps called for is an alternative, discontinuous genealogy, one that anchors the left not to the history of watchwords and names, but to practices and subjects who have borne them, taking up again the long history of the marginalized, the excluded (women, the racialized, subalterns, heretics . . .), the propertyless, the *popolo minuto*.[29] Here 'left' denotes those who are *outside* or who are *within* only to the extent that they are structurally *against*, who are *inside* but as the grist upon which power turns. This is the ambivalent moment of the negative, whether dialectical or not, of

---

27 Tronti, 'Sinistra', p. 132.

28 Tronti is not specific about where or when this happened, speaking merely of 'some decades ago', but one may assume that he is drawing upon analyses from the early decades of the twentieth century—such as those of Carl Schmitt—that situate this phenomenon temporally and geographically in Europe from the 1880s onwards, when the *potestas indirecta* of groupings such as mass parties, trade unions, etc., came to fragment the unity of state *auctoritas*.

29 A term denoting the urban poor in Italian communes between the thirteenth and fifteenth centuries, by contrast with the *popolo grasso*, the wealthy townsmen.

subjects who are sometimes subsumed, but only as subordinated moments whose subordination must be repeatedly renewed, in an infinite programme of integration; or who are sometimes expelled, but in their banishment are always circling and threatening the dominant order. And yet, one must beware of romanticism. Heidegger states that Nietzsche's breach with Wagner was inscribed from the start in the nature of the younger man's captivation by the older; whereas 'Wagner sought sheer upsurgence of the Dionysian upon which one might ride [...] Nietzsche sought to leash its force and give it form'.[30] The issue is not a celebration of the 'untamed' and of those who are always without. That would lead us to the defeatist (if for some comforting) conclusion that the left can never assume power; that wherever a hierarchy exists, the left cannot; that wherever an exclusive group establishes itself, it is by its very nature already on the side of the enemy. The risk of this position is to establish the untamed as the virtuous but ineffective—the 'good' by virtue of their futility, prophetic *because* disarmed.

While not gainsaying the critical importance of the encounter with the workers' movement—without which the global political history of the last 150 years remains indecipherable—it is imperative to reinsert it into *longue durée* and Blochian non-synchronicity of the 'tradition of the oppressed'. If the transformative encounter between progressive bourgeois or radical-liberal ideology, on the one hand, and the history- and value-making industrial masses, on the other, represents the event of the left's originary accumulation, so to speak, its modern synthesis, we also need to consider those left formations which escape, deflect or undermine the 1789 (or 1793) paradigm. Against a virtuous or progressive dialectic between bourgeoisie and workers' movement are those 'lefts', or those anti-systemic plebeian movements which would not necessarily identify

---

30 Martin Heidegger, *Nietzsche, Volume 1: The Will to Power as Art* (New York: Harper Collins, 1979), p. 88.

as 'left', which refused the 'encounter' with liberalism, parliamentarianism, natural law, the language of rights, or the state. From within the ranks of the workers' movement itself, one can think of Georges Sorel's steadfast anti-Jacobinism and radical suspicion of the nexus of parties, intellectuals, and elites—an illiberalism capable of inspiring both Benjamin's 'Critique of Violence' and sundry reactionary *dérives*. But, perhaps more pointedly, we can meditate on how a 'mis-encounter' or 'non-recognition' of the bourgeois filiation is a vital component of multiple non-European, anti-capitalist radicalisms.

An affirmation of the clash or missed encounter[31] between the 'bourgeois revolution' and anti-systemic movements from below is at the core, among others, of subaltern studies,[32] the Black radical tradition[33] and anti-colonial indigenous political philosophies,[34] as well as of Third World and anti-capitalist feminisms.[35] It is an open question whether a radical 'stretching' (to invoke Fanon's remarks on Marxism) of the notion of the 'left' to encompass, if not to synthesize, these insurgent currents requires rewriting or abandoning the framework of political modernity, especially as crystallized in

31 We are playing here with the notion of a *desencuentro* (between Latin American political history and Marxism) at the heart of José Arico's *Marx and Latin America* (David Broder trans.) (Leiden: Brill, 2012). See also Bruno Bosteels, *Marx and Freud in Latin America: Politics, Psychoanalysis, and Religion in Times of Terror* (London: Verso, 2012).

32 Ranajit Guha, *Elementary Aspects of Peasant Insurgency in Colonial India* (Durham, NC: Duke University Press, 1999).

33 Cedric J. Robinson, *Black Movements in America* (New York: Routledge, 1997).

34 Audra Simpson, 'The Ruse of Consent and the Anatomy of "Refusal": Cases from Indigenous North America and Australia', *Postcolonial Studies* 20(1) (2017): 18–33; Glen Sean Coulthard, *Red Skin, White Masks: Rejecting the Colonial Politics of Recognition* (Minneapolis, MN: University of Minnesota Press, 2014).

35 Brenna Bhandar and Rafeef Ziadah, *Revolutionary Feminisms: Conversations on Collective Action and Radical Thought* (London: Verso, 2020).

the short twentieth century.[36] Indeed, when it comes to these questions we may need to dwell in antinomy, recognizing, for instance, *both* that the Haitian Revolution was the intense apex of a transnational revolutionary phase, the 'coming-true' of the principles of the French revolution *and* that 'it never lived up to the schema by which revolution functions as a modernizing force catalysing technological advancement and the emergence of new, more sophisticated and efficient modes of capital accumulation'; that it was not a progressive act of emancipatory state making but the emergence of a 'profoundly entrenched counterinstitutional society', against state and capital.[37] What is evident is that thinking the left beyond the supposedly singular event, the originary political accumulation, of the meeting between the radical bourgeoisie (or even of 'philosophy', as in the young Marx) and the workers' movement, requires being open to the contingency, the novelty of the left's own formations. This is especially pertinent in our own moment of *polarization without orientation*, when the often-spectacular verbal or ideological antagonism that pervades an intensely mediated superstructure is not accompanied by a determination of political subjects with the collective consistency or cognitive coherence of classical lefts and rights. In the main, anti-communists without communism face off against social democrats bereft of social democracy's historical conditions of possibility. Meanwhile, and not least because of the lethal consequences of the 'metabolic rift' between capitalism and nature,

---

36 For an important effort to articulate an alternative political modernity open to a spectrum of subaltern and anti-colonial movements, see Massimiliano Tomba, *Insurgent Universality: An Alternative Legacy of Modernity* (Oxford: Oxford University Press, 2019).

37 Johnhenry Gonzalez, *Maroon Nation: A History of Revolutionary Haiti* (New Haven: Yale University Press, 2019), pp. 29–31. See also the review of Gonzalez's book, along with Julius S. Scott's *The Common Wind*, in David A. Bell, 'The Contagious Revolution', *The New York Review of Books*, 19 December 2019.

the philosophies of historical progress that made the '1789' encounter possible lie in tatters. Contrary to Joseph Stalin's entreaty at the 19th Congress of the PCUS in 1952 (the last he presided) for the communist movement to pick up the banners of the bourgeoisie, perhaps they are best left where we found them. Taking some distance from the icons and watchwords of the twentieth century, especially from the social democracy which is the real 'spectre' haunting our present (Green New Deal, etc.), might allow space for new encounters between political and organizational forms (which is, in a sense, to say *theory*) and collective movements and forms of life (that is, *practice*).

FIVE

Prometheanism

As the last echoes of a bullish neoliberalism fade, and we are asked to accustom ourselves, indefinitely, to austerity's hairshirts and the slow cancellation of the future,[1] it is worth reflecting on whether the attitudes of mind learnt over the past few decades retain within them the resources for effective opposition.

Whether the dominated think the thoughts of the dominant, or the dominant plunder and traduce those of the dominated, a certain affinity between pro- and anti-systemic ideologies is a common feature of discursive contests. Insofar as the forms of our social intercourse are recoded in our theories, this is no surprise. With the declaration that the age of extremes has drawn to a close, the spontaneous order celebrated by fervid marketeers found its counterpart in manifold resistances animated by those who felt that mutation was no longer to be mediated by orderly transition, that is by power and the state.

Though the genealogical threads that bind advocacy for and antagonism against the status quo are myriad, it would be difficult to underestimate the extent to which the sedimented effects of a long intellectual Cold War are still registered in the language of the left. Excoriations of the will, denunciations of the all-seeing state, grim warnings about the consequences of seeking mastery over nature and history: many of the main items in the dossier against 'the God

---

1 See Mark Fisher, *Ghosts of My Life: Writings on Depression, Hauntology and Lost Futures* (Winchester: Zero Books, 2014). Fisher takes the expression from Franco Berardi 'Bifo'.

that failed' are now intellectual reflexes, dependable and ubiquitous. Otherwise incompatible worldviews—authoritarian liberalism and subversive libertarianism—converge in descrying the political ills of a 'Promethean' desire to control collective destiny.[2]

The anti-Prometheanism of the right can mostly be taxed with hypocrisy: Burkean calls for cautious reform have rarely impeded policies that devastated the customs and commons of the oppressed; and the much-vaunted shrinking of the state has meant a hypertrophy of its repressive apparatus, a low-intensity war of the state against society on behalf of the markets.

The anti-Prometheanism of the left, instead, is most often marked by melancholy or illusion. Melancholy: the sense that emancipation is an object better mourned than desired; that the price of our principles is prohibitive. Illusion: the persuasion that the powerless can prevail over the powerful without concentrating and organizing their forces; the belief that the systems and capacities that now embody the dead labours of generations, and bear the traces of barbarisms past, can simply be abandoned, or destroyed, rather than, at least in part, appropriated. Such attitudes channel, more or less unwittingly, that crucial counter-revolutionary tenet, according to which political violence and catastrophe is a consequence of imposing abstract ideas (liberty, equality, fraternity . . .) upon complex and refractory human material.

---

2 I have explored other theoretical dimensions of the Promethean and its critique in 'In Praise of Prometheus', *Critical Horizons* 10(2) (2009): 241–56 (a critical review of Simon Critchley's *Infinitely Demanding*), and 'The Promethean Gap: Modernism, Machines and the Obsolescence of Man', *Modernism/modernity* 23(3) (2016): 593–609. For a capacious and incisive exploration of the contradictory globalization and racialization of the Prometheus myth, see Jared Hickman, *Black Prometheus: Race and Radicalism in the Age of Atlantic Slavery* (Oxford: Oxford University Press, 2016). The complex history of the reception, elaboration and refunctioning of the Prometheus myth in European culture is explored in Parts III–V of Hans Blumenberg, *Work on Myth* (Robert M. Wallace trans.) (Cambridge, MA: The MIT Press, 1985).

Prometheanism is a matter of knowledge, scale and purpose. The neoliberal Right has often based its apology for the omnipotence of markets, and the disastrous impossibility of planning, on the limits of our cognition. Refusing the point of view of, and on, totality, it likewise rejects modern conceptions of a political control over the scope and impact of decisions, namely in the figure of popular sovereignty, while abetting the most pernicious effects of the notion, dear to contemporary micro-sociologies, that scale is produced in specific locales and geographies. Consider the present power wielded by those formidable sites for the production of massive social and political effects, credit rating agencies: organizations entirely beyond the purview of any collective control whatever, before which the power of parliaments pales. As far as purpose is concerned, advocates of market supremacy will never tire of proposing some variant or other of the pre-established harmony between the amoral compulsion to accumulate come-what-may and human needs, conveniently reduced to a narrow repertoire of consumer reflexes and satisfactions. The abstract and inhuman domination of the form of value, commensurating all human activity under the imperative of surplus, is reputed to be compatible with the quaintest and most predictable of 'our values', to borrow from the numbing vocabulary of today's politicians.

But the enduring association of twentieth-century hecatombs with the state, science and socialism has meant that the most sincere and bitter farewells to Promethean ambitions originate with progressives despairing of progress, pleading, with fluctuating conviction, for the piecemeal. In these times of precautionary principles and unforeseen effects, it is second nature to perceive totalizing knowledge as a harbinger of catastrophe, especially when wedded to a vision of history or of humanity as endowed with a telos. Instead of querying the repeated suppressions of any popular control or democratic practice beyond the periodic acknowledgment of a pacified and passive citizenship, both collectivity and control have become targets of suspicion. Those who refuse to wean themselves off an enthusiasm for politics project insurrections without end, powers constituent or destituent but never durably constituted, interruptions that are never the prelude to less abject continuities.

But the forces and fractions that collude in perpetuating the current patterns of domination are equipped with their own organizing nodes and sorting centres, strategically sited in vast networks of complicity. If the reformist mirage of the state as the sole locus of social resistance against capital dies hard, so does the myth that, amid immensely asymmetric social warfare, the amorphous swarms of an uncoordinated multiplicity might somehow carry an advantage against the sclerotic infrastructure of power. Without control over the modalities of production and reproduction, cooperation is always cooperation for capital, and commonality merely a buffer, a positive externality socializing the costs of more direct forms of exploitation. Under the current management, anarchy will invariably be the false anarchy of the markets, and 'spontaneous' order will always tend to make it so that assets return to their rightful owners, as an American banker once quipped about the consequences of crisis.

In a world where mankind has truly become a geological agent, enjoying (and suffering) levels of logistical integration and technical capacity that would have made the shock workers of old blanch, we may wonder whether a diffuse anti-Promethean common sense expresses a dangerous disavowal rather than a hard-won wisdom. The problems of anti-Prometheanism are rendered particularly acute if we consider its promotion as the ideological complement to an ambient catastrophism. The irony of our present predicament is nicely conveyed by the conjunction between, on the one hand, a diffuse rhetoric that we must learn to live within our means, that progressivism and productivism must be abandoned, and, on the other, the proliferation of practices and proposals for planetary governance, regulation and control—though of the kind that are invariably delegated to the functionaries of an imposed consensus, those tasked with changing everything so that nothing will change (or, if the periodic sequence of COP fiascos is any indication, of changing nothing so that everything will change . . .). The widespread notion that we are acting under the pressure of time, goaded from expedient to emergency by time's arrow, reinforces, in subtly pernicious ways, the abdication of the very idea of collective control. On the side of established powers, it perpetuates a practice of crisis management, which from toothless moratoria and pollution credits to road maps and peace processes, is among the chief ingredients of catastrophe. Among the forces of opposition, when it doesn't council ecological compromises even more rotten than the historical compromises of old, it fosters anti-political survivalist fancies or misplaced hopes in the post-political virtues of 'civil society'.

Whether in economics, ecology or geopolitics, this numbing state of anxious and impotent mobilization serves to further entrench all the structures of power and accumulation that perpetuate and feed off crisis, demoralizing and depoliticizing a disenfranchised populace that can at best acquiesce to prohibitions, recycle and adapt. But a legitimate scorn for the modern Leviathan has meant that, within oppositional cultures, the sense of emergency has counselled either a desperate hope in the vivifying virtues of collapse or a retreat into enclaves intended to prefigure the very future they are powerless to bring about. But barbarism is an even less likely catalyst for emancipation than those parties and states whose own barbarities now shadow every call, however mild, for organization and centralism. And though small may occasionally be beautiful, defeat and insignificance aren't.

While the anti-Prometheanism of the Right conspicuously disavows the ballooning power of money, class and finance, together with the political concentration and centralization of this power in crucial pivots, that of the left reifies the historical context and content of control. Borrowing from the feebler end of the nineteenth-century critique of religion it rails against the State, Technology, Progress, and History, as if to repudiate them with the same rush of righteousness with which one could once deny God, and all, again, for the sake of an ill-defined freedom and singularity. But the problem is that in a world thoroughly hominized, in this inhospitable and even inhuman Anthropocene, a totalizing politics, capable of envisioning collective control, is an indefeasible requirement for emancipation. Withdrawal, secession and mere interruption—that is, revolts conceived not as inexorable moments but as ends in themselves—will barely register on the seismographs of domination.

A new Prometheus need not take the form of the 'Modern Prince', the party, if the latter is regarded as a commanding height and centre supervenient on any other council, association or organizational form. Collective control must involve the control and 'recall', to use that important slogan of delegation in communes and soviets, of its inevitable instances of centralization. But whether the horizon be one of radical reform or revolution, a systemic challenge cannot but take on, rather than blithely ignore, the risks of Prometheanism, outside of any forgetful apologia for state power or survivalist, primitivist mirage. Most significantly, the unreflective habit of associating power's corruption with certain seemingly intractable contents—the possibility of violence, the proliferation of bureaucracies, the mediation of machines—needs to give way to an engagement with the social forms and relations of control. Warning against the menace of Prometheanism at a time when the everyday experience of the immense majority is one of disorientation, powerlessness and opacity—that is, one where knowledge, scale and purpose are rent asunder—is simply to acquiesce in the exercise of power in the usual sites and by the usual agents, in that particular mix of anarchy and despotism that marks the rule of and for capital.

For better and for worse, the world we inhabit is an immense accretion of dominations, of the living labours of centuries mortified into the massive infrastructures that channel our daily lives, of natural processes at once subsumed and refractory—a vast accumulation of ends, endings and extinctions heterogeneous to original plans, when plans there were. In this regard, any politics today which is not merely a vapid accompaniment to dispossession and degradation, whether it claims the legacy of painstaking reform, desperate conservation or comprehensive revolution, cannot but confront the 'Promethean' problem of articulating action and knowledge in the perspective of totality, at multiple scales. To the extent that we regard Prometheus as 'the most eminent saint and martyr in the philosophical calendar' (as Marx wrote in his 1841 dissertation), the emblem of a refusal to serve abstract and alienated powers (God, State, Money, Capital), then Promethean should be a proud adjective for those who consider revolution not as a passionate attachment to some flash of negation or other, but as a process of undoing the abstract social forms that constrain and humiliate human capacities, along with the political agencies that enforce these constraints and humiliations.

SIX

The People

[E]ach time that the bourgeoisie has wished to subject a popular uprising to the constraint of a state apparatus a court has been set up.

—Michel Foucault, 'On Popular Justice'

In the secular work of the constitution and thus unification of the dominant bourgeois ideology, it is *juridical ideology that was determinant*, and *philosophy which was dominant*.

—Louis Althusser, *Être marxiste en philosophie*

So much of the contemporary discussion on the political valences of the people, including but not solely in terms of the vexed question of populism, has centred on the rhetorical and performative potentials harboured by this foundational category of political modernity.[1] Naming, more precisely *the name of the people*, returns ceaselessly as a leading concern when it is a question of thinking through the kinds of hegemony, antagonism or subjectivation that this figure of collectivity affords. This widespread theoretical preoccupation is also accompanied by the recognition, in varying registers, of how the political lemma 'people' is plagued by an ambivalence as foundational as it is ungrounding—between the legitimized, sovereign, normative *populus* or *peuple-nation*, on the

---

1 See Alain Badiou et al., *What is a People?* (New York: Columbia University Press, 2016).

one hand, and that accursed share or base stratum, the *plebs*, the *populace*, the insurgent mob, on the other.[2] It is of course precisely this ambivalence, the transmutation of base into high, remnant into ruler, nothing into all, that radical recoveries of the people have so often sought to leverage.

Yet efforts to capture or de-sediment the insurrectionary potentials of the popular often neglect the historical conditions of possibility of this 'return of the people' to the foreground of the radical imagination. In a Francophone European context, the so-called *pensée soixante-huit* ('68 thought), but also the various seams of insurrectionary and liberationist theorizing that traversed *les années rouges* (the red years), enjoyed a fraught relation to invocations of the people. Claims laid to the continuity of a revolutionary republican tradition, as well as to the heroism of the Resistance, meant that far from being subsumed by class—as some retrospective accounts seem to intimate—reference to the people was paramount in the political rhetoric of post-war French Communism (as it was, albeit for distinct reasons, in the Italian case). There is thus a considerable irony, even a kind of mirage, in a recovery of 'the people' nominally grounded in the impasses of Communist class politics and its attendant Marxist theoretical arsenal, as historical Communism often operated by giving primacy, in both rhetorical-electoral and practical-organizing registers, to the people *over* the class. The considerable affinity between post-Marxist theorizing of the 'populist hypothesis' and the politics of post-war Western European Communism—which never entirely practiced the workerism or economism targeted by post-Marxism—bears testimony to this. Rather than a horizon of proletarian self-abolition, or what these days may be termed 'communization', the dominant

---

2 See Gérard Bras, *Les voies du peuple: Éléments d'une histoire conceptuelle* (Paris: Amsterdam, 2018), as well as the entries 'People' (by Sandra Laugier) and 'People/Race/Nation' (by Marc Crépon, Barbara Cassin, Claudia Moatti), in Barbara Cassin (ed.), *Dictionary of Untranslatables: A Philosophical Lexicon* (Princeton, NJ: Princeton University Press, 2014), pp. 750–63.

ideological practice of Western European communism was that of the convergence (underwritten by a theory of class *alliances*) of the people-nation with the populace, *populus* with *plebs*, usually in the form of the subsumption or integration of the latter under the former, under the aegis of the *party of all the people*.

The left dissent from the Communist articulation of class, people and nation under the symbolic emblem of a resistant Republic can be seen to have taken, through the 1960s, 1970s and beyond, three distinct, if sometimes intersecting, trajectories.

The first, perhaps best crystallized in the kind of libertarian-populist Maoism of the Gauche prolétarienne (GP), involved the raising of a plebeian mass over a nationalized, gentrified 'people'. Inasmuch as it wished to retain a mobilizing reference to the Resistance (invoking a *nouvelle résistance*) and a horizon of the Party (or even, in deference to the Chinese Maoist model, the People's Army), this strand often ended up re-territorializing the plebeian moment (we will see below that Foucault intimated as much in his discussions of 'popular justice'). Some of the current return of the people to the forefront of radical theorizing, namely in the writings of Jacques Rancière, can be traced back to this moment, though now shorn of any symbolic or rhetorical nostalgia for revolutionary or resistant state forms, be they Chinese or French.

A second strand of critical responses to Communist national-populism, echoing the earlier efforts of left-communists and syndicalists in the face of the 'statization' of Marxism, emphasized the irreducibility of class antagonism to popular sovereignty. Mario Tronti formulated this position with trenchant lucidity in 'Il piano del capitale' (1963):

> *Workerism* [*operaismo*] can also be a real danger when waged industrial workers [*operai salariati*] are a stark minority among the labouring classes. But what of a process that tends to reduce every labourer to a worker?

True, in the name of not disavowing the old strategy, new *allies* are invented for the working class: the place left empty by the once-boundless masses of poor peasants is now filled by the refined elites of the new middle classes. Thus, the workers simultaneously free themselves both from any *sectarian* temptation and from any socialist *perspective*. The capitalists are well aware of this: the real generalisation of the condition of the working class can reassert the appearance of its formal withering away. This is the basis on which the *specificity* of workers' power is immediately absorbed into the *generic* concept of popular sovereignty: the political mediation here serves to allow the explosive content of the workers' productive force to function *peacefully* within the fine forms of the modern capitalist relation of production. So, at this level, when the *working class* politically refuses to become *the people*, it does not block but rather opens up the most direct path to socialist revolution.[3]

A third strand of opposition to the rhetoric and strategy of the national-popular came from an exaltation of groups, movements, masses, multiplicities acting beyond the nexus of party, class and people—what would retrospectively be captured in the limiting languages of *identity politics*, *social movements* and so on. *Plebeian*, *workerist* or *movementist* challenges to national-popular Communism—to summarize the three practical critiques all too hastily sketched out here—all struck against the *continuity*, dear to much mainstream twentieth-century communism, between the modern state and its foundations in bourgeois revolutions, on the one hand, and contemporary emancipatory insurgencies, on the other. The absence or critique of a popular referent in the left political theory and practice of the 'long 68' can be at least in part

---

3 Mario Tronti, *Workers and Capital* (David Broder trans.) (London: Verso, 2019), p. 57 (translation modified).

chalked up to this desire for rupture. Inasmuch as its concrete target was the national-popular horizon of European communism, the philosophical critique of the party form elaborated over this period was thus also, if implicitly, a critique of the category of the people understood as a category *immanent to the state*. The break with the national-popular continuum that a dominant strain of Communist thought drew between the bourgeois revolutions and a future communist transition took the form of an emphasis on the political centrality of collectives or groups that could not be subsumed under the aegis of party, people or state.

One interesting symptom within the philosophical field of this effort to theorize communist collectivity beyond the national-popular can be found in the peculiar convergence—given their underlying philosophical differend—of the critiques of the party form elaborated by Jean-Paul Sartre (in 1969) and Louis Althusser (in 1978) in response to interpellations by Rossana Rossanda and *il manifesto*. Sartre—whose own theory of the overcoming of seriality into the *group in fusion* and the ossification of the latter into institutional forms of party and state crucially transited through a critique of the history of the French Revolution and of its images of the people[4]—stressed the contradictory externality of mass (or group) and party. For the author of *Critique of Dialectical Reason*, the party developed

> as an ensemble of institutions, and therefore as a closed, static system, which has a tendency to sclerosis. This is why the party is always behind in relation to the fused mass, even when it tries to guide that mass: this is so because it tries to weaken it, to subordinate it, and may even reject it and deny any solidarity with it.[5]

---

4 See especially 'Sartre inédit', special issue, *Études sartriennes* 12 (2008), with Sartre's previously unpublished notes on the French Revolution, and the illuminating discussion in chap. 2 of Luca Basso, *Inventare il nuovo: Storia e politica in Jean-Paul Sartre* (Verona: Ombre Corte, 2016).
5 Jean-Paul Sartre, 'France: Masses, Spontaneity, Party' in *Between Existentialism*

And while 'the people', we might add, could serve to inflame and 'fuse' the mass, acting as a kind of affective condenser, it can also be a powerful operator of that delayed weakening or subordination.

Where Sartre, at Rossanda's prompting, moves towards a thinking of a dynamic externality of party and mass in the guise of 'dual power'—with neither being subsumed to the other—Althusser's reflections on 'finite Marxism' add to the externality of mass and party a claim about the necessary *externality* of the party to the state. They also stress how the state has expanded itself in a capillary, even molecular way, into dimensions neglected by a *restricted* conception of the political, which can only recognize the latter in the domains of government, party and (parliamentary) representation. Expanding Althusser's argument into the problematic terrain of 'the people', it is evident that the latter, especially as handled in the discourse of the Communist parties, would fall foursquare into the domain of the juridical ideology of politics that subtends the ideological state apparatus, especially in view of how the latter is capable of integrating and transforming elements that have not arisen from within the ambit of the state itself. As Althusser details, 'for bourgeois hegemony, it is *juridical ideology* which carries out this function of aggregation and synthesis. This is a process that must not be understood as completed but as contradictory, since the dominant ideology does not exist without the dominated ideology, which is in its turn marked by this domination.'[6] To which we may add that, within this juridical

---

and Marxism (J. Matthews trans.) (London: Verso, 2008[1969]), pp. 120–21.

6 Louis Althusser, 'Le marxisme comme théorie "finie" ' (1978) in *Solitude de Machiavel* (Y. Sintomer ed.) (Paris: P. U. F., 1998), p. 288. The version of this text recently translated into English ('Marxism as a Finite Theory' [Asad Haider trans.], *Viewpoint Magazine*, 14 December 2017 [available online: https://bit.ly/40GzbVl ; last accessed: 4 February 2023]), was based on Althusser's text published in French in the journal *Dialectiques*, which does not include the passage quoted here. On the Althusserian thesis according to which the dominant ideology is 'a specific universalization of the imaginary of the dominated', see Étienne Balibar, 'The Non-Contemporaneity of

ideology, 'the people' is, in its structuring ambivalence, a key oper-ator of the integration-transformation of the dominated ideology by the dominant one.

In what follows, I want to explore two philosophical episodes from this left critique of the national-popular imaginary of revol-utionary politics. My aim is to try and displace somewhat the con-temporary preoccupation with the radical potentialities of the *name* of the people, to think instead the twisted, halting dialectic of people and group, the better to explore what is at stake in the return of the people to the field of radical political theory after its seeming abandonment in the long '68 (with the qualified exception of what I've termed above the *plebeian* strand). I want to consider the relation between the people, the group and the law through a con-trastive reading of two indicative moments in the philosophical inquiry into the people that took place in France around May '68.

My first exhibit, critical for its exploration of the occlusion of the group by the people, is Louis Althusser's symptomatic reading of Jean-Jacques Rousseau from the mid-1960s. My second is Michel Foucault's encounter with the *gauchiste* practice of 'popular justice' in the early 1970s. As I hope to show, though the Althusser and Foucault problematize in distinct and divergent ways the nexus of people, group and law, jointly considered they can open lines of interrogation that remain pertinent to current debates, which often evade the question of the relation of the people to other collective formations while occluding its formative entanglement with the juridical.

___

Althusser' in E. Ann Kaplan and Michael Sprinker (eds), *The Althusserian Legacy* (New York: Verso, 1993), p. 13. On the question of juridical ideology in Althusser, see also Alberto Toscano, 'The Detour of Abstraction', *Diacritics*, special issue on Louis Althusser, 43(2) (2015): 68–90.

The Contract against the Group

The thwarted dialectic of people and group is among the themes emerging from Althusser's dense and sinuous symptomal analysis of the *Social Contract*, drawn from his École Normale lectures of the mid-1960s on Rousseau and his precursors, and published as an essay in the *Cahiers pour l'analyse*. For Althusser, the theoretical object 'social contract' functions through a series of *décalages* (lags, gaps, intervals) which are in turn masked, meaning disavowed and repressed. What I'm interested here is not so much the forensic dialectic of Althusser's reading, but his anatomizing of Rousseau's own presentation of that act whereby a people is or becomes a people, that 'first convention' of popular *unanimity* that provides the true foundation of society.[7] Among the foremost conditions for posing the problem of the social contract in terms of this founding act is the emergence of the category of *interest*, a category that can only arise in a generalized state of war which is in its turn the precondition for the socialization of human beings after the 'end of the forest' — that space without places which in Althusser's bravura reading proves central to Rousseau's political anthropology.[8] The rise of the *interested* individual, of the one who harbours 'goods' as one of his 'forces', shows that for Rousseau, when it comes to the 'dialectic of forced socialisation', *opposition comes first*. As Althusser comments:

---

7 Louis Althusser, 'Sur le "Contrat social"' (1967) in *Solitude de Machiavel*, p. 63; Louis Althusser, *Politics and History: Montesquieu, Rousseau, Hegel and Marx* (B. Brewster trans.) (London: New Left Books, 1972), p. 117. For a reading, at once incisive and comprehensive, that periodizes and contextualizes Althusser's Rousseau readings, see Panagiotis Sotiris, *A Philosophy for Communism: Rethinking Althusser* (Leiden: Brill, 2020), chap. 6.

8 On the forest as 'the truth of the state of nature', 'a space without places' and 'without *topos*', and ultimately 'the society of non-society', see the fascinating discussion in Louis Althusser, *Cours sur Rousseau: 1972* (Y. Vargas ed.) (Montreuil: Les Temps des Cerises, 2015), pp. 115–16, as well as his *Politique et Histoire, de Machiavel à Marx: Cours à l'École normale supérieure 1955–1972* (F. Matheron ed.) (Paris: Éditions du Seuil, 2006), pp. 116 and 311. See also Sotiris, *Philosophy for Communism*, pp. 99–101, 105–6, 113–22.

The objective content of particular interest links it directly
with the nature of the state of war. The category of particular interest immediately betrays its universal basis. One
particular interest can only exist as a function of the other
particular interests in rivalry, in universal competition
[. . .] particular interest is constituted by the universal
opposition which is the essence of the state of war. There
are not first individuals each with his own particular interest: opposition intervening subsequently as an accident.
The opposition is primary: it is the opposition that constitutes the individual as a particular individual.[9]

And the fruit of this opposition is alienation.

When the 'end of the forest' came and the whole earth came
under cultivation and was seized by its first occupiers or the
strong men who supplanted them, then there was no longer
any refuge for human liberty. Men were forced into the state
of war, i.e. into alienation. That is how they were trapped in
the very relations that their activity had produced: they
became the *men of those relations, alienated like them*,
dominated by their particular interests, powerless against
those relations and their effects, exposed at every moment
to the fatal contradiction of the state of war.[10]

This then generates the position of a problem, whose solution—the
contractual act whereby a people becomes a people[11]—constitutes

---

9 Althusser, *Politics and History*, pp. 120–21.
10 Althusser, *Politics and History*, p. 122.
11 In his 1965–66 ENS course, from which the 1967 essay is drawn, Althusser
refers to the social contract as 'the contract that is constitutive of the being
people of the people'. He continues, in a manner that complements the 'fear
of the group' that we will explore below:

It can be explicit or tacit, but it is always unanimous: opponents
exclude themselves from the city; and if they remain, they admit to
having contradicted their own vote. [The contract] constitutes the
internal essence of all the acts of the city . . . It constitutes a political
body among the contracting parties. It has an objective as well as a
moral reality. (Althusser, *Politique et Histoire*, pp. 349–50)

the first *décalage* in Rousseau's social contract. Yet how can a juridical device founded on individualized exchange, on the form of the legal person, render possible the emergence, indeed the self-founding of a sovereign collective?

For Althusser, Rousseau engages in a peculiar *détournement* of the operation whereby the philosophers of natural law had earlier adopted 'the juridical structure of the contract (an exchange between two parties)'. For the people to be inscribed in the contract, that contract must be exceptional, its structure *paradoxical*. The paradox stems from the fact, stressed by Rousseau himself, that all the contract's clauses are reduced to the *total alienation* of each associate member and his rights to the entire community. As Althusser underscores, Rousseau identifies a bifurcation in the very meaning of alienation, between *giving* and *selling* oneself—in other words between, on the one hand, a gratuitous act devoid of exchange and, on the other, a non-gratuitous if in its own regard paradoxical exchange, whose upshot is that *one cannot sell one's freedom* (a contract of enslavement in exchange for subsistence cannot serve as the model for a civil contract of political submission). And yet the birth of a free people seems to depend precisely on total alienation, that exceptional clause of the social contract. Having framed the state of war—in language that is not Rousseau's own—as a state of universal alienation, Althusser formulates the paradox as follows: 'the total alienation of the Social Contract is the solution to the problem posed by the state of universal alienation that defines the state of war, culminating in the crisis resolved by the Social Contract. *Total alienation is the solution to the state of total alienation.*'[12]

Beneath the paradox is a shift from the unconscious and involuntary alienation that governs the 'slavery' of the state of war (in which one gives one's freedom for nothing) to a conscious and voluntary (contractual) alienation. If the solution to alienation must be immanent to it, it involves a different *use*, a different *experience* of alienation; it must involve a change in its 'modality'. Alienation

---

12 Althusser, *Politics and History*, p. 127.

has, it could be argued, the structure of a *pharmakon*: 'This is what Rousseau very consciously states elsewhere when he says that the remedy of the evil must be sought in its very excess. In a word, a forced total alienation must be turned into a free total alienation.'[13]

But can a *free alienation* be? For this solution not to stand as a *mere* paradox, a *décalage* must obtain. To elucidate this, Althusser asks his readers to consider the form of this most peculiar contract. We have two 'recipient parties' (RP),[14] RP1 (the individual) and RP2 (the community). If RP1 gives everything (including his *freedom*), what is exchanged by RP2? To answer this, we must ask: what is the community? Well, it is the association of individuals and their 'forces' (including their goods, their interests). *But this association is meant to be the product of the contract itself.* The temporality of all other contracts, according to Althusser's Rousseau, presupposes that its parties are pre-existing, pre-formed, individuated, while here the existence of one of the parties is conditional on the completion of the contract.

In a word, here is the difficulty: in every contract the two Recipient Parties exist prior to and externally to the act of the contract. In Rousseau's Social Contract, only the RP1 conforms to these conditions. The RP2 on the contrary, escapes them. It does not exist before the contract for a very good reason: it is itself the product of the contract. Hence the paradox of the Social Contract is to bring together two RPs, one of which exists both prior to and externally to the contract, while the other does not, since it is the product of the contract itself, or better: its object, its end. It is in this difference in theoretical status between the two Recipient Parties to the contract that we inscribe: Discrepancy [*Décalage*] *I*.[15]

---

13 Althusser, *Politics and History*, p. 128.
14 *Partie prénante* can also be translated as 'stakeholder'.
15 Althusser, *Politics and History*, p. 129.

It is not that Rousseau ignores this paradox, rather that he masks and disavows it in the seeming recognition of its paradoxical character. Thus, when he says, in *Émile*, that the people only enters into contracts with itself (as though RP2 were tautologically contracting with RP2), or, in *The Social Contract*, that 'each individual is, so to speak, contracting with himself' (as though RP1 were tautologically contracting with RP1), he betrays (that is to say both avows and masks) the fact that the difference and *décalage* between RP1 and RP2, between the isolated individual 'in the form of isolation' and the individual 'in the form of community', is operated through the category of *individuality*. It is this category that oversees the suture or compression of the *time lag* between the isolated individual and the community in the *atemporal* act of the contract.[16] The *décalage*, the gap or lag, transpires in the very lexical moves through which Rousseau masks or annuls it, namely by referring to RP1 with the name of RP2 (the people contracts with itself) or RP2 with the name of RP1 (the individual enters into a contract with himself). As Althusser sums up: 'Rousseau's contract does not correspond to its concept. In fact, his Social Contract is not a contract but an act of constitution of the Second RP for a possible contract, which is thus no longer the primordial contract.'[17] From a different angle, we can also say that this is a contract without parties in which an exchange nevertheless appears.

But the key moment for our purposes in Althusser's decryption of the *Social Contract* is to be found in his exploration of another *décalage*, the one operative between *particular* and *general* interests (and wills). Althusser dwells on Rousseau's 'dream' in the dedication to the second *Discourse*, his wish that People and Sovereign be *the same person*, and comments that:

16 The aporetic time of the people will require Rousseau's 'forward flight into ideology'. See *Politics and History*, p. 155. It is also, more specifically, what requires the twin intervention of religion and the (external) legislator to ensure the institution of a people. Althusser, *Politique et Histoire*, p. 353.

17 Althusser, *Politics and History*, p. 131.

This dream is realized by the Social Contract, which gives Sovereignty to the assembled people. The act of legislation is indeed never anything but the Social Contract combined, repeated, and reactivated at each 'moment'. The primordial 'moment' which 'has made a people a people' is not a historical 'moment', it is the always contemporary primordial 'moment' which relives in each of the acts of the Sovereign, in each of his legislative decisions, the expression of the general will. But the general will only exists because its object *exists*: the general interest.[18]

At the heart of Althusser's investigation of the passage between particular and general interest—or better, of the fact that the particular interest is both the foundation and the contrary of the general interest—is the way in which it depends, like the *décalage* (or short circuit) between RP1 and RP2, on *the interdiction on any group formation*.

The individual can only rise to the collective so long as he is not ensnared in the group, namely if the immanent identification of citizen and people is not inhibited or deflected by other collective formations or investments. Althusser dwells on the passage from the *Social Contract* (Book II, Section III) where Rousseau observes that if '*citizens had no communication with one another*', then 'small differences' would always result in the general will, and deliberation would not stray from its correct path. Here lies the crux of Althusser's critical exploration of the figure of the people across the lags and gaps of the *Social Contract*. For Rousseau's 'people' to constitute itself through that founding act that is the social contract, and to reproduce itself in its deliberations as the general will, 'there must be no "factions" or "partial associations" in the State, above all no dominant partial association, for then what is "declared" will no

---

18 Althusser, *Politics and History*, pp. 147–48.

longer be the general will but a partial will, if not quite simply a particular will: that of the dominant group.'[19] What's more, there is an

> *absolute condition* for Rousseau: that the general will really is interrogated in its seat, in each isolated individual, and not in some or other group of men united by interests which they have in common, but which are still *particular* with respect to the general interest. If the general will is to declare itself, *it is thus essential to silence (suppress) all groups, orders, classes, parties, etc.* Once groups form in the State, the general will begins to grow silent and eventually becomes completely mute.[20]

Althusser's forensic investigation pushes further and finds in the homonym 'particular interest' another symptomatic *décalage*, which shows that Rousseau both recognizes and masks, which is to say disavows, the distinction between *groups* and *individuals*. As Althusser details:

> We have a total contradiction: particular interest is the essence of the general interest, but it is also the obstacle to it; now, the whole secret of this contradiction lies in a 'play' on words in which Rousseau calls the particular interest of each individual in isolation and the particular interest of social groups by the same name. This second interest, which is a group, class or party interest, not the interest of each individual, is only called particular with respect to the general interest. It is a 'play' on words to call it particular in the way the interest of the isolated individual is called particular. This 'play' on words is once again the index of a Discrepancy [*Décalage*]: a difference in theoretical status of the isolated individual and social groups—this difference being the object of a denegation inscribed in the

19 Althusser, *Politics and History*, p. 150.
20 Althusser, *Politics and History*.

ordinary use of the concept of *particular interest*. This denegation is inscribed in so many words in his declaration of impotence: human groups must not exist in the State. A declaration of impotence, for if they *must not* exist, that is because they *do* exist.[21]

The group is thus the *point of the real*, the disavowed obstacle, within Rousseau's construction of the people. The echoing or specular 'myths' of the individual and general interest, have their condition of (im)possibility in the repudiation or disavowal of the existence of groups (orders, estates, classes, etc.).[22] These political and juridical myths reveal the functioning of a (bourgeois) ideology that can present class interests to particulars (the dominated) in the guise of the general interest.[23] This disavowal or denegation is for Althusser no longer simply theoretical, it is practical: 'to denegate the existence of human groups (orders, classes) is to suppress their existence practically.'[24]

---

21 Althusser, *Politics and History*, pp. 151–52. This 'fear of the group' was also operative in the ideological battles within the French Revolution, for instance in the Abbé Sieyès' identification of a formidable risk in the possibility that political agents would call upon (fractions of) the people and undermine the unity of the Nation. See Bras, *Les voies du peuple*, p. 71.

22 Conversely, in the register, at once concrete and contingent, of history, not every group of men 'is destined at every moment to the vocation and destiny of becoming people, to receive laws'. Althusser, *Politique et Histoire*, p. 352. Althusser notes how, for Rousseau, Russia is a case of the premature institution of a people, while both Corsica and Poland are ripe for receiving laws, and thus for *becoming peoples*.

23 In his 1965–66 ENS, Althusser presents Rousseau's account of the origins of the contract in the second *Discourse* in terms whose classed nature is rather 'unmasked': 'The rich elaborated a well-pondered [*très réfléchi*] project: to demand from those who are subjected [*soumis*] and who threaten them that they transform their servitude into juridical alienation in order to preserve their liberties. The contract is thus born from an objective misunderstanding regarding the proposition of the rich, and thus from a differential reason'. *Politique et Histoire*, p. 325.

24 Althusser, *Politics and History*, p. 154. For an interpretation of the figure

The People against the Law

Towards the end of the 'red years' of French philosophy, Michel Foucault—responding to the 1978–79 Iranian revolution as a break with a European (and Marxist or *dialectical*) model of revolutionary action—would identify the vanishing of groups in the apotheosis of the general will as a kind of political epiphany experienced at first hand on the streets of Tehran.

> Among the things that characterize this revolutionary event, there is the fact that it has brought out—and few peoples in history have had this—an absolutely collective will. The collective will is a political myth with which jurists and philosophers try to analyze or to justify institutions, etc. It's a theoretical tool: nobody has ever seen the 'collective will' and, personally, I thought that the collective will was like God, like the soul, something one would never encounter. I don't know whether you agree with me, but we met, in Tehran and throughout Iran, the collective will of a people. Well, you have to salute it, it doesn't happen every day.[25]

Pressed by his interviewer to reflect on the resonances between the mass unanimity witnessed in the Iranian streets and the vicissitudes of the Chinese Cultural Revolution, Foucault further specified the importance, for him, of the *undivided* character of the Iranian people in revolt, vis-à-vis the Maoist masses:

---

of the people Rousseau that tries to counter Althusser's ideological reading for the sake of an emphasis the emancipatory rhetorical appropriations of 'the people', see Bras, *Les voies du peuple*, p. 34ff. Transposing Althusser's critique of Rousseau to the present, we could hazard the following thesis: *populism is an individualism.*

25 Michel Foucault, 'Iran: The Spirit of a World Without Spirit' in *Politics, Philosophy, Culture: Interviews 1977–1984* (Lawrence D. Kritzman ed., Alan Sheridan et al. trans.) (London: Routledge, 1988[1979]), p. 215.

the Cultural Revolution was certainly presented as a struggle between certain elements of the population and certain others, certain elements in the party and certain others, or between the population and the party, etc. Now what struck me in Iran is that there is no struggle between different elements. What gives it such beauty, and at the same time such gravity, is that there is only one confrontation: between the entire people and the state threatening it with its weapons and police. One didn't have to go to extremes, one found them there at once, on the one side, the entire will of the people, on the other the machine guns.[26]

I introduce this quote by way of contrast with the text I wish to focus on, namely Foucault's 1972 discussion with the Maoists of the Gauche prolétarienne on 'popular justice'. Though their registers and occasions vary, Foucault's political interventions of the 1970s allow us to discern the figure of the people as an operator of division and indivision, but also to perceive how Foucault, albeit in a very different vein than Althusser, could also thematize the ambivalent nexus of the people and the law, as well as the need to undermine our juridical illusions by attending to the antagonistic politics of groups and classes. The 'popular' moment in Foucault also reveals the presence of what we could term an *anti-strategic* moment amid his inquiries into the meshworks of power and the tactics of resistance—what he would identify in the figure of the *plebs* as a kind of 'limit' of the field of power.[27]

---

26 Foucault, 'Iran', p. 216.
27 Michel Foucault, 'Powers and Strategies' (1977) in *Power/Knowledge: Selected Interviews and Other Writings 1972–1977* (Colin Gordon ed.) (New York: Pantheon Books, 1980), pp. 137–38 (the text is an interview with the editorial collective of *Les révoltes logiques*, including Jacques Rancière):

The plebs is no doubt not a real sociological entity. But there is indeed always something in the social body, in classes, groups and individuals themselves which in some sense escapes relations of

The occasion for Foucault's debate with *les Maos* of the GP, first published in a special 1972 issue of *Les Temps modernes* on 'New fascism, new democracy', was a sequence of largely abortive or thwarted efforts to institute 'people's courts' against the impunity of bosses, cops and landowners—beginning with a widely publicized tribunal in Lens, in which Jean-Paul Sartre participated, that sought to inquire into the deaths of sixteen miners in a methane explosion.[28] In 1971, the GP had been involved in a project to establish a people's court against the police, which is explicitly indicated as the context for the discussion in a brief note at the beginning of the text.[29]

---

power, something which is by no means a more or less docile or reactive primal matter, but rather a centrifugal movement, an inverse energy, a discharge. There is certainly no such thing as 'the' plebs; rather there is, as it were, a certain plebeian quality or aspect [*de la plèbe*]. There is plebs in bodies, in souls, in individuals, in the proletariat, in the bourgeoisie, but everywhere in a diversity of forms and extensions, of energies and irreducibilities. This measure of plebs is not so much what stands outside relations of power as their limit, their underside, their counter-stroke, that which responds to every advance of power by a movement of disengagement. Hence it forms the motivation for every new development of networks of power.

The interviewers are in many ways pushing Foucault to distinguish himself from the use of the *plebs* by the *nouveaux philosophes*. See also Peter Dews, 'The Nouvelle Philosophie and Foucault', *Economy and Society* 8(2) (1979): 127–71.

28 For a rich account of this sequence see David Macey, 'The Militant Philosopher' in *The Lives of Michel Foucault* (London: Verso, 2019). As Macey notes, the Lens tribunal gave inspiration to Foucault's partner Daniel Defert to establish the Groupe d'informations sur les prisons (GIP). He also sees Foucault's discussion with the '*les Maos*' as haunted by the shadow of a clandestine tribunal the GP instituted against one of their very few Black members, Moussa Fofana.

29 Foucault, 'On Popular Justice: A Discussion with Maoists' in *Power/Knowledge*, p. 1. It is not insignificant that in the issue of *Les Temps modernes* in which it was first published, this text was preceded by a 70-page essay of André Glucksmann on old and new fascisms, in which the police and

As has been noted,[30] this discussion is rife with mutual incomprehension—the 'Maos' (especially the GP leader Pierre Victor, aka Benny Lévy) maintaining as their lodestar the articulation of mass insurgency and the People's Army in the Cultural Revolution, Foucault evading the strictures of 'Mao Zedong thought' to trace a genealogy of popular justice back to the French Revolution and further into the Middle Ages. And yet the misunderstanding is productive, as it obliges Foucault to speculate on the practical, political possibilities of those 'popular illegalisms' that so much of his work of the 1970s would explore[31]—from the inquiries of the Groupe d'information sur les prisons[32] to his Collège de France course on *The Punitive Society*, from his oblique engagement with E. P. Thompson[33] to his striking portraits of 'infamous men'. What's more, bending, or rather *breaking* the stick,[34] is that while his GP

---

the Interior Ministry were presented as the avant-garde of a counter-revolutionary process of 'fascisation'. See André Glucksmann, 'Fascismes: L'ancien et le nouveau', *Les Temps modernes* 310 (1972): 266–334.

30 See Macey, *The Lives of Michel Foucault*.

31 For an illuminating treatment of Foucault's thinking about illegalism in the 1970s, see Alex J. Feldman, 'Foucault's concept of illegalism', *European Journal of Philosophy* 28(2) (2020): 445–62.

32 See Alberto Toscano, 'The Intolerable-Inquiry: The Documents of the Groupe d'information sur les prisons', *Viewpoint Magazine*, 25 September 2013 (available online: https://bit.ly/3I8lY0h; last accessed: 5 February 2023).

33 Bernard Harcourt, 'Course Context' in Michel Foucault, *The Punitive Society: Lectures at the Collège de France 1972–1973* (Bernard Harcourt and Alessandro Fontana eds, Graham Burchell trans.) (New York: Palgrave Macmillan, 2015).

34 I am referring to this moment in the exchange with Victor/Lévy (Foucault, 'On Popular Justice' in *Power/Knowledge*, p. 32):

FOUCAULT: I had got the impression that you thought that only the existence of a state apparatus could change a desire for retribution into an act of popular justice.

VICTOR: At the second stage. At the first stage of the ideological revolution I'm in favour of looting, I'm in favour of "excesses". The

interlocutors are pushing in a (revolutionary) statist direction, Foucault takes the occasion to advance some of his most radical propositions about the need to have done with the entire juridical sphere, and he does so with reference to a certain figure of the people.

From the word go, Foucault questions the idea that one should presuppose the form of the court in thinking through the problem of popular justice. His point is indissolubly methodological and political: to frame popular justice through the court form is to prejudice one's understanding of this political phenomenon, and to channel mass acts of resistance into an institutional apparatus which, as he will sketch out, does not have a popular origin. On the contrary, his hypothesis is 'not so much that the court is the natural expression of popular justice, but rather that its historical function is to ensnare it, to control it and to strangle it, by re-inscribing it within institutions which are typical of a state apparatus.'[35] In an implicit disavowal of any linear vindication of popular sovereignty running from Jacobinism through the Resistance all the way to French Maoism, Foucault chooses to emphasize the passage from popular violence to the Terror in the French Revolution as the site of a capture and neutralization of popular justice by a classed juridical apparatus. With his characteristic penchant for provocation, Foucault presents a *plaidoyer* for the September Massacres of 1792 as 'at least an approximation to an act of popular justice; a response to oppression, strategically effective and politically necessary.'[36] Manifesting an anti-Jacobinism that will also colour

---

stick must be bent in the other direction, and the world cannot be turned upside down without breaking eggs . . .

FOUCAULT: Above all it is essential that the stick be broken . . .

35 Foucault, 'On Popular Justice', p. 1.

36 Foucault, 'On Popular Justice', pp. 1–2. The September Massacres will reappear in Foucault's work in the context of his analysis of the genesis of the 'political monster' in conjunction with the establishment of the penal system

Foucault's later sympathy for the *nouveau philosophes* and his appreciation of François Furet, the Terror emerges by way of contrast with these preventive acts of plebeian vengeance as a usurpation of popular energies and a crystallization of state power.

But, in a genealogical gesture familiar from Foucault's other historical anatomies of power, this rise of the judicial state and its mechanisms of power is precisely a relational emergence and not merely a vertical imposition of domination. In this case, it is men from the Paris Commune who, in response to the 'wild' executions, set up courts with judges behind a *table*—that symbol and spatial technology of the 'Third Party'—establishing truths, eliciting confessions and deliberating upon what is 'just'. On this stage, we see at work the three ingredients of a state judicial apparatus which 'ex-appropriate', to use a Derridean formulation, the very process of popular justice: '(i) a "third element"; (ii) reference to an idea, a form, a universal rule of justice; (iii) decisions with power of enforcement. It is these three characteristics of the courts which are represented in anecdotal fashion by the table, in our society.'[37] Looking over this small revolutionary stage of the law, Foucault poses a question that his Maoist interlocutors will ultimately elude:

> Can we not see the embryonic, albeit fragile form of a state apparatus reappearing here? The possibility of class oppression? Is not the setting up of a neutral institution standing between the people and its enemies, capable of establishing the dividing line between the true and the false, the guilty and the innocent, the just and the unjust, is this not a way of resisting popular justice? A way of disarming it in the struggle it is conducting in reality in favour of an arbitration in the realm of the ideal? This is why I am

in the late eighteenth century. Michel Foucault, *Abnormal: Lectures at the Collège de France 1974–1975* (Valerio Marchetti and Antonella Salomoni eds, Graham Burchell trans.) (London: Verso, 2003), pp. 99–100.

37 Foucault, 'On Popular Justice', p. 11.

wondering whether the court is not a form of popular justice but rather its first deformation.[38]

While not primarily concerned here with a juridical illusion, but rather with a juridical *dispositif*, Foucault's debate with his friends in the Gauche prolétarienne has an important affinity with Althusser's philosophical inquiry into the constitution of the people. In both cases—one organized by the form of the *contract*, the other by the form of the *court*—we see the nexus of the people and the law operate to control the risk posed by the actions of groups or collectives that evade or reject a juridical framing.

This nexus of people and law serves both to disavow and to intervene upon class antagonisms. Again, Foucault details this process by reference to the conflictual dynamics of the French revolution, and namely to the classed character of the emergence of the court as an instance of impartiality. As he observes, employing a language—that of *ideology*—which resonates with Althusser's, and which he would soon jettison:

> the people's court, as it functioned during the Revolution, did tend to act as a 'neutral institution' and, moreover, it had a very precise social basis: it represented a social group which stood between the bourgeoisie in power and the common people of Paris (*la plèbe*); this was a petty bourgeoisie composed of small property owners, tradesmen, artisans. This group took up a position as intermediary, and organised a court which functioned as a mediator; in doing this it drew on an ideology which was up to a certain point the ideology of the dominant class, which determined what it was 'right' or 'not right' to do or to be.[39]

---

38 Foucault, 'On Popular Justice', p. 2.
39 Foucault, 'On Popular Justice', p. 3. Also, p. 22: 'Penal law was not created by the common people, nor by the peasantry, nor by the proletariat, but entirely by the bourgeoisie as an important tactical weapon in this system of divisions which they wished to introduce.'

From this revolutionary scene, Foucault will step back to present a compressed history of the state judicial apparatus, delineating the passage in the Middle Ages from archaic systems of arbitration to modern institutions of judgement—a passage generated, first, by the 'fiscalisation of the judicial system', binding the legal power of judges to property (and varieties of tax farming), and second, by the 'increasing link between the judicial system and armed force'. In response to the commoners' uprisings of the fourteenth century, the fiscalization and militarization of legal processes would undergo powerful pressures towards centralization, generating an 'embryonic state judicial apparatus'.[40] What this abridged judicial history also allows us to perceive, in the chronicling of the dispossession of and war against the poor *through the law*, is that popular justice is embedded in a centuries-old 'anti-judicial' tradition. Such a tradition perceives 'in the judicial system a state apparatus, representative of public authority, and instrument of class power', and often has recourse to rituals of retribution drawing from archaic habits of 'private war'—among which Foucault pointedly mentions the thread linking the 'old Germanic custom to put the head of an enemy on a stake, for public viewing' to the parading of heads on pikes around the Bastille.[41]

Now, where, according to Althusser, the philosophical form of the contract served in Rousseau to displace and deny the reality of groups, in Foucault's account the legal form (and spatial technology) of the court functions to divide the people in the very process of presenting itself as neutral (as a 'third' party acting on behalf of the People and the Law). With an eye on the politics of incarceration in the present, and his own activist experiences with the GIP, Foucault declares that: 'The penal system has had the function of introducing a certain number of contradictions among the masses, and one major contradiction, namely the following: to

---

40 Foucault, 'On Popular Justice', pp. 5–6.
41 Foucault, 'On Popular Justice', p. 6.

create mutual antagonism between the proletarianised common people and the non-proletarianised common people.'[42] Advancing an historical hypothesis that will be fleshed out at great length in *The Punitive Society* and *Discipline and Punish*—namely in the analysis of the relation between the accumulation of capital and the 'accumulation of men', the articulation of infra-power and surplus-value[43]—Foucault presents the penal system both as an operator of proletarianization, 'fixing' the dispossessed to their workplaces, and as an apparatus to manage the remnants and the deserters of this 'making of the working class'—'the most mobile, the most excitable, the "violent" elements among the common people'.[44]

But the penal system also strives ideologically to regiment the proletarianized into a moral worldview that separates them from the rabble, the *Lumpen*, the mob, subjectivating them as other than the non-proletarianized. 'For the bourgeoisie it is a matter of imposing on the proletariat, by means of penal legislation, of prisons, but also of newspapers, of "literature", certain allegedly universal moral categories which function as an ideological barrier between them and the non-proletarianised people.'[45] Whether in regimenting the proletariat or in hounding the non- or de-proletarianized, the state judicial system in its long historical arc is above all an 'anti-seditious system' that operates by fostering class antagonisms among the common people.[46] Foucault, going against

42 Foucault, 'On Popular Justice', p. 14.

43 See Alberto Toscano, 'What is Capitalist Power? Reflections on *Truth and Juridical Forms*' in Martina Tazzioli, Sophie Fuggle and Yari Lanci (eds), *Foucault and the History of Our Present* (Basingstoke: Palgrave Macmillan, 2014).

44 Foucault, 'On Popular Justice', *Power/Knowledge*, p. 15.

45 Foucault, 'On Popular Justice', p. 15. It is difficult not to hear a denunciation here of the way in which post-war European Communist parties, drawing on nineteenth-century repudiations of the *Lumpenproletariat*, repeatedly enacted distinctions between the working class as the proper People and what Foucault terms 'the dregs of the population'.

46 Though Foucault, notwithstanding his involvement at the time with immigrant workers' struggles in France (as recounted by Macey), does not

the grain of the romantic populism and workerism that haunts the rhetoric of the GP, is stark about what he calls the 'ideological effects' of this system, not just in terms of its 'moral' capture of the proletariat, but in what concerns its shaping impact on the 'non-proletarianised plebs', which 'has been racialist when it has been colonialist; it has been nationalist, chauvinist, when it has been armed; and it has been fascist when it has become the police force.'[47]

Testifying to the Nietzschean inspiration that subtends so many of his writings, it is the connubium of morality and law that stands for Foucault as the ultimate adversary, and accounts for his formulation of the struggle between the people and the courts as *ideological*. Summarizing the crux of his intervention into the debate over people's courts, Foucault declares:

> the bourgeois judicial state apparatus, of which the visible, symbolic form is the court, has the basic function of intro-ducing and augmenting contradictions among the masses, principally between the proletariat and the non-proletarianised people, and [...] it follows from this that the forms of this judicial system, and the ideology which is associated with them, must become the target of our

thematize this at any length, the relevance of these speculations to a study of the relation between class, race and criminalization is evident enough. Interestingly, Foucault does touch on the nexus of race and class in settler-colonialism but only to conclude, all too hastily, that as the army and colonization have become obsolescent as mechanisms for dividing the non-proletarianized people and the proletariat, only the prisons remain. In a passage that curiously echoes debates on the 'wages of whiteness', from W. E. B. Du Bois to David Roediger, Foucault observes about the 'earlier' phase in the management of the non/proletarian difference: 'And it was certainly in order to avoid the forming of an alliance between these "lesser whites" and the colonized peoples—an alliance which would have been just as dangerous out there as proletarian unity would have been in Europe—that a rigid racialist ideology was foisted on them: "Watch out, you'll be living among cannibals". Foucault, 'On Popular Justice', p. 17. See also Feldman, 'Foucault's Concept of Illegalism'.
47 Foucault, 'On Popular Justice', p. 23.

present struggle. And moral ideology—for what are our moral values but those which are over and over again associated with and re-confirmed by the decisions of the courts—this moral ideology, just like the forms of justice operated by the bourgeois apparatus, must be submitted to the scrutiny of the most rigorous criticism.[48]

In later years, Foucault would not just entirely jettison the Marxist category of ideology, he would also develop an arguably far less 'Manichaean' conception of the politics of law. But in the militant crucible of the early 1970s, and especially of Foucault's prison activism—which also brought him into contact with the revolts of Black prisoners in Attica and with the emblematic figure of George Jackson[49]—a political figure of the people emerges in the throes of the conflict against the penal system and juridical ideology. As Foucault remarked to Deleuze:

> I think that it is not simply the idea of better and more equitable forms of justice that underlies the people's hatred of the judicial system, of judges, courts, and prisons, but— aside from this and before anything else—the singular perception that power is always exercised at the expense of the people. The antijudicial struggle is a struggle against power and I don't think that it is a struggle against injustice, against the injustice of the judicial system, or a struggle for improving the efficiency of its institutions.[50]

Now, while Foucault casts doubt on the idea of a counter-justice,[51] he does discern the possibility of a lived form of thought that would

---

48 Foucault, 'On Popular Justice', pp. 35–36.
49 See Toscano, 'The Intolerable-Inquiry'.
50 Michel Foucault and Gilles Deleuze, 'Intellectuals and Power: A Conversation between Michel Foucault and Gilles Deleuze' in Michel Foucault, *Language, Counter-Memory, Practice: Selected Essays and Interviews* (Donald F. Bouchard ed.) (Ithaca: Cornell University Press, 1977[1972]), p. 211.
51 Foucault, 'On Popular Justice', p. 34.

work to sap the very foundations of juridical ideology. In a 1973 preface to the writings of former convict and prison activist Serge Livrozet, Foucault provides an eloquent sketch of 'illegalism' as an intellectual attitude, which serves as a fitting endpoint to our exploration of the philosophical nexus between the people and the law in the environs of May '68:

> For a long time, there has been a thinking of lawbreaking [*infraction*] inherent to lawbreaking itself; a certain reflection on the law linked to an active refusal of the law [*loi*]; a certain analysis of power and law [*droit*] practiced among those who were waging an everyday struggle against power and the law. Strangely, this thinking seems to have been a greater menace than illegality itself, since it has been more severely censored than the facts that accompanied it, or of which it was the occasion [. . .] It now explodes with this book. It explodes because, in the prisons, among both those who leave and those who enter them, in revolts and struggles, it has gained the force to express itself. [This] book is the forceful and individual expression of a certain popular experience and a certain popular thinking of the law and of illegality. A philosophy of the people.[52]

The Problem of the People and the Limits of the Law

In distinct and divergent ways, both Althusser and Foucault would explore, throughout the 1970s and early 1980s, modalities of collective practice and political subjectivation irreducible to the frameworks of modern revolutionary and Republican traditions—inasmuch as these traditions hold 'the people' to be an indispensable referent. Many of their interventions would come to

---

52 Foucault, 'Préface' (1973) in *Dits et écrits I, 1954–1975* (Paris: Gallimard, 2001). See also Toscano, 'The Intolerable-Inquiry'.

be over-determined, especially towards the end of the 1970s, by the shadow of the French Communist Party and the Brezhnevite USSR—pushing Althusser towards a kind of heretical and movementist Leninism, searching out the 'virtual forms of communism' in the 'interstices of capitalist society',[53] while leading Foucault to uncertain alliances with the anti-totalitarian media strategies of *la nouvelle philosophie*, as well as perplexing oscillations between seemingly sympathetic analyses of neo-liberalism and enthusiasm for radical revolt (as in the Iranian case). In the vicinity and wake of '68, however, as I have tried to detail in this parallel reading, we encounter a striking affinity and partial convergence in these two philosophers' delineation of *the problem of the people*, one that remains fecund amid our current deliberations on populism and related matters.

For both Althusser and Foucault, notwithstanding their different framings, thinking through the people and its pitfalls involves a thorough critique (symptomal for one, genealogical for the other) of its entanglement with a juridical ideology that both asserts class power and profoundly masks or disavows it. Though, in his reflections on illegalism, Foucault does rescue a liminal figure of the people (even a 'philosophy of the people'), grounded in a pluri-secular history of popular anti-judicial movements, this appears to be a figure which, in its plebeian and insurgent character, remains beneath or beyond any modern figure of the sovereign people. For the late Althusser, the effort remained one of searching for a communist politics that could circumvent or undermine the 'forms officially consecrated as political by bourgeois ideology: the State, popular representation, political parties, political struggles for the power held by the existing State'[54]—all these were under-

---

53 Louis Althusser, 'Il marxismo come teoria "finita" ' in Louis Althusser et al., *Discutere lo stato. Posizioni a confronto su una tesi di Louis Althusser* (Bari: De Donato, 1978), p. 7.
54 Althusser, 'Il marxismo come teoria "finita" ', pp. 12–13.

written by the *juridical illusion of politics*, by the conviction that all politics is to be defined in and through law (or right). Recovering these textual remnants from a season of political and theoretical struggles that now seem so distant is perhaps not an entirely vain pursuit. It can perhaps make us sensitive to the fact that a wide swathe of contemporary radical thought rarely goes to the root, when it comes to the nexus between the people, the law, and the possible political forms of our collective life.

SEVEN

Resistance

Few terms in the language of the left are as frequent, or as ambiguous, as resistance. Among the reasons for its ubiquity and equivocity is no doubt the fact that it permits one to invoke oppositional energies and practices without having to wade into the often-intractable distinctions between rebellions, revolts, reforms and revolutions. Talk of resistance does this by fore-grounding antagonistic practices lying beneath the threshold, or beyond the radar, of formal, organized politics, be it on the side of the forces of order or of its adversaries. It is in this respect that the question of resistance is bound to that of the boundaries of the political, and in particular to what a number of thinkers have specified as pre-politics, or the pre-political.[1] Resistance also allows one to draw on forms of action whose historical origins and mani-festations are disparate, but which persist as more or less implicit paradigms for the anti-systemic imaginary. Two are particularly salient: on the one hand, the everyday forms of resistance of sub-alterns against overpowering domination (be this slavery, colonial-ism, or the subjugation of peasantries by central state powers); on the other, the formation of irregular or partisan armed bands against foreign occupation (from the 1808 Napoleonic war in Spain to contemporary Iraq or Afghanistan, though the intellectually formative reference—and one which, unlike the ones just

---

1 For further thoughts on this question, see Toscano, *Fanaticism*, pp. 48–52, and the second part of 'Resistance and Revolt in Pre-Political Times', *Pli: The Warwick Journal of Philosophy* 30 (2019): 1–22.

mentioned, seems unsullied by the taint of reaction—is to be found in the anti-Nazi resistances of the Second World War). There are obvious enough connections between these two paradigms: the presence of power as domination (or indeed occupation) and the seemingly reactive character of action are among them. We can even identify, especially in revolutionary anti-colonial writings, from *The Black Jacobins* to *The Wretched of the Earth*, synthetic treatments of these two strands. Yet in terms of how the term resistance is employed in their theoretical uptake, the differences are considerable. Due to its far greater role in current debates I will focus mainly on the first, subaltern resistance.

Everyday resistance against domination is most often juxtaposed to the restrictive standards imposed by an ideal-typical conception of political and/or revolutionary action which treats some dominant trajectory (be it that of bourgeois politics in liberalism, or of workers' revolutions in Marxism) as the standard, thereby expunging forms of action already silenced by the historical record from our thinking of politics. The writings of political scientist and anthropologist James C. Scott, the historian Ranajit Guha and much of the Subaltern Studies tradition, in different ways, contribute to this counter-paradigm, which could be seen, so to speak, to 'provincialize' a certain conception of revolutionary action—though we might also note that this is a strand of thought that has its sources (and critical targets) in Marxist social histories, namely Eric Hobsbawm's *Primitive Rebels* and E. P. Thompson's *The Making of the English Working Class*, *Whigs and Hunters* and various other essays. Scott observes that 'much of the politics of subordinate groups falls into the category of "everyday forms of resistance", that these activities should most definitely be considered political, that they do constitute a form of collective action, and that any account which ignores them is often ignoring the most vital means by which lower classes manifest their political interests'.[2]

2 James C. Scott, 'Everyday Forms of Resistance', *Copenhagen Papers in East and Southeast Asian Studies* 4 (1989): 33–62. Contrariwise:

Ordinary forms of class struggle under conditions of domination—in which outright rebellion is most often met with overwhelming force—are dissimulated,[3] aimed at securing material interests and giving one's group room to breathe and, while grounded on a communal climate of opinion and solidarity, are not accompanied by formal organization. The small arsenal of relatively powerless groups includes 'such acts as foot-dragging, dissimulations, false compliance, feigned ignorance, desertion, pilfering, smuggling, poaching, arson, slander, sabotage, surreptitious assault and murder, anonymous threats, and so on.'[4] Much of Scott's energies are expended in trying to counter those who emphasize the cumulative function of such acts in reproducing a structure of domination, providing a kind of safety valve.[5]

The case against moving everyday forms of resistance closer to the center of the analysis of class relations rests on the claim that these activities are marginal because they are 1) unorganized, unsystematic and individual; 2) opportunistic and self-indulgent; 3) have no revolutionary consequences and/or 4) imply in their intention or logic an accommodation with the structure of domination. An argument along these lines necessarily implies that "real resistance" is organized, principled, and has revolutionary implications. (p. 51)

3 Scott, 'Everyday Forms of Resistance': 54:

Much of the ordinary politics of subordinate groups historically has been a politics of dissimulation in which both the symbols and practices of resistance have been veiled. In place of the open insult, the use of gossip, nicknames and character assassination; in place of direct physical assault, the use of sabotage, arson, and nocturnal threats by masked men (e.g. Captain Swing, the Rebecca Riots, Les Demoiselles); in place of labor defiance, shirking, slowdowns, and spoilage; in place of the tax riot or rebellion, evasion and concealment.

4 Scott, 'Everyday Forms of Resistance': 34.

5 A clear and much-debated exemplar of this position is Eugene Genovese's discussion of slave revolt and resistance in *Roll Jordan Roll: The World the Slaves Made* (New York: Vintage, 1976). Saidiya Hartman has articulated a radical alternative to Genovese's framework, informed by Scott's notion of the

While the dialectic of resistance and accommodation is one that, at least for a time, partakes of the reproduction of hegemony and the endurance of domination, Scott's image of resistance is one that at least potentially heralds the possibility of a shift to something like a plebeian molecular revolution. The spectacular defeats of open challenges may be compensated by the aggregate effects of imperceptible erosions of power. Whether as implicit strategy or as what he calls 'tactical wisdom', everyday resistance may thus attain or prepare what a revolutionary surge on its own cannot produce (Scott gives the examples of uncoordinated mass desertions from the Confederate armies in the US civil war, and from the Tsar's divisions in 1917). In his own words:

> The small rebellion, the doomed slave uprising, may have a symbolic importance for its violence and its revolutionary aims, but for most subordinate classes historically such rare episodes were of less moment than the quiet unremitting guerrilla warfare that took place day-in and day-out. Everyday forms of resistance rarely make headlines. But just as millions of anthozoan polyps create, willy-nilly, a coral reef, thousands upon thousands of petty acts of insubordination and evasion create a political and economic barrier reef of their own. And whenever, to pursue the simile, the ship of state runs aground on such a reef, attention is typically directed to the shipwreck itself and not to the vast aggregation of actions which make it possible.[6]

'infrapolitics of the dominated', and centred on a conception of the 'practice' of the enslaved defined, *inter alia*, by 'the nonautonomy of the field of action; provisional ways of operating within the dominant space; local, multiple, and dispersed sites of resistance that have not been strategically codified or integrated; and the anomalous condition of the slave as person and property'. See Saidiya Hartman, *Scenes of Subjection: Terror Slavery, and Self-Making in Nineteenth-Century America*, REV. EDN (New York: W. W. Norton & Co., 2022), p. 103.

6 Scott, 'Everyday Forms of Resistance': 49. Consider also the following statement:

Here we can note one of the problems raised by present invocations in the capitalist heartlands of such a paradigm of resistance. For, even if when they are aware of the location of such resistances in situations of accumulation by dispossession or formal subsumption rather than under the integral sway of the value form, of capital's untrammelled domination, those who speak of the present in terms of this kind of resistance make a material, spatial and moral claim about contemporary groups. They approach them as having 'customs in common' to defend, even if said customs are not at all 'customary'. Perhaps the most explicit statement of this position can be found in Paolo Virno's attempt to resurrect the category of a right to resistance, employed in seventeenth-century political thought, for the purposes of the twenty-first. Against those who would pose the question of power and violence in terms of the seizure of the state and/or the negation of capital, Virno argues that:

> The 'right of resistance' consists of validating the pre-rogatives of an individual or of a local community, or of a corporation, in contrast to the central power structure, thus safeguarding forms of life which have already been affirmed as free-standing forms, thus protecting practices

---

Each of these small events may be beneath notice and, from the perpetrator's point of view, they are often designed to be beneath notice. Collectively, however, these small events may add up almost surreptitiously to a large event: an army too short of conscripts to fight, a workforce whose footdragging bankrupts the enterprise, a landholding gentry driven from the countryside to the towns by arson and assault, tracts of state land fully occupied by squatters, a tax claim of the state gradually transformed into a dead letter by evasion. (p. 37)

Scott also quotes this passage from Marc Bloch: 'Almost invariably doomed to defeat and eventual massacre, the great insurrections were altogether too disorganized to achieve any lasting result. The patient, silent struggles stubbornly carried out by rural communities over the years would accomplish more than these flashes in the pan'. Contrast the discussion of 'obscure leaders' in C. L. R. James, see 'Leadership' in this volume, pp. 196–213.

already rooted in society. It means, then, defending some-thing positive: it is a conservative violence (in the good and noble sense of the word.) Perhaps the *jus resistentiae* (or the right to protect something which is already in place and is worthy of continuing to exist) is what provides the strongest connection between the seventeenth century *multitudo* and the post-Ford multitude. Even for the latter 'multitude', it is not a question of 'seizing power', of con-structing a new State or a new monopoly of political decision making; rather, it has to do with defending plural experiences, forms of non-representative democracy, of non-governmental usages and customs.[7]

It's a strange right this, as it is not (nor, we might argue, could it ever be) sanctioned by any law or authority, except that of a collective defensive practice—thus bringing this concept closer to a problematic of dual power, as sketched out in the practices of the Panthers, some of the Italian *autonomia* or Zapatismo.[8] Though Virno knowingly qualifies his use of the term 'conservative', it may be worth dwelling more on its ambivalence.

After all, Locke's own defence of the right of resistance was founded on the non-negotiable imperative to conserve property, whilst, as Domenico Losurdo has argued, Kant's refusal of the right of resistance rested in large part on his opposition to the Vendée uprising against the French Revolution, and to the use of *jus resistentiae* as an argument to protect feudal privilege against the equalizing dimensions of centralized state power.[9] I am not disput-ing Virno's portrait of such a right to resist in terms of a defensive paradigm—which is no doubt apt for certain dimensions of

7 Paolo Virno, *A Grammar of the Multitude: For an Analysis of Contemporary Forms of Life* (Isabella Bertoletti, James Cascaito and Andrea Casson trans) (Cambridge, MA: The MIT Press, 2001), pp. 43–44.
8 See 'Dual Power' in this volume, pp. 170–95.
9 Domenico Losurdo, *Autocensura e compromesso nel pensiero politico di Kant* (Naples: Bibliopolis, 1983).

peasant, anti-colonial and anti-imperial struggles (though these often turn out to be much less 'conservative' and 'traditional' than they may at first appear, as the history of millenarian revolts demonstrates). Nor do I wholly reject the idea that, as struggles for social reproduction under the adverse conditions of a capitalist offensive, contemporary social movements could be deemed conservative in a non-pejorative sense.[10] Resistance, be it dissimulated or more open, is often, as Scott noted, 'a stratagem deployed by a weaker party in thwarting the claims of an institutional or class opponent who dominates the public exercise of power'.[11]

But the kinds of resistance envisioned by Virno suppose that a contemporary multitude has been able to produce plural experiences, forms of non-representative democracy, non-governmental usages and customs that it can defend. I don't deny the existence of interstitial spaces and practices, worth expanding and fighting for, but current struggles suggest that the most urgent battles are firmly on the terrain of social reproduction and the capitalist state— consider the post-2008 education struggles in Quebec, Chile or Puerto Rico, which took a mass resistance to marketization and austerity policies as the starting point for a more totalizing challenge to capitalist power. Plural experiences, forms of non-representative democracy, non-governmental usages and customs are part of this political equation, but they are products and dimensions of struggle, not independent or autonomous realities that one can defend. For though contemporary struggles are defensive, there is nothing to defend—in the simple sense that what we witness is not a valorization of the welfare state compact, but a sober recognition that this is the terrain of struggle, a terrain which, to paraphrase Shelley's essay on reform, is strewn with 'trophies of our difficult and incomplete victory, planted on our enemies' land'.

---

10 This link between resistance and conversation was also advanced by Pierre Bourdieu in 'The Essence of Neoliberalism', *Le Monde diplomatique*, December 1998 (available online: https://bit.ly/2RBEyVR; last accessed: 5 February 2023).

11 Scott, 'Everyday Forms of Resistance': 52.

In this respect, I think we can also voice suspicion about those positions that treat the positivity of resistance not in terms of (new) customs to defend—in what we could call an ethical (in the sense of *ethos*) model of resistance—but on the basis of an *ontology* of resistance. The most well-known statement of this position has been voiced by Michael Hardt and Toni Negri. As they declare in *Multitude*: 'resistance is primary with respect to power'.[12] This statement translates a particular social ontology in which, as against the negative correlation between domination and resistance in the works of Scott or Guha, there is something like a positive correlation between resistance and the modalities of capitalist power.[13]

Though Hardt and Negri's correlation of resistance and power flirts with widespread paeans to the 'network model of organization'[14], they also recast the workerist thesis about the primacy of class struggle (Mario Tronti's 'Copernican revolution'), arguing that capital 'depends on the multitude and yet is constantly thrown into crisis by the multitude's resistance to capital's command and authority'.[15] Though I don't wish to dwell on this overmuch, I think it is worth noting that for the two authorities on which Hardt and Negri

12 Michael Hardt and Antonio Negri, *Multitude: War and Democracy in the Age of Empire* (New York: Penguin, 2004), p. 64.

13 Hardt and Negri, *Multitude*, p. 68:

> The first principle that guides the genealogy [of liberation struggles] will refer to the historical occasion, that is, the form of resistance that is most effective in combating a specific form of power. The second principle will pose a correspondence between changing forms of resistance and the transformation of economic and social production: in each era, in other words, the model of resistance that proves to be the most effective turns out to have the same form as the dominant models of economic and social production. The third principle that will emerge refers simply to democracy and freedom: each new form of resistance is aimed at addressing the undemocratic qualities of previous forms, creating a chain of more democratic movements.

14 Hardt and Negri, *Multitude*, p. 87.

15 Hardt and Negri, *Multitude*, p. 90.

rely for the argument about the primacy of resistance—namely Tronti and Foucault—the primacy of resistance is a strategic and heuristic thesis, not an ontological one.[16] It allows a partisan or agonistic insight into the shaping of power by struggle, but does not translate into the speculative thesis that a creative or already emancipatory force is at the origin of power's mutations—which is to say, in a sense, the ultimate source of its own domination. Foucault's explicit rejection of what he calls the ontological conception—by which he understands the idea, erroneously attributed to him, of 'Power with a capital P' forever juxtaposed to minor and hopeless resistances[17]—should be extended to any vitalist conception of resistance as a generic, generative force.

---

16 And even the heuristic thesis about the primacy of resistance is qualified by the historical archive, as this comment of Foucault, cited by Scott, suggests:

> It was against the new regime of landed property—set up by a bourgeoisie that profited from the Revolution—that a whole peasant illegality developed . . . ; it was against the new system of the legal exploitation of labour that workers' illegalities developed; from the most violent such as machine breaking . . . to the most everyday such as absenteeism, abandoning work, vagabondage, pilfering raw materials . . . (Scott, 'Everyday Forms of Resistance': 38)

17 Michel Foucault, 'Précisions sur le pouvoir: Réponses à certaines critiques' (published in *aut-aut*, 1978), *Dits et écrits II, 1976–1988* (Paris: Gallimard, 2001), pp. 631–32:

> If I had an ontological conception of power, there would be on the one side Power with a capital P, a kind of lunar, supraterrestrial agency, and then on the other the resistances of the unfortunate who are forced to bend in the face of power. I believe that an analysis of this type is totally false; power is born from a plurality of relations that are grafted on something else, are born from something else and make possible something else. Whence the fact that, on the one hand, these power relations inscribe themselves into struggles that are for example economic or religious struggles—and it is therefore not fundamentally against power that struggles are born; but, on the other, power relations open up a space in which these struggles develop.

If we are to salvage a notion of resistance in order to think politically against the grain of the present, we will need to move beyond what remain its two leading variants: first, resistance as the always already of power, its secret virtuality, and, second, resistance as an ethical position of dissidence against power—as emblematized by the *nouveaux philosophes*.[18] The latter offers one of the great temptations for a left prone to transfigure its weaknesses into virtues, its powerlessness into *potentia*. This often amounts to celebrating resistance purely and simply as the defiance of or indifference to politics, the state, or more generically, mastery, in a manner that derides any directed collective project of transformation as tainted by the original sin of power taken and exercised. It is this 'angelism' of resistance (so alien, incidentally, to the wartime practices of anti-fascist partisans[19]) which a reflection on the next keyword in our brief lexicon, *transition*, should also serve to counterbalance.

---

18 Consider André Glucksmann's characteristic pronouncement, quoted in Julian Bourg, *From Revolution to Ethics: May 68 and Contemporary French Thought* (Montreal: McGill-Queen's University Press, 2007): 'The Russian dissidents can . . . help us to better understand ourselves . . . Keeping in view our own experience, we are free to meditate on the universal treasure of resistance to state violence' (p. 252). This ethical position has its *Ur-text* in Camus's *L'homme revolté*.

19 Claudio Pavone, *A Civil War: A History of the Italian Resistance* (Stanislao Pugliese ed., Peter Levy trans.) (London: Verso, 2014).

EIGHT

Transition

Tragedy and Transition

To speak of transition in these times—which may be times of riots, but are also times of stasis, reaction and counter-revolutions-without-revolutions—may appear in bad taste, as when, to use the old situationist turn of phrase, one speaks with corpses in one's mouth. Not only does such a discussion seem out of place and out of time, considering the global balance of forces, but all the major variants of emancipatory anti-systemic thought seem premised on the rejection of transition. This rejection concerns all the components of this concept.

The *time* of transition, understood in terms of the linearity of stages. The *space* of transition, whether state, commune, enclave, or liberated zone. The *political form* and *subjectivity* of transition, embodied by the party and related institutions. Accompanying these negations, these assertions of obsolescence, is a more encompassing ambient rejection of the 'progressive' philosophy of history that underlay the classical image of transition, with its analogies between the institution and the destitution of capitalism, between bourgeois and proletarian revolutions.

It would be relatively easy, though perhaps futile, to plunge into the messy archive of actual revolutions to show how the heroic stereotype of transition was openly declared by its supposed advocates to bear but a tenuous relationship to concrete revolutionary practice. It is all the more ironic that in some micro-habitats of the far left people still anxiously polish their Lenin fetishes ignoring how Bolshevik political practice broke, on multiple occasions, with almost all the ingredients of a linear logic of transition—skipping supposedly necessary stages, acknowledging the sociological disappearance of the very working class it was meant to represent, tactically re-establishing dimensions of capitalism after its accelerated suppression under war communism and so on.

This last remark hints at an important dialectical truth about transition in particular and political modernity in general: the symbolic force of a linear image of transition was the counterpart of conditions of unevenness and non-contemporaneity that marked all twentieth-century revolutionary experiences. Though they may have appeared as its stubborn shadow, twentieth-century revolutionary modernity was over-determined by the persistence of non-capitalist modes of production and especially of a non-capitalist peasantry. These revolutions were all revolutions 'against *Das Kapital*', in the young Gramsci's sense of remaining inexplicable for a purely 'economic' Marxism.[20] But it is also the partial kernel of truth behind the cynical statements that revolutions were but ruses of capitalist modernization—that communism, as the Hungarian joke went, was simply the longest path between capitalism and capitalism, with contemporary China as the massive confirmation of that punch line.

Conversely, what for some appears as the basis of a true revolution, the real subsumption of life by capital, the termination of all lags and outsides, reveals itself as revolution's Medusa. In Henri Lefebvre's formulation, from *The Production of Space*: 'the space that contains the realized preconditions of another life is the same one as prohibits what those preconditions make possible.'[21] So it

20 Antonio Gramsci, 'The Revolution against "Capital" ' in *Selections from Political Writings 1910–1920* (Quintin Hoare ed.) (London: Lawrence and Wishart, 1977), pp. 36–38.
21 Henri Lefebvre, *The Production of Space* (Donald Nicholson-Smith trans.) (Oxford: Blackwell, 1991), pp 189–90.

seems that transition was the order of the day when conditions were immature and is off the agenda now that capital has inundated our lifeworlds and terminated other modes of production. Beyond reflecting on this irony—hardly a recent discovery—are there reasons to retain the idea of transition?

My own response is affirmative. Notwithstanding the saturation, ossification and perversion of a classical twentieth-century schema, which often goes by the misleading syntagm 'Leninism', if transition without communism is empty, then communism without transition is blind. Even if we abandon, as we must, the conviction that even the 'bad side' of history carries with it, however secretly, all the seeds of transformation, that the seizing and accelerating of present tendencies has salvific powers, we cannot avoid trying to articulate the current mutations in the social forms of capitalism with tactics and strategies for its overcoming—that is, if we want to retain some practical content to our ideas of communism. Yet if capitalism is not pregnant with communism, and we can't simply indicate a political form that could oversee a phased passage from the one to the other in an expanding movement from one liberated territory to the next, how can we figure transition to ourselves?

One image of transition we may wish to avoid is that of an easily summarized, globally applicable plan. Transition today is not a programme. It is a problem. I mean this both in the negative sense—transition as the blind spot or 'bad object' of contemporary radicalism—and a positive one—meaning that theory is primarily a labour of problematization, of defining problems whose resolutions are a matter of practical, collective activity. To sketch the *problem* of transition and begin to reflect on how we can move beyond treating transition as a dogmatic talisman or a phobic object, I want to identify (in no particular order) four themes, four keywords in a contemporary lexicon of transition, which we could also call a political dictionary in a dialectical key.

145

First, *tragedy*. One of the principal ways to declare closed—even or especially from the left—the very question of transition, of oriented root-and-branch change, or of emancipation as something other than resistance or apocalypse, is to call for an acceptance of our tragic predicament, usually coded in terms of the lessons of defeat and the invariable fact of finitude. My proposal is that we not reject the tragic, but assume it as the element within which to recast our thinking of politics and communism. Thinking through tragedy as an experiential, narrative and political form can help us to break with a defeatist and deflationary reading of our baleful present, as well as to avert the curse of cruel and shallow optimism. The tragic as a modern political form—as made evident by the place of this notion in the writing of C. L. R. James about the Haitian Revolution and decolonization and of W. E. B. Du Bois on Black Reconstruction—emerges from reflecting on the trajectory of anti-systemic politics in a capitalist world riven by crisis and unevenness, in which subjective purity or collective will does not suffice to assure victory.[22] The political subject of transition must turn the apparatus of domination against itself, in full knowledge that the moment of emancipation may be transmuted into a vanishing mediator in the system's self-adjustment, but also that a rebellion without a transitional prospect is all too easily turned into an object lesson in futility by its adversaries or an aesthetics of defeat by its (false) friends—or even worse, as the 'Arab Spring' of 2011 reminded us, into an opportunity for the intensification of injustice. In his remarkable *Modern Tragedy*, Raymond Williams reminded us that a tragic perspective envisages the revolution as a long transition, immersed and entangled in the legacies and contradictions of the capitalist society it determinately negates. Tragedy lies both in the character of contemporary society and in the

---

22 For further reflections on the politics of tragedy, see Alberto Toscano, 'Politics in a Tragic Key', *Radical Philosophy* 180 (2013): 25–34, and 'Tragedy' in John Frow (ed.), *Oxford Encyclopaedia of Literary Theory* (Oxford: Oxford University Press, 2021).

unfolding of any process of abolition, that is to say of dismantling, refunctioning, and refounding: 'A society in which revolution is necessary is a society in which the incorporation of all its people, as whole human beings, is in practice impossible without a change in its fundamental form of relationships'—which is why revolutionary action must impel 'the change in the form of the activity of a society, in its deepest structure of relationships and feelings'.[23]

Second, *dead labour*. One of the most arresting representations of transition as tragedy is to be found in Jean-Paul Sartre's unfilmed 1946 script *L'engrenage* (*In the Mesh*), which depicts—in a manner only truly theorized in the French philosopher's later *Critique of Dialectical Reason*—the counter-finality of revolution. An uprising in a subordinate oil-producing country turns collective and individual action against itself, enmeshing it in the practico-inert, the materiality of a carbon-based imperialist order. Haunted by the work-energy crisis[24] and the deployment of the Anthropocene, but also by the related gigantism of fixed capital and the planetary installation of what Lefebvre presciently called the logistical state,[25] contemporary politics finds itself transfixed by the crushing disproportion between the scale of collective action and human experience, on the one hand, and the material conditions of social reproduction, on the other. This condition, which serves as a kind of paralysing social and economic unconscious, is to my mind the foremost reason—beyond an inherited suspicion of moribund, compromised reformisms—why contemporary radicalism tends to emphasize eventhood, disruption and interruption as the crux or at least the catalyst for any revolutionary transformation. The crushing scale of material and energy flows in the context of a

---

23 Raymond Williams, *Modern Tragedy* (Pamela McCallum ed.) (Toronto: Broadview Press 2006), p. 101.

24 George Caffentzis et al., *The Work/Energy Crisis and the Apocalypse*, *Midnight Notes* 2(1) (1980).

25 See Toscano, 'Lineaments of the Logistical State'.

world-market, along with the destructive dimension of this 'mega-machine', play a prominent role in the widespread scepticism towards transition. It appears as if first the total mobilization would need to be arrested and only then could the real task of emancipation commence.

The third term is *reproduction*. It is around social reproduction, both in its material supports and its social forms, that the critical problems of transition orbit. If certain assemblages of abstraction and exploitation—from the factory to money, from the army to the banks—are integral to the reproduction of capitalist social relations but also of the lives that radically depend on them, what happens to social reproduction in transition? Here we would seem to be faced with a (tragic) antinomy: maintaining the continuity of social reproduction risks perpetuating the very forms an anti-capitalist process is seeking to dismantle (using the state to abolish the state, money to abolish money, and so on); but a catastrophe of social reproduction risks being precisely that, a catastrophe. Capital constantly ventriloquizes its masks and bearers: 'Without me, you'll starve'. The historical connections between bread riots, famines and revolutions complicate that warning. Most theories and experiences of transition which don't have at their disposal the progressive optimism of socialist reformisms seem to depend on a radical break, but that break is often a rupture in the ideological and political facets of reproduction, not always the social and material ones—precisely the ones often left untouched by recent 'revolutions'.

Putting these three terms together, we may want to reflect on how the tragedy of transition is not just a matter of violence, that it does not just stem from the partial introjection of the enemy's instruments, or from the fact that the subjects of transition are shaped by the very world they wish to leave. It is not just that those who ignored this tragic dimension were dupes or dreamers. The tragic *form* of transition is also deeply embedded with the problem of the modalities and continuities of social reproduction and the vast hierarchically organized dead labours and apparatuses of domination on which most human life radically depends under capitalism. That is the lesson of Sartre's *L'engrenage*.

But it would be an insupportable speculative thesis, when it comes to reproduction, as the best of Marxist and Third World feminism has repeatedly shown, to treat this as a category wholly *internal* to capital, conceived as some kind of autopoietic and impermeable Moloch.[26] All human life might be forced to transit through capitalist forms, but the idea of a total subsumption is unduly dystopian and metaphysical. Indeed, capitalism combines structures of radical dependence with—especially in moments of crisis—the abandonment of social reproduction to circuits and sites and labours outside of accumulation, beyond the state.

Whence my fourth and final term, *dual power*.[27] A possible foothold for beginning to think transition concretely would be to take into consideration the crucial phenomenon of what we could call a kind of *dual biopower*—which is to say the collective attempt politically to appropriate aspects of social reproduction that state and capital have deliberately deserted or rendered unbearably exclusionary, from housing to medicine. These aspects—which incidentally are also the privileged sites for any non-reformist reforms one might propose in the current moment—are today the principal organizing bases of successful popular movements, whether progressive or reactionary. But they have also been the ful-crums from which to think the dismantling of capitalist social forms and relations without relying on the premise of a formal political break in the operations of power, without waiting for 'the day after', for the seizure or 'evaporation' of the repressive apparatus. Though they could be read in a merely ameliorative lens, I think the brutally repressed experiments of the Black Panther Party with health programmes among the Black 'lumpen'—to adopt their own

---

26 See Bhandar and Ziadah, *Revolutionary Feminisms*.
27 See 'Dual Power' in this volume, pp. 170–95.

terminology—are one such example, and their conception of self-defence not irrelevant to our own time. As we begin to see the emergence of spatial and temporal 'dualities' in the terrain of social reproduction and in the very uneven time-space of crisis, we can also start to think which of these experiences can be propagated or scaled up—not in fantasies of secession, nor in the illusion that post-capitalism is really possible now, but as ways of rooting the need to undo capitalist relations in the real if partial experience of efforts to limit capital's powers and repurpose its (our) dead labours. The realism of a 'tragic' conception of transition will be indispensable here, especially when the act of affirming a different standard of social reproduction comes up, in explicitly political forms, against capitalism's requirement to reproduce itself.

Of Horses and Locomotives

Ongoing debates about communism, communization and the commons remain haunted by the dilemma 'reform or revolution?' and the related alternative 'revolution or revolt?'[28] My hypothesis is that the intractability of these alternatives is bound up with the question of transition, the classical hinge between the theories of capital and revolution, and the blind spot of contemporary radicalism.

When it comes to revolt and revolution, the distinction proposed by the Italian mythologist Furio Jesi in *Spartakus: The Symbology of Revolt* is illuminating:

What principally distinguishes revolt from revolution is [. . .] a different experience of time. If, on the basis of the ordinary meaning of the two words, revolt is a sudden insurrectional explosion, which can be placed within a strategic horizon but which in itself does not imply a long-

---

28 See 'Reform' in this volume, pp. 75–83. I have tried to explore some of the limitations of the renaming of revolution as communization in 'Now and Never', in Noys (ed.), *Communisation and its Discontents*.

distance strategy, and revolution is instead a strategic complex of insurrectional movements, coordinated and
oriented over the mid- to long-term towards ultimate
objectives, then we could say that revolt suspends historical
time, suddenly establishing a time in which everything that
is done has a value in itself, independently of its consequences and of its relations with the transitory or
perennial complex that constitutes history. Revolution
would instead be wholly and deliberately immersed in
historical time.[29]

A contemporary defence of communist transition might be
tempted to uphold this distinction. Its rejection would instead
entail refusing the lamination of time and strategy, thereby absorb-
ing the sequenced instrumentality of revolution into the collective
experience of revolt. This second path is taken in Eric Hazan and
Kamo's pamphlet on the 'first revolutionary measures', in the
notion of a movement that would act immediately to 'create the
irreversible', not undoing the forms of state and capital but preventing their resuscitation after their collapse or 'evaporation' (for
instance, by repudiating the emergence of any kind of constituent
assembly).[30] Shifting to the reform and revolution axis, we can
discern a tendency for partisans of transition to consider non-
reformist reforms as a possible element of revolutionary politics,
while an anti-transitional stance would regard a transitional notion
of revolution as today indistinguishable from reformism, in all of
its impasses and anachronisms.

When it comes to transition, ossified doctrines and their
equally stale repudiations are always around the corner. So, we
should perhaps begin by jettisoning the scholastic debate, or at least

29 Furio Jesi, *Spartakus: The Symbology of Revolt* (A. Cavalletti ed., A. Toscano
trans.) (London: Seagull Books, 2014), p. 46.
30 Eric Hazan & Kamo, *Prèmieres mesures révolutionnaires* (Paris: La
Fabrique, 2013).

acknowledging the contemporary irrelevance of transition conceived in terms of a theory of stages, one that owes more to the civilizational schedules of eighteenth-century political economy and its philosophies of history than to communist critique. One path out of this impasse, which I will only gesture towards, would consist in accepting the historical and geographical heterogeneity of problems of transition, thereby complicating any containment of transition by the reform/revolution and revolt/revolution dichotomies. Consider some kinds of transition that have little do with our customary and schematic image thereof: the coercive elimination of capitalism under war communism[31]; the partial restoration of capitalist relations to reproduce the state but also to contain internal class struggle (in the USSR's New Economic Policy [NEP] period)[32]; the formal subsumption of capitalism by a socialist state, envisaging the employment of capitalist means to, as it were, boil the capitalist frog[33]; models of transition as non-reformist reform, from Karl Korsch's councilist vision of 'socialization', a cooperative crowding-out of capitalist competition,[34] to the Meidner plan in Sweden, and on to various recently resuscitated

---

31 See especially Nikolai Ivanovich Bukharin's 'Economics of the Transition Period' in *Selected Writings on the State and the Transition to Socialism* (Richard B. Day ed.) (Armonk, NY: M. E. Sharpe, 1982).

32 See Matteo Mandarini and Alberto Toscano, 'Planning for Conflict', *South Atlantic Quarterly* 119(1) (2020): 11–30.

33 See for instance the strategic role accorded to state credit in E. A. Preobrazhensky's 1921 science-fictional tract of political economy, *From N.' E. P. to Socialism: A Glance into the Future of Russia and Europe* (New York: New Park, 1973).

34 Karl Korsch, 'What is Socialization? A Program of Practical Socialism' (Frankie Denton and Douglas Kellner trans), *New German Critique* 6 (1975): 60–81. Korsch, while openly conscious of its potential pitfalls and reversals, presents a scenario in which capitalist competition would be sapped or defeated by the competition of workers' associations (this turning of competition against itself is also an element in the Leninist vision of the NEP).

visions of how to turn finance into a public utility.[35] The planetary record of revolutions, communes and uprisings also throws up a complex inventory of systematic attempts to undo and transform social relations of production which do not fit the impoverished terms of a homogenizing conception of transition, which continues to be fetishized by certain strains of the revolutionary left (while being stigmatized by others).

It is nevertheless evident that many visions of transition were shot through with a potent idea of historical-political linearity, arguably written into the very semantics of the concept. This was certainly at stake in early critiques of Bolshevism, for breaking with or anticipating a pre-set schedule of social transformation. The terms of this debate are strikingly, and symbolically, crystallized in an exchange between Leon Trotsky and Karl Kautsky, curiously echoed, however unwittingly, in some current discussions on strategy and communization. I offer it here by way of a dramatic interlude:

KAUTSKY: Would Trotsky dare to get on a locomotive and set it going, convinced that he would, during the journey, 'learn and arrange everything'? No doubt he would be quite capable of doing this, but would he have the necessary time? Would not the train be very likely soon to be derailed, or explode? One must have acquired something of the skills necessary to drive an engine, before one tries to set it going. In the same way, the proletariat must have acquired those qualities, which are indispensable for organisation of production, if it wishes to undertake this task.

---

35 On the Swedish economist Rudolf Meidner, see Blackburn, 'A Visionary Pragmatist'. On 'socialising' banking, see Leo Panitch, 'Rebuilding Banking', *Red Pepper*, January 2009 (available online: https://bit.ly/3YikhTe; last accessed: 5 February 2023).

TROTSKY: With infinitely more foundation one could say 'Will Kautsky dare to mount a horse before he has learned to sit firmly in the saddle, and to guide the animal in all its steps?' We have foundations for believing that Kautsky would not make up his mind to such a dangerous, purely Bolshevik experiment. On the other hand, we fear that, through not risking to mount the horse, Kautsky would have considerable difficulty in learning the secrets of riding on horse-back. For the fundamental Bolshevik prejudice is precisely this: that one learns to ride on horse-back, only when sitting on the horse.

KAUTSKY: It is true I did not learn to ride a horse before I mounted one, but the horse had learnt to carry a rider before I mounted it. And I did not ride alone, but with friends, who had learnt to ride, and gave me advice and directions. In the end, however, the challenge became easier because I exercised my body with gymnastics beforehand.[36]

Beyond these struggles within the linear conception of revolutionary transitions, it behoves us to reflect on the widespread disavowal in much of the classical Marxist debate of the fact that revolutions and transitions in the twentieth century were marked by the *absence* of a totalizing social homogeneity—they were transitions *in* and *of* unevenness.[37] There has been no social revolution which has not at least in part been a peasant revolution, even when it turns against this key wellspring of revolutionary politics; or, in Gramsci's sense, we could say that all revolutions have been revolutions against *Das Kapital*—though, as I'll suggest below, they are unthinkable without attending to Marx's critique of political

---

36 Marcel van der Linden, *Western Marxism and the Soviet Union: A Survey of Critical Theories and Debates Since 1917* (Jurriaan Bendien trans.) (Leiden: Brill, 2007), pp. 18–20.

37 I have tried to think through this question of uneven transitions in terms of C. L. R. James' conception of political tragedy in 'Politics in a Tragic Key', *Radical Philosophy* 180 (2013): 25–34.

economy. Parenthetically, we could ask if what ruins transitional imaginaries is not so much the dissipation of the mission of the industrial proletariat, appropriating the conditions of its exploitation (workers' control), but the tendential vanishing of the liminal, peripheral, uneven relationship of capital to other modes of production, and of the urban to the rural. In this regard, transition cannot be sundered from the fraught space-times of modernity and the desire for linearity that takes the name of modernization.

Mastering the Lag

A critical taxonomy of schemas of transition, and the practices they informed, is a worthwhile endeavour, if only to break through the nostalgic and caricatural turn often taken by this debate. What I want to sketch out here however is the theoretical question of transition—to see whether we can cut through dogmatic fidelities and doctrinaire dismissals by considering some of the more serious attempts to turn this somewhat threadbare Marxist watchword into a concept, or at the very least a problem.

My principal exhibit takes the form of a series of texts by the French philosopher Étienne Balibar, published between the mid-60s and the collapse of 'historical communism', texts that addressed the question 'Is there a Marxist theory of transition?'—Balibar's essay on the fundamental concepts of historical materialism from the collective volume *Reading Capital*; his 1973 rectification in response to queries posed by the journal *Theoretical Practice*; the discussion of transition and socialism in his 1976 *On the Dictatorship of the Proletariat*; an intervention on state, party and transition at a PCF conference; and a retrospect on transition as the crucial aporia of Marxist thought.[38]

---

38 See Étienne Balibar, 'The Basic Concepts of Historical Materialism' (1965) in Louis Althusser et al., *Reading Capital* (Ben Brewster and David Fernbach trans) (London: New Left Books, 1970); 'Self Criticism: Answer to Questions

A caveat: Althusserianism might appear the least felicitous source for such an inquiry. Its 'theoreticism' appears to suspend the practice of transition in analytical aether, and its hostility to value-form analysis makes it ultimately impossible to address the divisions in the concept of equality, which is critical to thinking transition.[39] But the conceptual anatomizing and relentless registering of humanist fallacies mean that Balibar's texts provide a useful source for avoiding resilient clichés and thinking the problem of transition with the requisite care and precision. It is tempting, following Balibar's own précis of the trajectory of Althusserianism, to see this critique (in a quasi-Kantian sense) of transition as moving through three levels: an 'economic' one, in which transition is figured through structural change in the mode of production; a 'political' one that foregrounds revolutionary transformations in the nature of state power; and an 'ideological' one, in which reproduction is emphasized, along with the obstacles confronting the changing of 'mindsets'.[40] But, as I hope will be evident in what follows, while attending to the centrality of self-criticism and rectification in the 'Althusserian moment',[41] we should also be mindful of its own potent criticism of periodization, acknowledging how, with differences of emphasis, these dimensions of transition are present at every step.

Balibar's methodological proviso—that Marx's periodization effects a break with the stageist periodization of the bourgeois history of modes of production—remains vital. The arguments for and against transition are usually confined within the bounds of a

from "Theoretical Practice" ', *Theoretical Practice* 7–8 (1973): 56–72; *On the Dictatorship of the Proletariat* (G. Lock trans.) (London: New Left Books, 1977); 'État, parti, transition', *Dialectiques* 27 (Spring 1979): 81–92; 'Les apories de la "transition" et les contradictions de Marx', *Sociologie et sociétés* 22(1) (1990): 83–91.

39 See my 'The Politics of Abstraction: Communism and Philosophy'.

40 Balibar, 'Les apories', pp. 83–84.

41 Balibar stresses this element in 'Les apories'.

linear conception that runs roughshod over many of Marx's insights about the contradictions and disequilibria of capitalism. For all their limits, the semi-structuralist concepts advanced by Balibar to ground Marx may serve as antidotes to a thinking of transition as a homogeneous 'expressive' totality in historical development. In particular, in presenting the 'science of history' as focused on a study of the variation of elements of a mode of production as well as on a 'differential determination of forms', Balibar reveals *temporal difference* as a key factor in transition.[42] The principal analytical principle in the delineation of transition within *Reading Capital* is the lag (*décalage*) between different components of a social formation (for instance, the lag between the social relations of appropriation and production, on the one hand, and the legal forms of property, on the other).[43]

Balibar's thesis at this juncture is that *décalage* is a feature of periods of transition, conceived of as times of unevenness and conflict. This is also linked to the repudiation of an *endogenous* understanding of transition, as manifest in the hydraulic or tectonic models of forces breaking through relations—a conception alien to a Marxism in which certain social and juridical relations (for instance concerning property) are presented as often being in advance or anticipation of forces of production and modes of exploitation. Transition is not part of a logical dialectic: 'the concept of passage (from one mode of production to another) can never be the passage of the concept (to another of itself by internal differentiation)'.[44] It cannot be subsumed under the common time of periodization that underlies the 'ideological theory of time', the

---

42 Balibar, 'Basic Concepts of Historical Materialism', p. 211.

43 Balibar, 'Basic Concepts of Historical Materialism', p. 223.

44 Louis Althusser, Étienne Balibar, Roger Establet, Pierre Macherey and Jacques Rancière, *Lire le Capital* (Paris: PUF, 1996[1965]), p. 522. The English translation renders both the French *passage* and *transition* as 'transition', losing some of the nuance of the original.

liberal philosophy of history through which bourgeois thought grasps social change.

Balibar views the tension or overlay between formal and real subsumption, the lag evident in the development of manufacturing into great industry, in particular, as opening up into a 'theory of the forms of transition [*passage*]'.[45] Such a theory would be a sub-component of history as a 'science of discontinuous modes of production, as the science of a variation'.[46] Here the stress on synchrony flips over into a much keener attention to discrepant temporalities than those of a linear, developmentalist, teleological Marxism—a Marxism whose legacy is arguably still strong, even in some of the more heterodox contemporary theories of communism (namely *operaismo* and post-*operaismo*, but also so-called communization theory).

It is questions of continuity and discontinuity that permeate Balibar's protracted struggle to elucidate the theoretical and political meanings of 'transition'. The foregrounding of the question of *reproduction* lends a welcome complexity to his inquiry. Understood to comprise the connection between different economic subjects (different capitals), as well as distinct levels of the social structure, and assuring the continuity of production— operating as the transformation of things but also the conservation, or even 'eternalisation' (*Verewigung*) of relations[47]—reproduction is, in *Reading Capital*, 'the general form of permanence of the general conditions of production, which in the last analysis englobe the whole social structure', meaning that '*it should be the form of their change and restructuration, too*'.[48]

---

45 Balibar, 'Basic Concepts of Historical Materialism', p. 234.
46 Balibar, 'Basic Concepts of Historical Materialism', p. 257.
47 Balibar, 'Basic Concepts of Historical Materialism', p. 272.
48 Balibar, 'Basic Concepts of Historical Materialism', p. 259.

We can interpolate here Balibar's self-criticism from 1973. In retrospect, Balibar sees—I think rightly—the original framing of reproduction as obscuring the problem of transition. In *Reading Capital*, reproduction was conceived of quite narrowly in terms of the *continuity* of relations of production, with little attention to other levels of *social* reproduction. Against this restricted under-standing of reproduction,

> transition requires the analysis of *other* material conditions and other social forms than those implied in the concept of mode of production alone (in this case: of the capitalist mode of production). Or else the analysis of material results and social forms (re)produced by the development of the capitalist mode of production *in another respect* [*sous un autre rapport*] than the capitalist relation of production alone.[49]

Attention to the gendered and racialized character of capitalist social reproduction would accordingly transform the discussion of transition—so much is acknowledged, if not necessarily corrected, by Balibar in noting that the social form of the reproduction of labour power was left out of his original account.[50]

Reproduction can also be understood all too monolithically to imply a kind of seamless autopoiesis of capitalist social relations, creating an untenable dualism between transitional and non-transitional periods. This dehistoricizes the reproduction of capital and regenerates a kind of ideology of periodization—in the key of

---

49 Balibar, 'Self Criticism': 64.

50 Expanding the scope of the reproduction of labour-power, especially as concerns the questions of race and racism, would come to the fore in Balibar's work of the 1990s, having already been central to his critique of the PCF. See his *Les frontières de la démocratie* (Paris: La Découverte, 1998). See also his recent genealogy of Marxian debates on reproduction, in dialogue with other theoretical traditions: Étienne Balibar, 'Reproductions' (David Broder trans.), *Rethinking Marxism* 34(2) (2022): 142–61.

catastrophe rather than gradualism. Balibar's later exploration of the aporias of transition would reiterate this self-criticism in striking terms, linking it to the symbolic power of the link between communism and notions of intensification or acceleration, of a 'struggle to the death':

> Chased from the definition of contradiction, the metaphor of a 'struggle to the death' or of 'escalation to the extreme' then reappears in the definition of transition, or of history inasmuch as it would be a permanent transition, surpassing all structures. A transcendence as well as a finality are thereby reintroduced: because you must always fictionally give yourself the 'point of arrival', if only in the *names* of 'socialism' and 'communism', in order to think the meaning and the motor of the historical transition in process. Under these conditions, there is nothing either surprising or original in the fact that structuralism called upon, as its necessary complement, a revolutionary decisionism and voluntarism, even if it refused the category of the subject (and *a fortiori* that of the 'subject of history'). Regulation as the *invariance* of the mode of production and rupture as irreducible revolutionary *event*, exterior to and symmetrical with one another, are reciprocally completed and justified. We could even say that the one's *raison d'être* is in calling upon the second as its negation.[51]

Balibar's self-criticisms portray as untenable the distinction made in *Reading Capital* between the synchrony of reproduction and the diachrony of the passage. Reproduction is not to be confused with the *self-identity* of a mode of production. This would merely reify the theoretical *fiction* of 'simple reproduction'. In the final analysis,

---

51 Balibar, 'Les apories' p. 90. We're allowed to wonder, given the date of the text's publication, whether Balibar is not refunctioning Althusserian self-criticism into a polemic against the then recently published *Being and Event* by Alain Badiou.

to treat reproduction in this way is to reify capitalism as an order, to bury its lags and strains in the presupposition of stability and its repetition—to which we would then counterpose the putative radicality of an absolute novelty and the pure will of a decision. It is imperative instead to realize that the endurance and resilience of the capital relation, and its specific forms, remains an explanandum, not a presupposition.

It is the incomplete theory of reproduction that stops Marx from building on his genealogical account of primitive accumulation as a form of transition, leaving the critical problem of Marxist theory—the historical connection between the development of capitalism and proletarian revolution—ultimately unanswered. In other words, Balibar would seem to suggest, we have no theory of revolution that integrates the lessons of *Capital*. What I understand by this is that it is the inability to project the complex problem of reproduction back onto the caesura and encounters that made capitalism possible that leads either to feeble *analogies* between transitions to and from capitalism, or to a merely logical or dogmatic consideration of the problem of transition. I want to return to this question of reproduction, but first we need to develop the account of discontinuity or *décalage* in *Reading Capital*. This should allow us to see why Balibar concludes that there is no general theory of transition.

In his contribution to that collective project, Balibar had already warned against the view of transition as an event. 'The transition,' he wrote, 'cannot be a moment of destructuration, however brief'. It is 'a movement subject to a structure which has to be discovered'.[52] This is the abiding problem: is there a structure or general theory of transition? Key to any reply is ascertaining whether all passages, all transitions are of the same type. Balibar suggests that in Marx we sometimes can perceive the presence of a general model, a logical dialectic of the social (his example is *Capital*, VOL. 1, chap. 32, on

---

52 Balibar, 'Basic Concepts of Historical Materialism', p. 273.

the 'historical tendency of capitalist accumulation'). Yet Balibar also proposes that we can think Marx against the grain of this general logic and of a never-exorcized tendency to an evolutionist period-ization—namely by posing the model of primitive accumulation (in which the elements of the encounter, free labour and capital, have different genealogies) as alien to the conception of endogenous change. In the force field of primitive accumulation, we can think of 'passage' or transition not as an inner metamorphosis of structures but as a contingent recombination of elements. This recombination is then thought by contrast with capital's *tendencies*, in which limits are internal but never encountered, and where true transformation cannot partake of the structural time of capital's dynamics, including the time of its crises.[53] In other words, the immanent limits of capital do not *delimit* their negation, they do not bear the time of transition *in potentia*.

How then is transition to be defined? In *Reading Capital*, Balibar still maintains a rather unstable double Marxian reference to primitive accumulation (the genealogy and encounter of elements) and the period of manufacture (formal subsumption) as sources for thinking transitional periods. What remains critical in the end is that transition is to be defined by a *décalage* or 'non-correspondence' between different levels or components of the social formation. The contradictory character of these temporally and formally unstable formations is deemed, by analogy with the role of the state in so-called primitive accumulation, to give a *primacy to politics*. As Balibar writes: 'In a transition period, there is a "non-correspondence" because the mode of intervention of political prac-tice, instead of conserving the limits and producing its effects within their determination, displaces them and transforms them.'[54] Politics is no longer a domain of integration and reproduction, but of *dis-location*. Though it is not explicitly addressed, we could discern here a complex parallelism or entanglement between the theory of dual

53 Balibar, 'Basic Concepts of Historical Materialism', p. 291.
54 Balibar, 'Basic Concepts of Historical Materialism', p. 307.

power and that of the 'double reference' of the period of transition to two or more modes of production, in volatile coexistence.[55]

That coexistence is the leitmotiv of Balibar's return to the question of transition in *On the Dictatorship of the Proletariat*. The problem that frames this return is that of socialism. Against the conviction, both Stalinist and social democratic, that something like a stable socialist society could be envisaged, in Balibar's interpretation of Lenin it is simply incoherent to consider socialism as a classless society. Though the transition period combines mixed transitional social relations with capitalist ones, it is not in any way an independent economic and social formation, or a mode of production in its own right. Neither evolutionary staging post nor stable phase, socialism is the organization, under the political control of the party and the state, of this contradictory coexistence. In Lenin's words, it is 'a phase of struggle, of contradiction between the surviving elements of the capitalist mode of production and the nascent elements of communist relations of production'.[56] The party would here be a kind of master or organizer of *décalage*. Socialism is from this vantage *the existence of two worlds in one*, for it 'is always based on commodity production and circulation in course of transformation towards non-commodity production', which includes 'a permanent *tendency* to the re-constitution of relations of exploitation, and of the development of the still existing forms of exploitation'.[57]

Building on Balibar's mapping of the problem, we could say that just as Marx's theory of transition may been seen to suffer from its insufficient attention to *reproduction-in-transition*—to the antagonistic interleaving in political time of schemas of reproduction and 'schemas of non-reproduction'[58]—a Leninist image of socialism is undermined by its inability fully to confront

55 See 'Dual Power' in this volume, pp. 170–95.
56 Quoted in Balibar, *On the Dictatorship of the Proletariat*, p. 144.
57 Balibar, *On the Dictatorship of the Proletariat*, p. 148.
58 Balibar, 'Reproductions', p. 158.

what it would mean to undo the forms of reproduction, forms bound (as Lenin himself recognized in the wake of Marx's *Critique of the Gotha Programme*) to abstract labour in its multiple economic, legal and social dimensions. As Robert Linhart incisively details in *Lenin, the Peasants and Taylor*, the party as master of the lag itself mutates into a schizoid or tragic form, treating this lag as one in which *political* communism is to master the *social* endurance of commodity relations, with the bitter irony of workers split between their political roles as agents of transition (or even of pre-figurative communist relations) and their subsumption to the residual coercive forms of the law of value.[59] What's more, the phase of socialism as state capitalism implies an indefensible faith in the capacity of political power to subsume and progressively neutralize capitalist relations—while the material, economic conditions of those state capacities result in the reinforcement, or even intensification, of relations of exploitation and domination. The absence of a theory of reproduction-in-transition is thus shadowed by the lack of a critical political economy of the state.[60] The consequence of this unfinished business with reproduction and the state is a twofold over-estimation: of culture and of politics.

First, as evidenced for instance in Korsch's proposal of socialization, inordinate idealist weight is placed on the cultural

59 Robert Linhart, *Lénine, les paysans et Taylor* (Paris: Seuil, 2010[1976]).

60 Balibar suggests as much in 'État, parti, transition', where he delineates how Lenin's theory of transition tends to isolate the party from the internal contradictions of the bourgeois state—a state which, in political-economic and sociological terms, is by no means 'smashed' by the mere fact of revolution. But see also, for a more nuanced historical reflection on the relationship between economic and political forms in Lenin's provisional balance-sheet of the Bolshevik Revolution, Charles Bettelheim, *Les luttes de classes en URSS: 1ère période, 1917–1923* (Paris: Seuil/Maspero, 1974), pp. 402–3. Bettelheim also argues elsewhere for the primacy of politics, but of *class* and not just party politics, in his contribution to Paul M. Sweezy and Charles Bettelheim, *On the Transition to Socialism* (New York: Monthly Review, 1971), pp. 15–24.

formation or pedagogy of the proletariat, on the development of socialist habits that would somehow thwart the reproduction of capitalist relations. That said, it would also be unwise to neglect how the notion of a *cultural revolution*, through and beyond its reference to Maoist China, draws its impetus and determinacy from the effort to respond to some of the deadlocks in the thinking of transition, especially as concerned the thwarted dialectic between party, state, classes, and masses. It is indeed from the vantage point of the aporias of transition, and from attempts at 'rectifying' the theory of transition, that we can understand the significance of the 'internal critique of Stalinism' even for a thinker like Balibar, who had little affinity for the organizational models of Maoism, with their stress on will and enthusiasm.[61]

Second, as evidenced especially by Althusser's posthumously published book manuscript on reproduction, we encounter the temptation to give priority to the conquest of the *state* institutions that oversee and regulate the reproduction of capitalist relations of production. A revolution is depicted as what 'interrupts' and appropriates the conditions of reproduction.[62] Here the radical, enduring core of the state is taken to be its repressive apparatus, whereas Ideological State Apparatuses are 'infinitely more vulnerable'.[63] It is struggles in the latter that *prepare* revolutions, which is why reproduction is central to the concrete history of revolutions. Balibar's own rectification of the Althusserian theory

---

61 On 'cultural revolution' as a rectification of the Leninist theory and practice of transition, see 'État, parti, transition', for an ampler discussion in Balibar on Maoism and cultural revolution, which stresses the question (itself of considerable significance for 'transitional' questions) of the division of intellectual and manual labour, see Étienne Balibar, 'Mao: critique interne du stalinisme?' in 'Sociétés occidentales / Idée du socialisme', special issue, *Actuel Marx* 3 (1988): 145–54. See also Fredric Jameson, 'Cultural Revolution' in *Valences of the Dialectic*.

62 Louis Althusser, *Sur la reproduction* (Paris: PUF, 1995), p. 182.

63 Althusser, *Sur la reproduction*, p. 184.

of transition in his intervention at a 1979 conference at the Centre d'Études et de Recherches Marxistes on 'The Contemporary State in France', identified the limitations of such an understanding of transition, which would overburden the party with the subjective tasks of the passage out of capitalism while not confronting how deep the infrastructure of reproduction goes. The state, in its juridical rather than extended meaning, is for Balibar a relatively *weak* element. As we've witnessed across multiple revolutions and regime changes over the past decades, the state can change hands without fundamentally troubling the vicissitudes of accumulation and social power. This also relates to the limitations of the party, which, while sometimes excelling in the struggle against *centralized* political power (say, in the figure of the despot), is found wanting when it is a matter of confronting the *concentration* of social power, in the interlinking of economic control, the division of labour, and the mechanisms of ideological subjection.[64]

Lenin beyond Lenin?

Where Balibar's polemic against the post-Stalinist or Euro-communist understanding of socialism underscored its Leninist image as a phase of social struggle and reconfiguration under political oversight, Toni Negri's reflections on communism and transition, roughly contemporaneous with the PCF debate on the dictatorship of the proletariat,[65] deny any continuity between socialism and communism. Partially resonating with what Henri Lefevbre was writing at the time about the state mode of production in the 4-volume *De l'État* (On the State), Negri deems socialism not a pre-communist phase, however contradictory, but the superior form of the economic rationality of capitalism. The target here is

---

64 See Balibar, 'État, parti, transition'. This article's concern with the Marxist aporias of the party/state dyad is expanded upon in 'Les apories'.

65 Negri was hosted by Louis Althusser in his seminar at the École normale supérieure, where the lectures that make up Negri's *Marx Beyond Marx* were first delivered.

both the rightist teleological linearity of stages and a leftist penchant for communism as utopia or catastrophe—for both, communism comes *after*. For Negri instead, communism is only ever given *in transition*, as the practical negation of capitalist categories, which he articulates in a dense but ultimately incisive formulation: 'it is not the transition that reveals itself (and eliminates itself) in the form of communism, but rather it is communism that takes the form of transition'[66]—a form that involves the planned liberation from labour.

Though we might see the jettisoning of the idea of socialism as an advance, it is not evident that Negri has resolved, or even convincingly posed the problem of reproduction-in-transition emerging from Balibar's reflections.[67] His starting point is a collapse in the difference between productive and reproductive labour—in that sense opening up reproduction beyond both simple reproduction and its political over-determination in Balibar. But despite protestations against teleology, we could argue that the model of living labour's 'productivity' straining against the obsolescent, parasitic limits of capitalism and its state still retains a schema of transition as the resultant of the contradiction between content and form, forces and relations, or indeed needs and exploitation—something that Balibar's differential analysis had warned us against.

---

66 Antonio Negri, *Marx Beyond Marx: Lessons on the 'Grundrisse'* (New York: Autonomedia, 1991), p. 153.

67 Though I cannot do it any justice here, any contemporary consideration of the problem of transition as a problem of political practice must take into consideration the reflections on the 'state in times of transition' that arose out of the now largely thwarted political processes that unfolded in Venezuela and Bolivia in the 2000s. It is telling, in this respect, that the attempt to theorize the transitional state by the former Bolivian vice-president, Álvaro García Linera, is explicitly formulated in terms of *reproduction*: 'In moments of *state crisis*, what are the mechanisms of the reproduction and amplification of the new correlation of forces emerging from social insurgency, collective movements and elections?' See 'Bloque de poder y punto de bifurcación' in *La potencia plebeya* (La Habana: Fondo Editorial Casa de las Americas, 2011), p. 353.

What both Balibar and Negri leave us with is not a theory but a problem of transition, one in which the idea of a socialist phase is in abeyance and the question of reproduction comes to the fore. This pushes us beyond the *analogy* in transition between modes of production—especially the analogy between the passage from feudalism to capitalism and the transition *from* capitalism. The critical difference between the two philosophers can be located in their way of confronting unevenness and its temporalities. We could see *Marx Beyond Marx* as answering the question of what transition becomes when it does not draw on unevenness—on the coevalness of different temporalities, the stress and strain between different modes of production. But the result is an overly linear and homogenizing conception of revolutionary change, which in its attention to the material realities of cooperation underplays their insidiously capitalist forms. This makes it possible for Negri to postulate the insurgent autonomy of an antagonistic class, which fails—precisely at the level of reproduction, of the capillary resilience of capitalist relations and ideologies—the test of realism.

Against the temptation to flee the aporias of transition through the exaltation of subjectivity or political decision, in recasting this pivotal problem today we should especially attend to the interlinked dimensions of time, space, and reproduction. Though the stasis of the present has turned the imaginary of a radical caesura into a lodestar for political theory, we should work against this theoretical desire, and return to a thinking of the *long* transition, of transition not as a programme of construction but a contradictory tendency—as Marx wrote in *Civil Wars in France*, a time of 'long struggles [. . .] a series of historic processes'.[68] These processes must be thought in their social and geographical unevenness, against capital's own fantasies of homogeneity and smoothness. Lastly, it is perhaps time to turn away from the lures of enthusiasm and wilfulness, from the desire for a break with a present that we

---

68 See 'État, parti, transition', where Balibar cites this passage from Marx.

imagine as self-identical, moving instead towards developing the kinds of analyses and actions that might be able to confront the thorny question of what I've termed reproduction-in-transition. We may therefore have more to learn today from the Lenin who soberly recognized that revolutionary Russia was still capitalist— in the depths of its social relations, by the compulsions of the world market, through the very parameters of its social reproduction— than from the Lenin who scrawled in the margin of his Hegel: 'Leaps! Leaps! Leaps!'[69]

---

69 Quoted in Daniel Bensaïd, ' "Leaps, Leaps, Leaps": Lenin and Politics', *International Socialism* 95 (2002).

NINE

Dual Power

From now on your first imperative should be: 'Imagine!'
And your second, immediately connected to the first:
'Fight against those who cultivate the weakening of this
faculty'.

—Günther Anders, *The Molussian Catacomb*

The present, due to its staggering complexities, is almost
as conjectural as the past.

—George Jackson, *Blood in My Eye*

The Spectre of Reformism

Reformism is our utopia. That would be a reasonable conclusion to
draw from the discourse that accompanied the recomposition, electoral surge, impasse and retreat of electoral Lefts in Southern
Europe (especially Greece and Spain) in the second decade of the
twenty-first century. It also speaks to the broader structure of feeling belonging to progressive movements worldwide. Politicians
who came of age in the neoliberal nineties, and whose image of
antagonism was durably shaped by the so-called anti-globalization
movement, addressed their ideological constituencies with a
simple, sober message: what constituted the common sense of the
post-war Western European compact between state, capital and
labour, across the Christian-Democrat and social-democratic (or
even communist) divide—namely a welfare state animated by a

regulative ideal of expansive social citizenship—was now both the 'point of the impossible' (to borrow Alain Badiou's formulation) of the European order, and the only basis to build a national- popular consensus against austerity, not so much beyond but *before* left and right.[70]

In 'An American Utopia', Fredric Jameson, faithful to his conviction that one must struggle indefatigably for social democracy to learn the lessons of its bankruptcy,[71] inscribes this moment of opposition not as a component of a transitional programme for the present, but as a 'discursive struggle' that might be waged in the representational sphere by a retooled party-political cadre, a struggle that is ultimately distinct from the business of materially challenging capitalist power.[72] This predicament is a product not only of what Jameson frames as the twin implosion of the revolutionary and reformist paths, of Leninist wars of manoeuvre and social-democratic wars of position—which is to say of the strategic horizons of all the Internationals of the socialist and communist movements—but of the seeming collapse of André Gorz's framing distinction between reformist and non-reformist reforms: all reformism, understood as a durable if gradual transformation of the status quo in the direction of greater equality and freedom, is stamped by neo-liberalism with the mark of impossibility. The depressing pantomime of Eurogroup meetings with Greece's SYRIZA-led government in 2015 certainly testified to this. Yet the fact that contemporary radicalism must fashion its mass appeal by

---

70 See Pablo Iglesias Turrión, *Disputar la democracia. Política para tiempos de crisis* (Madrid: Akal, 2014). See also my review article on Iglesias: Alberto Toscano, 'Portrait of the Leader as a Young Theorist', *Jacobin*, 19 December 2015 (available online: https://bit.ly/411J000; last accessed: 17 February 2023).

71 Fredric Jameson, 'Lenin and Revisionism' in Sebastian Budgen, Stathis Kouvelakis and Slavoj Žižek (eds), *Lenin Reloaded: Toward a Politics of Truth* (Durham: Duke University Press, 2007), p. 69.

72 Fredric Jameson, *An American Utopia: Dual Power and the Universal Army* (Slavoj Žižek ed.) (London: Verso, 2016).

confrontationally refunctioning the non-utopian features of reformism as the basis for a rupture with the status quo is instructive. It
appears to corroborate Jameson's diagnosis of the imaginative and
ideological closure of the present, even as it instantiates the very
discursive struggle he gestures towards.

At the crux of Jameson's essay is the conviction, which I think
unimpeachable, that to unblock the atrophied strategic imaginary
of the Left a new conception of transition is necessary. It is striking
nevertheless that transition is so closely associated here with the
problem of *positive* utopia (and not just of the negative utopian
impulse towards another future). After all, with relation to the
Marxist tradition, it could even be argued that the problem of
transition—as formulated in Marx's 'Critique of the Gotha
Programme', Lenin's *State and Revolution*, and many other tracts
and programmes—was profoundly anti-utopian in intention,
delineating the strategic outlines of how the power of state and
capital could be disarticulated while side-lining frameworks that
would regard revolution as a matter of implementing a utopian
schema.[73] This is even more the case for what Jameson presents here
as the 'third' transition (after the revolutionary war of manoeuvre
and the reformist war of position), *dual power*. In Lenin's
formulation, the latter appears as an extreme anomaly or
aberration, a true Russian exception that expresses the extremely
unique conditions in which the deficiency of the bourgeois revolution and the premature irruption of the proletarian one came to
overlap. There is a kind of delightful dialectical perversity in
Jameson's choice of dual power as the lever through which to
refunction both transition and utopia for a seemingly closed
present. To gauge its effects, a detour through some figures of dual
power is required.

---

73 Here one would need to dwell on how the partial Bolshevik achievement
of transition led to an explosion of concrete and speculative utopias, from
projects of de-urbanization to orchestras without conductors. See Richard
Stites' wonderful *Revolutionary Dreams: Utopian Vision and Experimental Life
in the Russian Revolution* (Oxford: Oxford University Press, 1991).

Power in the Interregnum

In 1917, during the tumultuous interregnum between the collapse of Tsarism and the October revolution, Lenin stressed the unprecedented emergence of a wild anomaly in the panorama of political forms: dual power. As he remarked in Pravda, 'alongside the Provisional Government, the government of the bourgeoisie, another government has arisen, so far weak and incipient, but undoubtedly a government that actually exists and is growing—the Soviets of Workers' and Soldiers' Deputies'.[74] The often sterile disputations over the evils and virtues of the seizure of state power tend to obscure the far greater challenge posed by thinking revolutionary politics in terms of the *sundering* of power—not just in the guise of a face-off between two (or more) social forces in a situation of non-monopoly over violence and political authority, but in the sense of a fundamental *asymmetry* in the types of power. The power wielded by the Soviets is incommensurable with that of their bourgeois counterpart, however 'democratic' it may be, because its source lies in popular initiative and not parliamentary decree; because it is enforced by an armed people and not a standing army; and because it has transmuted political authority from a plaything of the bureaucracy to a condition wherein all officials are at the mercy of the popular will and its power of recall.

The model for this power of a new type is the Paris Commune. And it is the incipient, *larval* form of 'a state of the type of the Paris Commune' that, in the spring and summer of 1917, coexists with the parliamentary type of State, the 'dictatorship of the bourgeoisie'. In the tradition that draws from Lenin's texts—yet another case in Marxism where ephemeral and exceptional categories are, for better and for worse, turned into trans-historical or at least trans-situational ones—this notion of dual power as the consolidation of embryonic institutions of the proletariat's 'non-state state' is critical.

---

74 Vladimir Lenin, 'The Dual Power' (9 April 1917) (Isaacs Bernard trans.) in *Lenin Collected Works*, VOL. 24 (Moscow: Progress Publishers, 1964), pp. 38–41 (available online: https://bit.ly/2FHtjTL; last accessed: 17 February 2023).

Antonio Gramsci will speak of a state *in potentia*. From the juridical standpoint, dual power as an embryo of workers' power is also a site of legitimacy without legality, and thus the incubator or political condenser of a new legality, which is also to say new relations of power based on the direct initiative of the masses.[75] But for such a preparation of new power to take place, the notion of dual power demands a deeply rooted prior form of collective identity—no doubt one politically mediated and consciously intensified by these institutions, but nevertheless grounded in class belonging or even tradition.

To return to the context of interregnum, the Soviets, which were not yet under Bolshevik hegemony, lived under the constant menace, exacerbated by the advocates of reform, of a neutralizing absorption into a state power that in principle suffers no duality (in this sense, Lenin and Trotsky are 'Weberian', and the great German sociologist will indeed return the favour by quoting Trotsky himself to back up his canonical formulations on the monopoly of violence). In such a conjuncture, the only strategy is to strengthen the new type of power, 'clarifying proletarian minds . . . emancipating them from the influence of the bourgeoisie', since 'as long as no violence is used against the people there is no other road to [State] power'. The problem of constituting a potent communist bloc and consolidating the new type of power into a force that can truly sap the dictatorship of the bourgeoisie is thus a problem of autonomy and separation, of the disciplined, painstaking constitution of a proletarian political capacity that takes its distance from the apparatus of the state in order to prepare its 'smashing'. This process of constitution is marked by an inexorable temporal determination. The 'interlocking' of two dictatorships gives rise to an exceedingly volatile amalgam, whence the axiom: 'Two powers cannot exist in a state'.[76]

---

75 Riccardo Guastini, 'Materiali per una teoria del doppio potere' in *I due poteri: Stato borghese e stato operaio nell'analisi marxista* (Bologna: Il mulino, 1978).
76 Vladimir Lenin, 'The Tasks of the Proletariat in Our Revolution' [Draft

Dual power is thus both an opportunity and a menace, the terrain where autonomy and initiative can be quashed or squandered. This is the sense in which, in June 1917, Lenin, facing a capitalist offensive in the domain of production itself, declares: 'The root of the evil is in the dual power'.[77] And the culprits of this crisis, the harbingers of the 'evil', are precisely those who seek to serve as hinges between the two powers, the 'Narodniks and Mensheviks' who lead the Soviets (the power of the majority) in the interests of the bourgeoisie (the dictatorship of the minority). In any case, 'this dual power cannot last long'. This merely transitory *kairos* or occasion that dual power represents, founded on the lethal contest between two dictatorships—two types of power—means that Lenin cannot accept the 'fetishism' of the Soviet as an organ of self-government but will seek, through the fundamental instance of the party, in Antonio Negri's gloss, to 'fix in the Soviets the immediate expression and political form of class insubordination to the general experience of exploitation' and to maintain the dyad 'autonomy-organization'.[78] For without class autonomy there is no organization and without organization, class autonomy— independent proletarian political capacity—dissipates. In this

Platform for the Proletarian Party] (September 1917) (Isaacs Bernard trans.) in *Lenin Collected Works*, VOL. 24 (Moscow: Progress Publishers, 1964), pp. 55-92 (available online: https://bit.ly/3YuCc9z; last accessed: 17 February 2023).

77 Vladimir Lenin, 'Has Dual Power Disappeared?' (May/June 1917) (Isaacs Bernard trans.) in *Lenin Collected Works*, VOL. 24 (Moscow: Progress Publishers, 1964), pp. 445-48 (available online: https://bit.ly/3xsshoW; last accessed: 17 February 2023). As Lenin notes:

> Meanwhile the crisis is growing. Things have reached a point where the capitalists—the coal mine owners—are brazenly committing outrageous *crimes—they* are *disorganising and stopping* production. Unemployment is spreading. There is talk of lockouts. Actually they have *started* in the form of disorganization of production by the capitalists (for coal is the *bread of industry!*), in the form of growing unemployment.

78 Antonio Negri, *Factory of Strategy: Thirty-Three Lessons on Lenin* (Arianna Bove trans.) (New York: Columbia University Press, 2014), pp. 123-24.

context, dual power, as Negri notes—contrary to the Menshevik vision of incorporating the Soviets within the state as a 'regional' instance of worker's self-government and self-management—is 'not a juridical relation that can be institutionalized'.[79] For Negri, the 'ambiguity of dual power must therefore be confronted and resolved from the workers' standpoint: first and foremost, the proletarian moment of the antithesis must be emphasized and thus exalted until it founds the dictatorship of the proletariat in its Soviet form'.[80]

While for Jameson dual power is marshalled for the critique of political theory, of the political as a theoretical and practical chimera, it could be argued that in Lenin's work, precisely as an anomaly, aberration, or exception—albeit one that demands to be seized upon strategically—dual power marks out the space for a specifically Marxist political thought. This is not a vision of transhistorical normativity, or of the state's foundational antinomies, but a thinking of the necessary invention, in situations of crisis, of political forms oriented towards the abolition of capital. In his *Dual Power in Latin America*, the Bolivian theorist René Zavaleta Mercado, writing through the unravelling of the truncated experiments in dual power in Bolivia and Chile while attending to the conceptual and political history of the notion in Russia and South America, signalled this singular status of dual power by referring to it as 'a Marxist metaphor that designates a special type of state contradiction or a state conjuncture of transition'.[81] I take this to suggest that, unlike the concepts of classical political theory, dual power, as a term that tries to approximate the uniqueness of a social and state crisis, does not cover or subsume its cases. In stressing (and indeed, perhaps overstressing) the difference between Lenin and Trotsky on this matter, Zavaleta argues that while in Lenin the

---

79 Negri, *Factory of Strategy*, p. 127.
80 Negri, *Factory of Strategy*, p. 127.
81 René Zavaleta Mercado, *El poder dual en América Latina: Estudio de los casos de Bolivia y Chile* (México: Siglo XXI, 1974), p. 18.

phenomenon of dual power *between* February and October is an extremely singular exception to antecedent theories of revolution, an overdetermined *fact* that demands the invention of an organization and strategic response, for Trotsky's later systematization of the notion of dual power in his history of the Russian revolution, dual power is a regularity, a social law of revolution instantiated in conjunctures as dissimilar as the opposition of Parliament and King in pre-revolutionary England, or the confrontation between Constituent Assembly and Monarchy in pre-revolutionary France. Notwithstanding the brilliance of Trotsky's play of historical analogies, for Zavaleta turning dual power into a social law ultimately dissolves the distinctiveness of Lenin's proposal, which lay in giving the name dual power to a phase of *qualitative contemporaneity and antagonistic development* of two asymmetrical, incommensurable powers, and even more precisely, of *two revolutions*, a congenitally malformed bourgeois one and a larval but powerful proletarian one. A qualitative asymmetry of powers and a quantitative conflict. Of this *political* unevenness there isn't really any 'law', but only, I would suggest, *figures*. It is one of the extreme weaknesses of 'Leninism' as a *forma mentis* and fetish that it has sought to turn the extremely exceptional circumstances of 1917 and the Bolsheviks' forced choices into a cookbook or algorithm for revolutions and insurrections to come. In this respect, dual power—like, albeit in a different vein, transition itself—is a *problem* (or a metaphor in Zavaleta's sense) not a general concept or theory.

As Negri presents it in his *Factory of Strategy*, Lenin's is a constant struggle against the 'constitutional mummification' of dual power, the transmutation of the Soviets into organs of democratic representation rather than class dictatorship. Communists must always reject this transformation; the movement must continue; it must surpass itself. Indeed, some of Negri's most interesting pages in his lessons on Lenin bear on the way the politics of capital, in its high reformist moments (especially the New Deal), inoculated itself with the Soviet form; how it institutionalized apparatuses of self-government in the guise of self-management and workers' collaborative insertion into the mechanisms and ideology of industrial labour. Against this recuperative dialectic, the autonomist imperative is that of an institutionalization of antagonism, the creation of 'class institutions, for the class, in the class', the 'institutionalization inside capital of what capital can only institutionalize for the purposes of domination, the consolidation of struggle for the purposes of power, and the irreversibility of struggles from the standpoint of struggle itself, of the process of the destruction of the existing'.[82]

Negri's wager is that the task of repeating Lenin must pass through a reckoning with the transformation in class composition (both in the subjective capacity of the class and its place in the dynamics of capital accumulation) as well as in the very meaning of power. Dual power retains its pertinence, but it is no longer thought exclusively in terms of the state as apex and possessor of power but in view of a 'tendential identification of capital and the State (a total fusion of organization and command)'.[83] Under these conditions of real subsumption, there is a plenitude of both capitalist and workers' power: the capitalist unification of society and its totalizing organization reproduce, over the entirety of the social fabric, the full potency of class antagonism, which is essential to the definition of capital. But if the overall concept of power under conditions of the real subsumption of society under capital cannot be identified with the seizure of state power per se, then, following Negri's argument, we could say that there emerges yet another 'new type' of (proletarian) power. For Lenin's vision of dual power as a critical and explosive but still transitory stage depended on a certain conception of power that Negri calls a 'non-dialectical absolute', not so distant from the bourgeois theories of power qua monopoly

---

82 Negri, *Factory of Strategy*, p. 142.
83 Negri, *Factory of Strategy*, p. 145 (translation modified).

exemplified by Weber and presaged in classic doctrines of sovereign *raison d'état*. On the contrary, the workers' struggles of the 1960s and 1970s, according to Negri (who does not flinch, in these pages, from invoking Mao as a distant witness), determine a new experience and a new concept of power, understood as a 'dialectical absolute that unfolds in the long term of the dualism of power, as a struggle that subverts the capital relation by introducing the worker's variable as a conscious will of destruction'.[84]

This newer type of proletarian power is paradoxically qualified as a form of *extremist gradualism*, a 'gradualism of power, of its seizure and management, [which] is the gradual nature of the destruction of capitalist power and capital relations'.[85] Whence the thesis that underlies the new Sovietism which Negri, at the time immersed in the experience of the extra-parliamentary group Potere Operaio, proclaims to be 'the transformation of the concept of insurrection into that of permanent civil war'.[86] Without entering into the virtues of such a provocative proposal, or indeed how it might relate to a strategic (mis)calculation of class forces and class composition, it is worth remarking that the vision of this permanent civil war, and of its new type of prolonged, gradual/ destructive dual power, led to an attempt to practice an appropriation and defence of physical areas of autonomy and 'self-valorisation'—'red bases' or liberated zones.[87] The presence of these Maoist concepts points to a key aspect of the autonomist theorization of dual power under conditions of real subsumption, namely its fusion of two models and practices of dual power: first, the intensive and metropolitan 'general strike scenario' (the model of urban insurrection manifest in the Paris Commune, the Petrograd Soviet, or the uprisings in Hamburg, Guangzhou, and

---

84 Negri, *Factory of Strategy*, p. 152.

85 Negri, *Factory of Strategy*, pp. 152–53.

86 Negri, *Factory of Strategy*, p. 153 (translation modified).

87 See Alberto Toscano, 'Factory, Territory, Metropolis, Empire', *Angelaki: Theoretical Journal of the Humanities* 9(2) (2004): 197–216.

Barcelona in the 1920s and 1930s), which might lead us to inter-rogate Jameson's distinction between dual power and uprising; second, the extensive and territorial prolonged 'popular war scenario', for which the Chinese revolution serves as a paragon, and which might lead us to qualify Jameson's demarcation of dual power from the figure of the enclave.[88] On the basis of a conviction in the power of the metropolitan proletariat in its new class com-position, the long duration of the people's war is projected onto the texture of the city.

Dual Biopower

In his more recent work with Michael Hardt, Negri has given a biopolitical twist to these earlier reflections on dual power. Writing of the legacy of guerrilla warfare, they note that it

> increasingly adopted the characteristics of biopolitical production and spread throughout the entire fabric of society, it more directly posed as its goal the production of subjectivity—economic and cultural subjectivity, both material and immaterial. It was not just a matter of 'win-ning hearts and minds', in other words, but rather of creat-ing new hearts and minds through the construction of new circuits of communication, new forms of social col-laboration, and new modes of interaction. In this process we can discern a tendency toward moving beyond the modern guerrilla model toward more democratic network forms of organization.[89]

88 See Daniel Bensaïd, 'On the return of the politico-strategic question' (August 2006), *International Viewpoint Online* 386 (February 2007) (available online: https://bit.ly/3YV8KJM; last accessed: 17 February 2023); *La politique comme art stratégique* (Paris: Syllepse, 2010). See also Ben Brewster's reflections on the Comintern's manual on *Armed Insurrection*, signed Neuberg but written by a team including Ho Chi Minh, Mikhail Tukhachesvsky and Hans Kippenberger, in 'Armed Insurrection and Dual Power', *New Left Review* 66 (1971): 59–68.

89 Hardt and Negri, *Multitude*, p. 81.

Is the contemporary horizon for a recovery and recasting of the theme of dual power a 'biopolitical' one? It is difficult to ignore that whether we are talking about the non-antagonistic forms of participatory dual power in the Porto Alegre model of urban self-government, the Zapatista attempt to defend zones for the self-organization of 'civil society' against oligarchic repression,[90] or the attempts to articulate forms of democracy-from-below with national-popular projects in Bolivia and Venezuela, the biopolitical element (understood both in the sophisticated sense of Hardt and Negri, but also in the simpler sense of welfare) is conspicuous.

The Lebanese Hezbollah is an interesting figure in this respect, representing the rise of a kind of 'biopolitical Islamism' in a context of dual power. Determined by a very unique historical and political constellation—which combines the anti-Israeli national resistance struggle, a Khomeinist party ideology profoundly modulated by the conditions of a multi-confessional Lebanon permanently threatened by relapse into bloody sectarianism, the contradictory support of Syria and Iran, and a wide proletarian Shi'ia social base—Hezbollah has thrived at different moments in the systematic use of the duality power (military, territorial, moral) and could be seen to represent a variant of this political form which is irreducible both to the model of the Leninist *kairos* as well to that of the people's war. This variant of dual power instead functions within something like a *permanent interregnum*, where its power is wielded forcefully but not in the sense of a unilateral seizure. Within this volatile geometry of forces, the 'biopolitical' element provides much of dual power's substance. In the planet of slums anatomized by Mike Davis we could even say that the 'biopolitical supplement' to the neoliberal evacuation of services and solidarity is both inextricable from and primary vis-à-vis any mere military strategy. Hezbollah's hegemonic strivings have depended on addressing key questions of the government of life, adopting a

90 See Zapatista Army of National Liberation, 'Second Declaration of the Lacandon Jungle' (June 1994) (available online: https://bit.ly/3xvriVc; last accessed: 17 February 2023).

'process of advocacy based on extensive-fact finding and teamed with grass roots support.'[91] In these Islamist inquiries of sorts, issues such as water problems are addressed through scientific-academic methods (Hezbollah's Center for Developmental Studies) and by encouraging 'the formation of residential and professional groups'[92] that can provide the territorial rooting for these welfare ventures. In a situation of prolonged dual power where the stakes, contrary to those envisioned by Negri, are precisely based on averting civil war whilst gaining relative hegemony over a population (what Judith Palmer Harik simply calls 'the abandoned') side-lined by a fragmented, unequal, and threadbare state, dual power is biopower, and daily garbage collection, large-scale health service provision, and emergency water delivery are weapons of the first order. Though little if anything can be directly extrapolated from a unique situation in which the notion of balance of power takes on an intense and tragic if quotidian connotation, Hezbollah's variant of biopolitical Islam hints at some of the contemporary conditions for the rethinking and exercise of dual power, where the separation of an autonomous political capacity and the generation of new types of power (whether revolutionary, conservative, or reactionary) cannot bypass the dimension of the production and reproduction of social life—in short, the question of survival. These interstitial, secessionist or parallel figures of para-state power are in turn bound to mutations in the state-form itself, which increasingly, especially as concerns territories targeted by neo-liberal, neo-colonial, and neo-imperial operations, no longer translates into the lamination of government, territory and population, but instead devolves into a violent governance by 'zones', indexed to the shifting requirements of extraction and security.[93] It is this context of neoliberalism which

91 Judith Palmer Harik, *Hezbollah: The Changing Face of Terrorism* (London: IB Tauris, 2005), p. 89.

92 Harik, *Hezbollah*, p. 89.

93 Badiou stresses this question of zones in his lecture course *Images du temps présent (2001–2004)* (Paris: Fayard, 2014). For an architectural and geographic reflection on these phenomena, see Alessandro Petti, *Arcipelaghi e enclave:*

is altering the link between capital and the spaces of governance and jurisdiction, and allowing for a proliferation, in various regions of the world, of violently overlapping authorities and enclaves in conjunctures of incomplete sovereignty.

A possible foothold for beginning to think transition concretely would then be to take into consideration the crucial phenomenon of what we could call a kind of *dual biopower*—which is to say a collective attempt politically to appropriate aspects of social reproduction that state and capital have abandoned, degraded, or rendered unbearably exclusionary, from housing to medicine. These aspects—which are also the privileged sites for any non-reformist reforms one might propose in the current conjuncture— are today the principal organizing bases of successful popular movements, whether progressive or reactionary. But they have also been the fulcrums from which to think the dismantling of capitalist social forms and relations without relying on the premise of a political break in the operations of power, without waiting for 'the day after', the seizure or evaporation of the repressive apparatus. Though they could be read in a merely ameliorative lens, the brutally repressed experiments of the Black Panthers with breakfast programmes, sickle-cell anaemia screening, and an alternative health service for the Black 'lumpen'—to use their own ter-minology—are one such example, and their articulation with a con-ception of self-defence not irrelevant to our own time.[94] This also relates to the 'epidemiological dual structure' of which Jameson beguilingly speaks[95]—and which now resonates so intensely in the

---

Architettura dell'ordinamento spaziale contemporaneo (Milan: Mondadori, 2007).
94 See Alondra Nelson, *Body and Soul: The Black Panther Party and the Fight Against Medical Discrimination* (Minneapolis, MN: University of Minnesota Press, 2013). See also Joshua Bloom and Waldo E. Martin, *Black Against Empire: The History and Politics of the Black Panther Party* (Berkeley, CA: University of California Press, 2014).
95 As he writes: 'it may not be impossible to imagine crisis situations in which physicians are able to wield social power of considerable significance, in a kind of epidemiological dual structure'. Jameson, *American Utopia*, p. 17.

protracted Covid-19 pandemic. We cannot but remark the centrality of health to transitional imaginaries in a phase plagued by crises of social reproduction (the critical and rational core, to my mind, of discussions on biopolitics): from the Solidarity for All initiatives that accompanied SYRIZA's rise in Greece to Hazan and Kamo's utopian speculations on how health could be a prominent locus of 'first revolutionary measures'.[96] As we witness the proliferation of spatial and temporal 'dualities', the sheer fragmentation and zoning in the domain of social reproduction, and the formation of mutual aid collectives through the uneven time and space of crisis, we can also start to think which of these experiments can be propagated or scaled up—not in fantasies of secession, or in the illusion that post-capitalism is really possible now, but as ways of rooting the need to undo capitalist relations in the real if partial experience of attempts to limit capital's powers and repurpose its (our) dead labours.

Crisis Politics

Even if, following Zavaleta, we treat dual power as a metaphor or problem, rather than a universal whose particulars we could inventory, it is still possible to identify some of its elements. It is in light of these that I want to address Jameson's anchoring of his utopian speculation in the 'universal army' as a concrete institution of dual power. Whether we identify the space-time of dual power as that of a punctual, if uneven, crisis of the state, or in the protracted or 'permanent' (if also uneven) crisis of social reproduction, the great majority of invocations of dual power follow Lenin's lead in seeing it as inextricable from crisis. While war is certainly on the horizon, mediate or immediate, of these debates, to the extent that

---

96 Hazan & Kamo, *Prèmieres mesures révolutionnaires*. See the extremely perspicuous critical comments in Jason E. Smith's extended review of this pamphlet, 'The Day After the Insurrection: On *First Revolutionary Measures*', *Radical Philosophy* 189 (2015): 37–44.

it is the crisis of the state and its functions that they address, we could say that all the figures of dual power surveyed above already, to different degrees, respond to Jameson's important entreaty: 'we must invent better temporal models of crisis, long- and short-term, than those afforded by war.'[97]

The second element, along with crisis, is evidently the state: whether they are shadowed—as Bolshevik debates certainly were— by a conception of the state as a unified monopoly of violence that cannot tolerate duality, or whether they conceive the duality (or multiplicity) of powers in terms of a waning or fragmentation of the state, shedding areas of control or reproduction, the image of dual power is intimately bound to the extant modalities of state power. It is, to quote Zavaleta again, 'a special type of state contradiction or a state conjuncture of transition'.

This contradiction is exacerbated by the third element I'd like to stress, that of dual power as determined by the emergence of an *embryo of alternative power*, a *qualitatively different* power (and state) which shares and shapes the space-time of the official and legitimate power, and which sinks its roots in the *capacity* of an emergent class, so that—at least in 'classical' theories of this ultimately non-classical notion—dual power as a political reality is foreshadowed by a dualism of power emerging from the domain of production itself.

Jameson's American utopia of dual power appears to foreground this third element, the identification of an institutional embryo of a power other than that of the capitalist state, to the detriment of the other two. Against the classic, namely Leninist, figure of dual power, which links this hopeful but unstable strategic aberration to the specificity of a general crisis of the state, Jameson stages his search for a contemporary candidate for dual power in terms of the apparent impossibility of the very break in the structures of the state that was the condition of possibility for classic dual power in the first

---

97 Jameson, *American Utopia*, pp. 21–22.

place. Where the latter signalled an uneven qualitative interlocking of bourgeois and proletarian revolution, war of position and war of manoeuvre, dual power as speculative utopia is occasioned by the seeming occlusion of the very horizon in which these distinctions originally obtained. Crisis, both in the sense of a more or less punctual political rupture, and of the aforementioned implosion of social reproduction, certainly shadows this valiant speculative effort, but it is not as such integrated into the concept of dual power, save in the form of an indispensable symbolic ingredient, an analogue of war as mobilizing 'fetish' for a collective.

Jameson's communist fabulation shares with many of the utopias he's so brilliantly analysed elsewhere a curious relation to political time, which the terminology of dual power exacerbates: on the one hand, the turn to a revised notion of dual power is required by the absence of a prospect of revolutionary crisis, and thus suggests itself as a mechanism to unblock a situation of cognitive and practical paralysis; on the other, as the reference to Terry Bisson's splendid speculative abolitionist novel *Fire on the Mountain* intimates, such a dual power in real 'competition' with the state could only be envisaged *after* a rupture (and it is telling that utopian texts, projects and experiences proliferated *after* the Bolshevik revolution, rather than preparing its outbreak). No doubt, classic dual power itself was both *after* a rupture (February) and *before* the decisive one (October), but dual power as speculative utopia shifts from this determinate indeterminacy—which binds the dualism of power to the interregnum—to a rather different scenario, in which the background conditions of the classic form seem to be missing. Today, we are after October—still dragging along shards of the Bolshevik explosion, some as futile relics others as potential weapons—but we remain, in most of the world, before February, without a rupture in state domination yet in sight (the Arab Februaries grimly demonstrated that the incompleteness of revolution in no way moderates the brutality of counter-revolution).

This displacement or blackboxing of dual power as a state crisis of transition can be approached through the debates and shifts the concept has undergone from its initial formulations—in particular by addressing its resurgence in the 1970s in Latin American and European debates, and the set of theories and practices, already alluded to, which stress a duality or plurality of powers surfacing out of the state's abdication of many of its social reproduction functions in the ambit of the neo-liberal counter-revolution. In both these historical and conceptual clusters, we could speak of something like *diffuse* dual power, while recognizing, in the wake of Zavaleta's warnings, that any such diffusion, or indeed generalization, of dual power, risks fatally dissolving the notion, watering down its anomaly.

While maintaining a classic emphasis on the institutional duality of powers in the 'same' space-time (namely against the enclave and the 'riot-commune' as potential candidates of dual power), Jameson's American utopia inherits from the post-Leninist mutations of dual power the problem of how to think transitional institutions outside of a decisive rupture. In this respect, despite opting to retain the terminology of dual power, Jameson's proposal seems to share more with the strategic horizon of Nicos Poulantzas' democratic socialism—which envisaged a kind of erosion of the bonds between the bourgeoisie and the state—than with the Trotskyist vision of dual power advanced against the Greek philosopher by the young Henri Weber, for whom a military-political rupture was indispensable to retain any conception of revolution— a rupture that would be precipitated by the consolidation of diffuse social dual powers (the plurality of embryos of self-organization and popular power emerging in a protracted situation of social crisis) into a frontal challenge to the capitalist state.[98] Weber thus

---

98 See their 1977 debate on 'The State and the Transition to Socialism', now in Nicos Poulantzas, *The Poulantzas Reader: Marxism, Law and the State* (James Martin ed.) (London: Verso, 2008).

reasserts the classic perspective that a clash, a decisive rupture with some military dimension cannot be circumvented, and suggests contra Poulantzas that without full-blown dual power, no rupture is possible. Viewed from the vantage point of these 1970s debates, Jameson's speculative utopia of dual power is somewhat of a centaur—trying to articulate the duration of a long march *of* the institution (in this case the universal army) with a firm commitment to duality (against Poulantzas' far more 'molecular' conception of democratic struggles). Moreover, no doubt due to its US vantage point, which quickly puts paid to any parliamentary illusion, it entirely side-lines the problematic of representation and the party form that dominated earlier debates.[99]

What then of the scandalous proposal that we should seek the fulcrum of dual power in the army? Set against the often-disavowed anarcho-individualist or radical-liberal tendencies of much *soi-disant* contemporary anti-capitalism, this provocation is of course, as Jameson eventually concedes, the very point of the exercise, serving as a kind of reactant to reveal our deep-seated fear of the organized collective. Yet Jameson has anchored his utopia in a concrete question of revolutionary analysis and strategy, so we can be excused for also approaching it in that register. The first comment to make in that respect is that Jameson's search among *existing* institutions for his experimental subject of dual power goes against the grain of many of the debates we've already touched upon. Whether in the *cordones industriales* of Chile, the Panthers' health programmes, the *shura* councils of the Iranian revolution or the Asamblea Popular in Chile, or indeed the Petrograd Council of Workers' and Soldiers Deputies, embryonic revolutionary power is organized around *new* institutions, which from the start assert their asymmetry and incommensurability with the extant institutions of the state. Not that the

---

99 The party is of course the element of the classical-Leninist theory of dual power which serves as a kind of *point de capiton* (Jacques Lacan's 'quilting point') for the other three elements: the situation of crisis, the challenge to the state, and the embryos of power.

refunctioning of established institutions is a theme absent from revolutionary theory—far from it, since, notwithstanding de rigueur nods to the smashing of the state, most revolutionary practice is nothing but such a refunctioning, with all the contradictions, setbacks, and counter-finalities that entails. And yet that is not the unique problem that dual power has generally been invoked to articulate, or rather not so much to solve as to describe.

Now, and this is the second comment I want to make on the proposal of the universal army, Jameson's utopia turns the classic problem of dual power—in a nutshell, there exist but there cannot be two repressive apparatuses in one state, which is also to say *two states in one state*—into its own solution, by transmuting the army into the dual power itself. And yet in his own description of this utopian army, which emerges in a situation of dual power, and 'which begins life as a parallel force alongside the state *and its official army* (my emphasis) and finds its first tasks and indeed its vocation in the fulfilment of neglected social services and in a coexistence with the population of a wholly different type',[100] we sense that the figure of the *situation* of dual power is wholly unlike that faced by Lenin, for whom *by definition* an army couldn't be a locus of dual power. A 'parallel' force (rather than one embroiled in a frontal struggle) could only emerge once a rupture has taken place, be it only in the rise of the kind of *governmental* power that could decree universal conscription as a first transitional measure. But we are arguably here in a rather different terrain than classic dual power; more perhaps in that of a contradictory polity in which the duality of powers is experimented both from above and from below, in which (parts of) the state and (parts of) society are involved in a transitional effort that does not take the guise of a head-on conflict (a clash would be *immediate* given the existence of two armies representing different social and political imperatives in the same territory).

---

100 Jameson, *American Utopia*, p. 56.

Whether we want to call this an expanded or diffuse dual power or abandon the terminology altogether (as Poulantzas urged), it is nevertheless evident that we are in a post- or non-Leninist horizon. It is a horizon in which the state is neither an instrument nor a fortress, but a field of struggles[101] (and whatever Jameson's universal army might be, it still remains in many ways *of* the state, even or especially as it is envisaged as sapping the anti-emancipatory features of US *states*). This diffusion (and potential dissolution) of the problematic of dual power can be located in many disparate moments across the twentieth century: Korsch's councilist proposals for socialization from above and from below; the debate on *poder popular* in the last months of Salvador Allende's Unidad Popular government in Chile[102]; but also the theoretical efforts by the likes of Sartre or Althusser to think how the party could be reimagined no longer as the monopolist of power, but in a novel articulation with mass initiatives and forms of self-organization that would permit envisaging a non-Leninist politics which is still resolutely anti-liberal, preventing dual power from devolving into a balance of powers.[103] In our own century, this is

---

101 See Panagiotis Sotiris, 'Neither an Instrument nor a Fortress: Poulantzas' Theory of the State and his Dialogue with Gramsci', *Historical Materialism* 22(2) (2014): 135–57.

102 See Franck Gaudichaud (ed.), *¡Venceremos! Analyses et documents sur le pouvoir populaire au Chili (1970–1973)* (Paris: Syllepse, 2013).

103 Responding to Rossana Rossanda, also Althusser's interlocutor in the interview on 'Marxism as a Finite Theory' in which he advanced rather similar views, Sartre says: 'At any rate, what seems to me interesting in your schema is the duality of power which it foreshadows. This means an open and irreducible relation between the *unitary* moment, which falls to the political organization of the class, and the moments of self-government, the councils, the fused groups. I insist on that word "irreducible" because there can only be a permanent tension between the two moments. The party will always try, to the degree that it wants to see itself as "in the service" of the movement, to reduce it to its own schema of interpretation and development; while the moments of self-government will always try to project their living partiality upon the contradictory complex of the social tissue. It is in this struggle,

how some have sought to theorize the institutional experiments of the Bolivarian revolution in Venezuela.[104]

Another way to pose this question, which perhaps resonates with Jameson's bracing reflections on envy, is whether *stasis*, the division fracturing a polity, can somehow be institutionalized. Though post-Marxists have unconvincingly interpreted late liberalism as bearing this *agonistic* politics within it, surely it would be a task of any transition towards communism to invent modalities of antagonism not steeped in belonging, identity, or class. One might take inspiration here from Solon's 594 BCE decree against neutrality, which provided for punishment for any citizen who had not taken sides in a civil war. Of course, Solon's proposal depended on the politically-reproduced identity of citizen, and one of the questions we need to ask ourselves in gauging the pertinence of dual power today is whether the link between the emergence of an embryonic power and a pre-existing identity—be it of class, ethnos, or community—can be broken. After all, another way that Jameson's proposal moves beyond revolutionary classicism is by seeing the function of the universal army not only as that of undoing class distinction but to make possible a dual power that is not itself grounded on class difference—unlike most of those we can encounter in both classical and diffuse figures of dual power. This question is even more urgent since what I've called dual bio-power can root itself in ethnic, religious, or racialized communities, distant from the modernity of nation-state identity formation that still appears to operate as the background of Jameson's reflections.

It is if course the US context of Jameson's utopia that lends the seemingly classical modernity of a national-popular army its anti-systemic charge, as though a kind of anticipatory nostalgia for a

---

maybe, that can be expressed the beginning of a reciprocal transformation'. Jean-Paul Sartre, 'Masses, Spontaneity, Party', *Socialist Register* 7 (1970): 248.
104 See especially the stimulating analysis in George Ciccariello-Maher, 'Dual Power in the Venezuelan Revolution', *Monthly Review* 59(4) (2007) (available online: https://bit.ly/3Iv072X; last accessed: 17 February 2023).

Jacobinism pre-empted by US federalism suffused Jameson's vision. Here Jameson's excision of a whole welter of American utopias of secession should not go unremarked. The abrogation of any radical reference to the Constitution or the Declaration of Independence that preceded it doesn't just cut off the problematic tendency among some US progressives to echo Hannah Arendt's positioning of a US revolutionary tradition against the supposed trap of a quintessentially French 'social question'; it also distances the persistence of these references among practitioners of embryos of dual power in the US—not least the Black Panther Party, whose Ten-Point Programme concludes with an acute *détournement* of the Declaration of Independence: 'when a long train of abuses and usurpations, pursuing invariably the same object, evinces a design to reduce them under absolute despotism, it is their right, it is their duty, to throw off such government, and to provide new guards for their future security'. There is an even stronger opposition in Jameson—and I would argue a salutary one—to the frontier anarcho-communism (contaminated with disavowed settler-colonialism) which serves as the political unconscious of much of the US extreme left, and which can be traced back not so much to the militia ideal which is most active on fringes of the white supremacist right, but to that whole host of experiments—often promoted by the escapees of the failed European revolutions of the nineteenth century but also permeated by the sectarian exuberance of American Christianity—which was inventoried in Charles Nordhoff's classic volume *The Communistic Societies of the United States*.

Cultural Revolution Redux

Though it is a utopia that tries to refunction against political theory a notion around which Marxists tried to invent a *sui generis* communist politics for a 'non-state state', the heart of Jameson's proposal is evidently not strategic in any customary understanding of that term. The bold attempt to refashion a Fourierism for our time, largely autonomous from the wilfully paradoxical hypothesis of a dual power army, shows that the core of this 'therapeutic' utopia is *cultural revolution*—a theme that punctuates Jameson's work[105] and is encapsulated in the idea of the 'programming and retransformation of subjects trained in one society for functioning in a different one'.[106] The terms of this inquiry—like Jameson's quoting of Trotsky's bleak directives on militarization, which in turn hearken back to Engels' bluntly realist 'On Authority'—are precisely selected to elicit a libertarian reaction that Jameson rightly connects, in the US context, to the deep tendrils that anti-communism discourse has projected into the mental habits of radicals and progressives.

We can extract from Jameson's essay a salutary antidote to what has almost become common sense in contemporary far Left discourse, to wit that today's struggles—all the everyday ruptures, all the cracks in capitalism—already presage the sloughing off of the whole integument of alienated life. We might thus wish to balance the consoling notion that 'we are the change we were waiting for' with Franco Fortini's poetic counsel: 'Among the enemies' names / write your own too' ('Translating Brecht'). Whether because of a (partially justified) horror at the spectre of the state or a kind of ontological optimism about the human condition (which Jameson nicely punctures), today's 'communisms' (of the commons, communization, or the commune) largely reject the problem of what we could call an *anthropological transition*.[107] In the end, Jameson has refunctioned the strategic singularity of dual power into a speculative tool to pose this very question, repressed along with Stalinist nightmare of the New Man (but also the Fanonian discourse of a new humanity). This is a vital contribution that no amount of pseudo-iconoclastic invocations of communism as the

---

105 Fredric Jameson, 'Cultural Revolution' in *Valences of the Dialectic*.
106 This formulation is from an earlier unpublished draft of Jameson's essay.
107 On this question, see also Alberto Toscano, ' "Everything can be made better, except man": On Frédéric Lordon's Communist Realism', *Radical Philosophy* 2(12) (2022): 19–34.

image-less movement of the destruction of the ruling order of things can substitute for. For the destruction of the status quo will also need to be the destruction, the 'programming and retransformation', of ourselves, of our own status.

I can't exhaust the wealth of speculative suggestions in Jameson's piece—from the tantalizing invention of the Psychoanalytic Placement Program to the problematic bracketing of the self-management of *producers* (surely not an insignificant question given the vastness of today's global proletariat)—but to conclude I wanted to touch on two of its features that I think would be deserving of further . . . speculation. The first is the theme of a 'Utopia of the double life'. Here I think Jameson is right to eschew the fusional imaginaries that would see freedom and necessity merge into a seamless socialization of play. Not only should a utopia for today fully assume and mobilize negativity (as the theme of 'envy' hammers home), but it should also attend to what we may term, echoing Herbert Marcuse's *Eros and Civilization*, necessary as opposed to surplus alienation. And yet the double life needs to contend with the tragic, shattering duality that has often accompanied revolutionary efforts, none perhaps more so than the Bolshevik one. As Robert Linhart showed in his incisive *Lenin, the Peasants and Taylor* the political pedagogy and emancipation of workers *qua* administrators of the new state went hand in hand in Lenin and Trotsky's writings and directives with an exceptional, extreme regimentation of production. How would the double life not revive the punishing schizophrenia where the worker is politically (or libidinally) liberated only to be productively shackled (no matter for how few hours) by an agency that speaks in his name? No Leninist 'habit' is going to happily square this circle, nor provide an answer to the psycho-political question of the persistence of the state in the transitional period, of its transcendence, not only as an institution, but as a super-egoic agency.

I fear that Jameson's animus against politics and the political—despite serving as a healthy bending or breaking of the stick—might make it difficult indeed to pose these questions, or to address the fact that a thinking of transition, as Lenin himself showed in forging the weird and unstable 'metaphor' of dual power, demands the *invention* of a communist politics which, like dual power itself, must ·be asymmetrical to its bourgeois counterpart. Such an invention can, I think, take inspiration, and this is my second point, from a theme that pervades 'An American Utopia', namely Jameson's attempt to imagine various modalities for *disactivating* political (and we could say *sovereign*) power, linked to his attention to the enduring need for fetishes even 'after' the transition. Our political anthropology of transition will need to face not just the bond of the state with fear, but another Hobbesian theme, the persistence of politics as a *desire for domination*, and an associated drive towards conflict. Will this require politics in its classical acceptation to continue in the mode of the 'as if,' as a kind of vestigial ritual shadowing true cultural revolution? Doesn't this slip towards a cynical reason which is hardly conducive to the efficacy of these rituals and fetishes? The horizon of Jameson's utopia would thus be not that of a constituent power (as his objections to the US Constitution make clear) but, to echo Agamben's most recent investigations, that of a *destituent* power, where what is to be deposed, hollowed out, sapped, is politics itself. I would suggest however that destitution is not just an anti-political but an anti-strategic concept, a messianic one. In order to retain the fecund tension between the utopian and the strategic that traverses Jameson's American utopia, I believe—to borrow from Zavaleta's *El poder dual* one last time—that we need to turn our speculative and practical attentions towards building a *disorganizing power*, a power to disorganize not just the institutions of the capitalist state but, as Jameson rightly notes, the manner in which capital pervades the very structure of our desires, including our desires for revolution—or the lack thereof.

TEN

Leadership

[T]he people were generally far superior to their leaders. The more I have dug into this history, the more I have found that what really mattered was below, in the obscure depths . . . The chief actor is the people. To find them once more, to replace them in their role, I have been compelled to reduce to their true proportions the ambitious marionettes, of whom the people pulled the strings, and in whom, up to now, we thought we could seek and find the inner movement of history. The recognition of this, I have to confess, has struck me with astonishment. To the degree that I have entered more profoundly into this study, I have found that the party leaders, the heroes of conventional history, have foreseen nothing, that they did not take the initiative in any of the things that really mattered, and particularly of those which were the unanimous work of the people at the beginning of the revolution. Left to themselves at these decisive moments, by its pretended leaders, it worked out what was necessary to be done and did it.

—Jules Michelet, Preface to *History of the French Revolution* (quoted in C. L. R. James, *Nkrumah and the Ghana Revolution*)

The seats of power are very warm and very comfortable.
—C. L. R. James, 'Lectures on *The Black Jacobins*' (1971)

When I hear people arguing about Marxism versus the nationalist or racialist struggle, I am very confused. In England I edited the Trotskyist paper and I edited the nationalist, pro-African paper of George Padmore, and nobody quarrelled. The Trotskyists read and sold the African paper and . . . there were (African) nationalists who read and sold the Trotskyist paper. I moved among them, we attended each other's meetings and there was no problem because we had the same aim in general: freedom by revolution.

—C. L. R. James, 'Towards the Seventh: The Pan-African Congress' (1976)

If we are to survive, we must take nothing which is dead and choose wisely among the dying.

—Cedric J. Robinson, *Black Marxism* (1983)

The times when the cause of democracy and socialism was associated only with Europe alone have gone for ever.

—V. I. Lenin, 'On the Slogan for a United States of Europe' (1915)

At the end of the first chapter of *The Black Jacobins*, 'The Property', C. L. R. James recounts a famous and theoretically charged biographical vignette about the Haitian revolutionary leader Toussaint Louverture, which seems to inscribe the emergence of Black revolutionary leadership at the radical margins of the European Enlightenment frame. In the Abbé Raynal's anti-slavery tract *Philosophical and Political History of the Settlements and Trade of the Europeans in the East and West Indies*, Toussaint came across the following lines, which, according to James, he would often repeat to himself:

Already are there established two colonies of fugitive negroes, whom treaties and power protect from assault. Those lightnings announce the thunder. A courageous chief only is wanted. Where is he, that great man whom Nature owes to her vexed, oppressed and tormented children? Where is he? He will appear, doubt it not; he will come forth and raise the sacred standard of liberty. This venerable signal will gather around him the companions of his misfortune. More impetuous than the torrents, they will everywhere leave the indelible traces of their just resentment. Everywhere people will bless the name of the hero who shall have reestablished the rights of the human race; everywhere will they raise trophies in his honour.[108]

And James comments: 'It is the tragedy of mass movements that they need and can only too rarely find adequate leadership.'[109] Tragedy—as David Scott[110] and Jeremy Matthew Glick[111] have recently explored—is indeed the recurrent name for the historical grandeur and dramatic limits that accrue to the relationship between political leadership and mass action in the writing of James, from his parallel reconstructions of the Haitian and Bolshevik revolutions to his writings on decolonization and Black Power in the 1960s and 1970s. The fateful demand and fatal limits of leadership are a function of historical transitions or crises in which mass action is not *synchronized*, so to speak, with its material

108 Quoted in C. L. R. James, *The Black Jacobins: Toussaint L'Ouverture and the San Domingo Revolution*, 2nd REV. EDN (New York: Vintage, 1969[1963]), p. 25.
109 James, *Black Jacobins*, p. 25.
110 David Scott, *Conscripts of Modernity: The Tragedy of Colonial Enlightenment* (Durham, NC: Duke University Press, 2004); *Omens of Adversity: Tragedy, Time, Memory, Justice* (Durham, NC: Duke University Press, 2014). For some critical reflections on Scott's thesis, see Toscano, 'Politics in a Tragic Key'.
111 Jeremy Matthew Glick, *The Black Radical Tragic: Performance, Aesthetics, and the Unfinished Haitian Revolution* (New York: NYU Press, 2016).

and ideological determinants, and where leadership—though repudiated by James for 'advanced' temporalities and geographies of class struggle—seems an inevitable synthesizing and empowering instrument. Whether in *The Black Jacobins* or four decades later in *Nkrumah and the Ghana Revolution*, the historical, strategic and dramatic question of political leadership is at the nexus of Marxist proletarian politics and Black liberation struggles, in ways that I hope to sketch out below. In that regard it presents a privileged prism to revisit Cedric J. Robinson's own encounter with James' work, both in *Black Marxism* and in the 1992 essay 'C. L. R. James and the World-System'. Of the radical Black thinkers treated by Robinson, James—whom he appositely hails as a 'too rare example of a living, active, grappling Marxism'[112]—is arguably the one for whom the sustained interrogation of the theory and practice of Black struggles, whether in the West Indies, the US Black Belt or across the Pan-Africanist movement, was inseparable if not indistinguishable from his profound revision of and fidelity to a Marxist and *sui generis* Leninist tradition. If, from a certain angle, the making of the Black radical tradition is also the unmaking of a precarious ideological amalgam called 'Black Marxism', then James' trajectory poses perhaps the most generative challenge to Robinson's proposition that said tradition is a creative negation of a Western paradigm of political thought that *comprises* Marxism, including James' own.

I want to begin by briefly gauging the force of Robinson's demolition of the myth and social epistemology of political leadership in his first book, *The Terms of Order: Political Science and the Myth of Leadership* (1980), which, albeit in a more 'archaeological' and quasi-transcendental vein than *Black Marxism*, sets many of the guidelines for his later work. In *Terms*, Robinson already challenges the possibility of a successful immanent overcoming of

---

112 Cedric J. Robinson, *Black Marxism: The Making of the Black Radical Tradition* (London: ZED Books, 1983), p. 384.

the limits of Western political thought as an ideology of domination embedded in the complex legacies of racial capitalism—casting doubts on anarchism's capacity to challenge the nexus of authority, order and leadership while broaching, through a study of Tonga society, the possibility of an *antipolitical utopia*.[113] In a captivating reinterpretation of Max Weber's notion of charisma, *Terms* also displays Robinson's insistence on the creative power of mass resistance and the derivative nature of leadership. In *Black Marxism, Black Movements in America*, and incisive essays on Fanon, Du Bois and especially Amilcar Cabral (the one twentieth-century political thinker who appears as a kind of revolutionary model in Robinson in the early 1980s) this deconstruction of political leadership is enhanced by a class critique, which connects the problem of political leadership to that of the contradictions besetting the petty bourgeoisie and the formation of that Black intelligentsia to which James himself belonged. Instead of evaluating Robinson's theoretical and biographical diagnosis of the tensions traversing C. L. R. James' encounters with the Black radical tradition, I want to touch on the striking convergence between themes that criss-cross Robinson's work and James' own attempts at self-criticism or self-revision in his lessons on *The Black Jacobins* from 1971, as well as his revisiting of the leader-masses problematic in his critical history of the Ghanaian revolution. It is at this point of closest affinity that we can also see where Robinson's understanding of the Black radical tradition and James' Black Marxism retain their political and theoretical discrepancies, which we could summarize as a difference between the political autonomy of revolutionary Black struggles and the metaphysical autonomy of an antipolitical tradition of resistance.

---

113 The Tonga (or Batonga) are a Bantu people principally inhabiting contemporary southern Zambia and northern Zimbabwe.

Presaged by a 1972 study on the place of charisma in the political thought of Malcolm X,[114] Robinson's first book is a dense, intricate and intransigent destruction of what the subtitle of the book (a revised version of his doctoral dissertation) identifies as the political myth that structures Western political science. Though Robinson musters an impressive arsenal to 'abuse the political consciousness'[115] of the West (in ways, incidentally, not reducible to the spectrum of contemporary decolonial and postcolonial perspectives, and even less to Afro-pessimist invocations of Blackness), the underlying claim is stark: Western political thought and political science are based on two fallacies—that leadership is necessary for order and that hierarchy can be rationally legitimated. As Robinson observes: 'The presumption that political leadership is a concept through which the *event* of social organization can be made recognizable is a specious one. Yet it is this same presumption which underlies both liberal and radical attempts at social reorganization and "perfection".'[116] But the illusion of the political remains bafflingly unshaken by a historical record which provides abundant proof that politically consolidated and enforced authority is *not* a source of social stability and order. A Western political worldview persists in presenting leadership as the 'solvent-object' of that 'problem-object' that is the periodic crisis of stability. As Robinson observes: 'The literatures of sociology, political science, history and social psychology stridently substantiate through the plethora of analytical instruments, the metaphysics of leadership.' As he concludes, in a bitingly florid turn of phrase: 'It is, indeed, difficult to escape the mischievous tyranny of a mind which cannot only declare but also sculpture the physique of its error into reality.'[117]

---

114 Cedric J. Robinson, 'Malcolm Little as Charismatic Leader' in *On Racial Capitalism, Black Internationalism, and Cultures of Resistance* (H. L. T. Quan ed.) (London: Pluto Press, 2019), pp. 267–94.
115 Robinson, *Terms of Order*, p. 6.
116 Robinson, *Terms of Order*, pp. 4–5.
117 Robinson, *Terms of Order*, p. 36.

In the Western political frame this error-become-reality imposes leadership as the instrument to represent and articulate the objective phenomena of order and authority, over-coding them with a political metaphysic born of a mixed paradigm that combines the parameters of geometric order with the urgency of salvific narratives, while presenting the leader as 'an instrument of rational action where rational action is understood as collective action which extends the survival of a community',[118] such that the 'illusion of pure decision [subsidizes] the belief in the select nature of the decision-maker'.[119] The political heart of *The Terms of Order* is to be found in the nuanced juxtaposition of the immanent critique of this political paradigm in the European anarchist tradition, on the one hand, and the alternative to leadership deposited in the ethnography of antipolitical societies, on the other. While it is worth noting that this critique of anarchism serves as a template of sorts for Robinson's demarcation of Marxism's limits, I want to home in on his recasting of the Weberian concept of charisma. The latter serves as a kind of hinge in *Terms*: it is both the blind spot of a political science obliged to make surreptitious recourse to the irrational derivations of authority *and* an opening to rethink leadership not as that which authoritatively orders a mass into a socially stable and obedient people, but as what springs forth from mass movements and cannot be contained by authority or order. Leadership derives from movement, not vice versa. Pulling at the contradictions inherent in Weber's view of charisma as the 'specifically creative revolutionary force of history',[120] Robinson instructs us that: 'It is, in truth, the charismatic figure who has been selected by social circumstances, psychodynamic peculiarities, and tradition, and not his followers by him.'[121] The phenomenon of

118 Robinson, *Terms of Order*, p. 39.
119 Robinson, *Terms of Order*, p. 65.
120 Robinson, *Terms of Order*, p. 83.
121 Robinson, *Terms of Order*, p. 151.

charisma is a kind of residue or indivisible remainder that a rationalist political science cannot metabolize, and must both presuppose and treat as pathological. Outside of the mixed paradigm of Western political science, charisma draws its authority from beyond the leader, and the charismatic chief is himself a 'charismaticized follower' of his followers. Thus, the historically dominant image of political authority is 'the perversion of charisma' and 'the alienation of the mass authority of charisma', with the latter understood as 'a psychosocial force constructed by a people who have undergone an extended period of traumatizing stress" '[122]

Almost two decades after *Terms*, Robinson would reiterate this figuration of charisma to situate Martin Luther King (and Malcolm X) in the Black liberationist politics that found their taproot not in the experience of free Blacks in the North, as was the case for an accommodationist elite racial politics, but in slave resistance: 'King's charismatic authority was tributary of the Afro-Christian tradition embedded in the consciousness of the now mostly urban Blacks in the South and elsewhere . . . In this performance, he was less a person than a social and historical identity.'[123] This stood in contrast with those 'representative colored men,' who Robinson deems largely irrelevant to Black masses fashioning their alternative forms of communal life. The 'charismatic phenomenon' instead remains in Robinson's estimation, 'the only instrument of survival and liberation organic, that is, authentic, to the circumstance, tradition, and psychic nature of the bulk of human beings living in oppression'[124]—with the leader operating as a 'finely tuned' instrument sensitive to the suffering and aspirations of masses who have charismaticized him in a conjuncture of crisis.[125] As Erica

---

122 Robinson, *Terms of Order*, p. 156.
123 Robinson, *Black Movements in America*, p. 144.
124 Robinson, *Terms of Order*, p. 152. On Robinson's conceptualization of charisma, see also Joshua Myers, *Cedric Robinson: The Time of the Black Radical Tradition* (London: Pluto Press, 2021), pp. 91–105.
125 Robinson, *Terms of Order*, p. 151.

Edwards notes in her incisive cultural critique of the gendered logic of Black leadership as both reality and myth: 'One of the founding problematics of black political modernity is [the] double potential of the charismatic leadership role: to discipline, on the one hand, and to disrupt, precisely by way of charismatic performance, the disciplinary machinations of the capitalist order, on the other.'[126]

Now, though C. L. R. James was himself wary of the notion of charisma, the belief that leadership draws its dynamism (and its limits) from mass movements, and not vice versa, and that it is a function of crisis (and more, particularly, of revolutionary transition), is deeply Jamesian. It is striking in this respect that Robinson chooses to present James' analysis of Toussaint's *hamartia* or tragic flaw as an implicit recognition of the limitations attaching to the class perspective of a diasporic Black intelligentsia—the perspective that had also allowed James, along with Du Bois and Padmore but also Cabral and Fanon, to make the theoretical leap from the Western political paradigm to the Black radical tradition. Commenting on what James suggestively referred to as Toussaint's 'failure of enlightenment', the combination of an authoritarian project of state modernization with deafness to the demands of the very Black toilers who had made him leader ('to bewilder the masses is to strike the deadliest of all blows at the revolution', James admonished), Robinson displays his clinical insight:

> We, of course, recognize James (and perhaps even his impressions of Padmore) in these assertions. We can see the declared identification of a Black revolutionary intelligentsia with the masses; the willingness to continue the submission to 'scientific socialism' by denying the material force of ideology while indicating a bitter disappointment with the Communist movement; the patronizing attitude toward the organic leaders of the

126 Erica R. Edwards, *Charisma and the Fiction of Black Leadership* (Minneapolis, MN: University of Minnesota Press, 2012), p. 5.

masses; and the ambivalent pride of place presumed for the Westernized ideologue. Moreover, it is clear that James was looking critically at his own class. *Unlike his confederates, he was compelled to face up to the boundaries beyond which the revolutionary petit bourgeoisie could not be trusted. For that reason he was to insist often that the revolutionary masses must preserve to themselves the direction of the revolutionary movement, never deferring to professional revolutionists, parties, or the intelligentsia.*[127]

Robinson further excavates how in *Notes on Dialectics* and related writings, James had supplemented his tracing of the historical logic of the class struggle between proletariat and bourgeoisie with an attention to the transformation of the petty bourgeoisie. Recognizing the latter's transmutations was necessary *'because this strata had presumed the leadership of the proletarian movement and then betrayed it'.*[128] James' anti-vanguardist axiom—'There is nothing more to organize'—was also to be read as the product of a vital (self-)criticism of the petit-bourgeoisie, in other words as a class analysis of the composition and orientation of revolutionary leadership. That this was an abiding concern of James, especially as concerned the question of Black and Pan-African leadership, is eloquently testified by the Trinidadian thinker's reflections on the need to trust in the masses against the collusions and prevarications of petty bourgeois leaders. Drawing on George Lamming's *Season of Adventure*, James muses:

> I don't know anywhere, where any intellectual, any member of the intellectual élite, has taken upon himself complete responsibility for what has happened to the people he has left behind him. The people will make their way. We who have had the advantages must recognise our

---

127 Robinson, *Black Marxism*, pp. 388–89.
128 Robinson, *Black Marxism*, p. 395.

responsibility . . . there are not many intellectuals who realise what they are doing and the social crimes they commit, who say: 'I won a scholarship, I joined the élite and left my people behind, and I feel that that action on my part is responsible for what is happening to them'.[129]

In Robinson's own work, the sharpest political lessons to be drawn about the ambiguous but critical situation of the Black petty bourgeois intelligentsia—'mediators between Black workers and the social tapestry woven by capitalist-determined forms of production'[130]—is to be found in his article 'Amilcar Cabral and the Dialectic of Portuguese Colonialism', originally published in the journal *Radical America* in 1981. There, Robinson links the brilliance of Cabral's anticolonial leadership to his capacity deftly to anatomize the contradictions of colonized society, namely the problem of the revolutionary petty bourgeoisie. That of Guinea-Bissau and Cabo Verde was a revolutionary situation in which all the traditional class actors in the of European revolutions were stunted or absent: no industrial proletariat, no developed bourgeoisie, not even a mass peasantry. Rather, it was the transfiguration of the petty bourgeoisie on which the revolutionary impetus depended. As Cabral declared in La Habana in 1966: 'The revolutionary petty bourgeoisie must be capable of committing suicide as a class in order to be reborn as revolutionary workers, completely identified with the deepest aspirations of the people to which they belong'.[131] A creative adaptation of the received class schema of revolutionary politics (a 'stretching' we could say, paraphrasing Fanon on Marxism) was demanded by the conditions of Guinea-Bissau and Cabo Verde, a transformative nexus between petty bourgeoisie and the people.

---

129 C. L. R. James, 'Towards the Seventh: The Pan-African Congress' (1976) in *At the Rendezvous of Victory* (London: Allison & Busby, 1984), p. 249.
130 Robinson, *Black Marxism*, p. 257.
131 Quoted in Robinson, *On Racial Capitalism*, p. 323.

In *Nkrumah and the Ghana Revolution*, C. L. R. James would foreground this very problem, both fully recognizing the contribution of ordinary Africans to the emergence of anticolonial emancipation (most prominently Ghanaian 'market-women'), and portraying personal political leadership, much as he had done in *The Black Jacobins*, as a necessity in the context of a 'backward' society. Contrary to Robinson—even to the latter's interpretation of James' affinity with the Trinidadian-American sociologist Oliver Cromwell Cox and the latter's break with the linear historical logic of Marxist class struggle—and notwithstanding his recognition of the critical contribution of ordinary Africans and their traditional political institutions to the liberation struggle, James does appear to present the advanced/backward distinction as crucial to the centrality of leadership to anticolonial politics, by contrast with class politics in advanced capitalist countries. The question of 'backwardness' is also constitutive of the tragedy of leadership, with Kwame Nkrumah seeming to repeat, in a different guise, the mistakes of Toussaint, losing his sense for the masses whilst being entangled in the apparent necessities of modernization. It is particularly remarkable that here, as in his texts on the autonomy of Black struggles in the United States, James turns, in a kind of heterodox dogmatism, to the authority of Lenin, returning to the Bolshevik leader's remarks on the vitality and relative independence of non-proletarian struggles (especially in Lenin's writings on Ireland), to ground the Marxist credentials of a revolutionary politics that does not have the proletariat as its exclusive (or in the case of Pan-African struggles, even its strategically key) subject. Thus, just as in the 1940s James would underscore Lenin's observations in the 1920 Second Congress of the Communist International, on the 'motley' character of struggles in which different non-proletarian groups and classes play an indispensable role,[132] to shore up his

---

132 See C. L. R. James, 'The Historical Development of the Negroes in American Society' (1943) in Scott McLemee (ed.), *C. L. R. James on the "Negro Question"* (Jackson, MS: University Press of Mississippi, 1996), pp. 72–73.

arguments for the autonomy of Black struggles, so in reflecting on the impasses of Nkrumah's Ghana in the 1960s, he would interpret Lenin's late writings on the administration of the state as a courageous recognition of the marginality of the classically conceived proletariat to the politics of 'backward' countries, be this the Soviet Union or Ghana.[133]

Parenthetically, we can note that while *personal* leadership is side-lined in James' 1940s writings on Marxist organizing and the 'Negro Question', what takes centre stage is the question of the leadership of the proletariat as a class—a class about which we can say that the more it leads the less it requires leaders or even a vanguard. In James' estimation, as stated with polemical lucidity in 'Key Problems in the Study of Negro History' (1950), among the ideological crimes of Stalinism was the lip service played to mass action, sugar coating an authoritarian conception of leadership and traducing the fact that true leaders were 'men whose every step is conditioned by the recognition that they represent the deepest instincts and desires of the mass'.[134]

From *The Black Jacobins* to *Nkrumah* and his essays and talks on Black Power, C. L. R. James would continue to maintain a shifting balance between spontaneous mass struggles for self-emancipation and the (often tragic) role of personal leadership. Prolonging the method of dialectic biography first broached in his study of the West Indian labour leader Captain Cipriani[135] and

133 See C. L. R. James, 'Lenin and the Problem' (1964), appendix to *Nkrumah and the Ghana Revolution* (Leslie James ed.) (Durham, NC: Duke University Press, 2022[1977]). It is worthy of note, in terms of Robinson's emphasis on James' auto-critique of the revolutionary petty-bourgeois intelligentsia, that James proposes that one can model the independence of 'racial' and national-minority struggles on that of non-revolutionary classes.

134 McLemee (ed.), *C. L. R. James on the "Negro Question"*, p. 128.

135 C. L. R. James, *The Life of Captain Cipriani: An Account of British Government in the West Indies, with the pamphlet The Case for West-Indian Self Government* (Bridget Bererton intro.) (Durham: Duke University Press, 2014[1932]).

masterfully developed in his study of the revolutionary sequence in Saint Domingue/Haiti, James would orbit around the question of Black leadership, not just in African or West Indian context (in recurrent reflections on Marcus Garvey, George Padmore, Frantz Fanon, Julius Nyerere and others) but in the US too, as his laudatory portraits of Stokely Carmichael and George Jackson testify.[136] But in the 1960s and 1970s his abiding concern with the autonomy of mass popular struggles and his related focus on the distinction between class leadership and personal authority would issue into treatments of Black struggles that not only move closer to Robinson's abiding emphasis on the 'capacities for resistance of ordinary black people'[137] as embedded in autonomous traditions of resistance, but largely undermine the very recourse to the phenomenon of charisma. In 'Black Sansculottes,' a short piece written in 1964 for the Newsletter of the Institute of Race Relations a year after the second edition of *The Black Jacobins* (which traced the arc from the Haitian to the Cuba revolutions), James homes in on Toussaint's tragic error, whereby recourse to French culture and capital meant sapping 'the newly-created energies of his own followers'.[138] Displaying that deep instinct for historical analogy that he shared with Trotsky, and which allowed him to present a history of the Haitian revolution both modelled on and foreshadowing the Russian as a crucial object lesson for the Pan-African movement— all in turn read through the prism of the radical historiography of the French revolution—James declares: 'the dilemma of Toussaint

---

136 C. L. R. James, 'George Jackson', *Radical America* 5(6) (1971): 51–54. C. L. R. James, 'Black Power' in *Spheres of Existence: Selected Writings* (London: Allison and Busby, 1980), pp. 221–36. Though it is interesting to note the provocation, so antithetical to Robinson's take on Black movements, to foreground the figure of Lincoln. See 'The Black Scholar Interviews: C. L. R. James', *The Black Scholar* 2(1) (1970): 39. See also J. R. Johnson, 'The Two Sides of Abraham Lincoln', *The Militant*, 14 February 1949, reprinted in McLemee (ed.), *C. L. R. James on the "Negro Question"*, pp. 108–11.

137 Robinson, *Black Marxism*, p. 383.

138 James, *At the Rendezvous of Victory*, p. 160.

was an elemental and primitive form of the dilemma which faces all newly-independent backward territories today'.[139] In particular, it is from the preface of Jules Michelet's multi-volume history of the French revolution (quoted as the epigram to this chapter), and in its elaboration by the historian Georges Lefebvre, that James would draw a key lesson for the critique of revolutionary leadership, namely that attention should be dislocated from the spectacular feats of the manifest leaders—Michelet's 'ambitious marionettes'— and redirected to the agency of the popular masses and to what Lefebvre called their 'obscure leaders'.

While James did not relent on the notion that great men[140] do make history (though not under conditions of their own choosing and on the sufferance of mass movement and feeling), the 'entry of the chorus' into history's tragic drama is crucial to his self-critical reflections on *The Black Jacobins*, as signalled by the repetition of Michelet-Lefebvre's admonition to attend to obscure leaders, augmented by a recognition of the relative superiority of Du Bois' *Black Reconstruction* over *The Black Jacobins* in recognizing to the role of Black culture and religious consciousness in the political psychology of resistance, as well as by the treatment of the 'leaderless' phenomenon of the general strike against the plantocracy. What's more, recognizing the critical role that African political culture and marronage had in the formation of slave resistance, James emphasizes how, in rewriting *The Black Jacobins*, he would have wanted to reconstruct the voices of the slaves in revolt, not just the record of their actions as sedimented in white metropolitan archives:

---

139 James, *At the Rendezvous of Victory*, p. 160.
140 For a powerful feminist critique of the gendering of Black leadership in C. L. R. James and other Black radical theorists, see Hazel Carby, *Race Men* (Cambridge, MA: Harvard University Press, 2000).

> I don't want today to be writing and say that's what *they*
> said about how *we* were being treated. Not any longer, no.
> I would want to say what we had to say about how we were
> treated, and I know that that information exists in all the
> material . . . We have had enough of what *they* have said
> about us even when sympathetic.[141]

The significance of Michelet's praise of the obscure leaders and the
people to James' shifting meditations on the complex problem of
revolutionary leadership is evident in critical role it plays in the
pivotal chapter of *Nkrumah and the Ghana Revolution* on 'The
People and the Leader', where James also takes the opportunity to
chide Trotsky for both misunderstanding and over-emphasizing
the 'very difficult question, the relationship of the leader to the mass
movement in a revolution' in his *History of the Russian Revolution*,
one of the key templates for *The Black Jacobins*. Though it may be
argued that James remains altogether too captivated by the vicissitudes of the great male leader, his anti-colonial critique of the petty
bourgeois intelligentsia and attention to the obscure leadership
and self-activity of the masses offers a rich avenue beyond the
repetitions—be they tragic or farcical—of the mass-leader dialectic.
And while never crystallizing into the idea of a distinct Black
radical tradition that would constitute a discrete and 'total' theory
of liberation, founded on a 'single historical identity', nor making
the clean break with the Marxian dialectic that Robinson glimpses
in James 1953 essay on Herman Melville, *Mariners, Renegades and*

---

141 C. L. R James, 'Lectures on *The Black Jacobins*', *Small Axe* 8 (2000): 99.
Carolyn Fick's superb *The Making of Haiti: The Saint Domingue Revolution
from Below* (Knoxville: University of Tennessee Press, 1990)—which makes
considerable thematic use of the notion of the 'obscure leader', and was in part
spurred by a dialogue with James—comes very close indeed to this imagined
rewrite of *The Black Jacobins*. For a recent study which complements Fick's
history with an exploration of the anti-statist moral economy of the Haitian
peasantry *after* the Revolution, see Johnhenry Gonzalez, *Maroon Nation*.

Castaways[142]—with its pathological figures of totalitarian leadership (Ahab) and petty-bourgeois intellectual complicity (Ishmael)—James' writing on Black revolutionary mass politics

---

142 Consider this remarkable if disputable passage from 'C. L. R. James and the World-System' (*Race & Class* 32(2) (1992): 59–60), where Robinson tries to merge Oliver Cromwell Cox's break with the Marxist historical logic of capital and James' writings on state-capitalism and the catastrophism inherent in Western civilization, while reflecting on the pathologies of personalistic leadership:

> In his apocalyptic interpretation of *Moby Dick*, James had fused the bureaucratic strata of the theory of state-capitalism with Hegel's 'world-historical' heroes, 'whose passionate belief in the legitimacy of their own private aims and interests is such that they cannot abide *any* disparity between what they desire for themselves and what the public morality and legal system demand of men in general'. And, in so doing, he had doubly damned the world-system, collapsing on to a perverted stasis of the class struggle (the rule of the bureaucrats) the tragic spectacle of the self-extinguishing and self-possessed individual. Without achieving synthesis, James had juxtaposed conflicting historical paradigms: one orderly, the other entropic and chaotic. In a generation when dictators had knifed through the fabric of history, James had retrieved from Hegel's philosophy of history a figure genetically linked to the mytho-ideology of Judaeo-Christian messianism, a figure that appears in Hegel's frustrated expectations of Fredrich Wilhelm and Napoleon, reappears as Nietzsche's Superman, and again as Weber's charismatic leader. Marx had imagined that the industrial proletariat was the hero of capitalism and had invented a theory of history whose narrative justified this presumption. James honoured that faith in the breach: choosing to represent the destructive and chaotic impulses of the capitalist world-system by the appearance of a new totalitarian personality from whom the world could be salvaged only by the mobilized working classes. The paradigms were irreconcilable. Ahab possessed the will and the institutional authority to destroy his crew and annihilate their social order. In James' own exposition of Melville, the dialectic to which Marx had adhered, between master and slave, between capitalist and proletariat, between man and nature, had proven itself inadequate to the task of disrupting the horrendous forces of capitalism.

resonates in illuminating ways with Robinson's abiding and multi-faceted attention to the 'capacities for resistance of ordinary black people' and his keen vigilance against the trap of leadership as socio-political authority and metaphysical fetish of order. But it does so while bypassing the phenomenon of charisma, one that for James is not, or no longer[143] indispensable to channelling the energies of popular struggles. If there is nothing more to organize, perhaps there is also no one to follow.

143 See C. L. R. James, 'Marcus Garvey' (1940) in McLemee (ed.), *C. L. R. James and the "Negro Question"*, pp. 114–16.

ELEVEN

Freedom

[A]s with the twentieth, the problem of the twenty-first century is freedom; and racialized lines continue power-fully, although not exclusively, to define freedom's contours and limits.

—Ruth Wilson Gilmore, 'Race and Globalization'

They seemed to want to get closer to freedom, so they'd know what it was—like it was a place or city.

—Felix Haywood, from *Federal Writers' Project: Slave Narrative Project, Volume 16: Texas* (1936)

Freedom is a homonym. This is the initial proposition of the mapping exercise I want to undertake in this final chapter. But unlike 'bat', 'right' or 'watch', where the same signifier can be contextually attached to distinct signifieds, to approach freedom as homonymic can prove a far trickier exercise in discernment and demarcation. The French philosopher Jacques Rancière has written perceptively about philosophy's thorny relation to homonymy:

> Philosophy . . . is this place and this activity, bound, owing to its own problematic homonymy, to work on the homonymies: man, politics, art, justice, science, language, freedom, love, work and so on. Only there are two ways to deal with homonyms. One is to proceed to purify them, to identify the good name and the good sense and disperse

the bad. Such is often the practice of the so-called human and social sciences, which boast that they only leave to philosophy empty or definitively equivocal names. Such is often the task that philosophers also give themselves. The other way considers that every homonymy arranges a space of thought and of action, and that the problem is therefore neither to eliminate the prestige of homonymy, nor to take names back to a radical indetermination, but to deploy the intervals which put the homonymy to work.[1]

What are the spaces of thought and action in which the political problem of freedom is embedded today? Or, what are the critical determinants of freedom's problem space, now? To reject the easy demarcation between good and bad freedom, to 'deploy the intervals' as Rancière suggestively puts it, is also to recover the centrality of contradiction, antinomy, paradox and tragedy to the intellectual adventures and impasses of freedom.

In what follows I want to consider three variants of freedom as homonym. The first is the saturation of our political discourse with authoritarian imaginaries of freedom that pit themselves explicitly against a protean nemesis that combines the freedom of capital, the freedom of movement, as well as the raced and gendered freedoms of multiple 'others'.[2] This is where we might be tempted to find comfort in the notion that *their* freedom has nothing to do with *ours*: just a homonym. The second variant is the conceptual counterthrust that seeks to disentangle mobile practices of liberation from a conception of freedom as possession, property, substance—the abolitionist figure of freedom. The third and last

---

1 Jacques Rancière, *Dissensus: On Politics and Aesthetics* (Steven Corcoran trans. and ed.) (London: Continuum, 2010), p. 218.

2 For further reflections on these matters, see Alberto Toscano, 'Fascists, Freedom and the Anti-State State', *Historical Materialism* 29(4) (2021): 3–21, as well as *Late Fascism: Race, Capitalism and the Politics of Crisis* (London: Verso, 2023).

variant of freedom's homonymy concerns the critical proposition according to which, in light of the material grounding of modern conceptions of freedom in unsustainable relations to energy and the Earth (let's call this 'fossil freedom'), it is urgent and imperative radically to reinvent (or perhaps even jettison) this pivotal if vexed term in our political vocabulary, to free ourselves from freedom, so to speak.

The Nationalization of Freedom

'I want to talk about freedom'. These are the first words of the closing monologue from Tiago Rodrigues's 2020 play *Catarina and the Beauty of Killing Fascists*. The play, set in 2028, centres on a Portuguese family that has been convening in an old rural house to preserve a bloody tradition inaugurated by the protagonist's great-grandmother: assassinating a fascist every year for 74 years by way of political revenge and prophylaxis after the murder of a sharecropper by the name of Catarina Eufémia—the name assumed by all the members of the family, men included. One of these Catarinas will cast doubt on the morality of antifascist violence, in dialogues that seem to bend Brecht towards Camus. The fascist politician will eventually emerge unscathed, triumphant, and his plethoric victory speech won't be unfamiliar to any earwitnesses to the planetary surge of authoritarianism: Rodrigues composed the monologue with splices from 200 hours of speeches he valiantly subjected himself to, delivered by Matteo Salvini, Jair Bolsonaro, Viktor Orbán, Donald Trump and the far-right Portuguese politician André Ventura. Recently, in response to her electoral triumph and coronation as Italian prime minister, a number of clips of Fratelli d'Italia (Brothers of Italy) leader Giorgia Meloni circulated online. These included a compilation of speeches enthusiastically supporting what is arguably *the* core racist myth of today's neo-fascist international, namely the Great Replacement (rootless financiers conspiring to enact the ethnic substitution of white European peoples through weaponized mass migration), as well as youthful declarations of admiration for Benito Mussolini. But one speech especially could have fit snugly in Rodrigues's rhetorical collage, a dextrous and politically sinister philippic delivered at the 2019 World Congress of Families in Verona. Towards the end of her speech, before quoting G. K. Chesterton, Meloni declaims:

> Why is the family an enemy? Why is the family so frightening? There's a single answer to these questions. Because it defines us. Because it's our identity. Because everything that defines us, is now an enemy for those who would like us to no longer have an identity, and simply be perfect consumer slaves. And so they attack our national identity. They attack our religious identity. They attack our gender identity. And family identity. I can't define myself as an Italian, Christian, woman, mother, no. I must be a citizen X, gender X, parent one, parent two. I must be a number. Because when I'm only a number, when I no longer have an identity or roots, then I will be the perfect slave at the mercy of financial speculators. The perfect consumer . . . We'll defend it, we'll defend God, country, and family. Those things that disgust people so much, we'll do it to defend our freedom, because we will never be slaves and simple consumers at the mercy of a financial speculator.[3]

As demonstrated by the historian Tyler Stovall—who is also instructive on the fascist love of freedom—reference to slavery by partisans of 'white freedom'[4] is indeed a rather timeworn trope.

---

3 My translation; video available online: https://bit.ly/3YZwL23 (last accessed: 17 February 2023).

4 Tyler Stovall, *White Freedom: The Racial History of an Idea* (Princeton, NJ: Princeton University Press, 2021). This 'white freedom' has also manifested itself in the context of the gendered, classed and racialized distribution of

And so, of course, is the defence of capital and the obfuscation of class through the pitting of patriotic producers against deracinated speculators. What Meloni rather perfectly exemplifies is the explicit *nationalization* (and not so implicit racialization) of freedom, as well as the way this operation anchors itself in the sexed and sexual body. The enemy of national freedom is freedom as license, flight, deracination, while the nemesis of the national family, of the nation *as* family, is the triptych of international speculative capitalism, so-called 'gender ideology', and migration, or the devilish plot woven by the rootless financier, the trans woman and the Black refugee. It is difficult to ignore the irony in this narrative of ethnic substitution: turning citizens into mere consumers has been central to the political project of Meloni's chief enabler, Silvio Berlusconi, while many of the migrants making the perilous journey across the Mediterranean, far from being docile subjects of finance, were part of the revolutionary wave of 2011.

Free to Be Free

But it's too comforting, if undoubtedly tempting, merely to polarize the homonym of freedom, marking the freedom dreams of the far right as our own freedom nightmares (the inverse is clearly the case, as evident from daily dispatches in our so-called culture wars or from those tutorials in the evils of 'critical race theory' and 'cultural Marxism', which sometimes clinch their prosecutorial case with an image of Angela Davis sitting side-by-side with Herbert Marcuse). As I've already suggested, I think it is more instructive, theoretically

---

vulnerability to the pandemic, and its attendant ideological and discursive struggles. As Robyn Maynard has noted, we can see a splitting, a homonymy of freedom in this instance too: 'There are two different visions of freedom at stake here. One is the freedom to evade, to deny one's responsibility to a collective social body; the other forwards a freedom that is relational, holds up freedom as collective safety.' Robyn Maynard and Leanne Betasamosake Simpson, *Rehearsals for Living* (Toronto: Alfred A. Knopf, 2022), p. 76.

and politically, to tarry with freedom's ambiguities, paradoxes, and contradictions. The predicament that any critical student of freedom's political and intellectual history finds themselves in may be captured with a passage from Hannah Arendt's essay 'What is Freedom?' She frames her inquiry in the following terms:

> To raise the question, what is freedom? seems to be a hopeless enterprise. it is as though age-old contradictions and antinomies were lying in wait to force the mind into dilemmas of logical impossibility so that, depending which horn of the dilemma you are holding on to, it becomes as impossible to conceive of freedom or its opposite as it is to realize the notion of a square circle.[5]

Her solution, however, involves a whole set of dyads and distinctions—public versus inner freedom, freedom to begin versus freedom from want, the political freedom of the American Revolution versus the social capture of freedom in the French and Russian Revolutions—which close the space of thought and action in which we may reflect and act upon the meanings of freedom.

But there is one distinction crucial to Arendt's argument that deserves greater consideration—not least because of how it crops up in some thinkers of freedom I will touch on momentarily—namely the distinction between freedom and liberation. For Arendt, liberation, associated with violent rebellions against domination, is a negative moment 'whose fruits are absence of restraint and possession of "the power of locomotion" '[6]—recalling Thomas Hobbes' definition of freedom in *Leviathan*: 'Liberty, or freedome, signifieth (properly) the absence of opposition; (by opposition, I mean externall impediments of motion)'. Freedom,

---

5 Hannah Arendt, 'What is Freedom?' in *Between Past and Future: Six Exercises in Political Thought* (New York: The Viking Press, 1961), p. 143.
6 Hannah Arendt, *On Revolution* (New York: Penguin, 1965), p. 32, quoted and discussed in Neil Roberts, *Freedom as Marronage* (Chicago, IL: The University of Chicago Press, 2015), p. 32.

the foundation of freedom or *constitutio libertatis* is something other. Liberation alone, however momentous, for Arendt could only generate (negative) liberties, civil rights. Yet these, as she suggests in a lecture from the mid-1960s on 'Revolution and Freedom', are 'by no means the actual content of freedom, whose essence is participation in public affairs and admission to the public realm'.[7] The time of revolution, which Arendt articulates in a two-stage model, spans both a time of liberation—a struggle to slough off a system of domination which is, as a rule, already disintegrating—and the time of freedom, which includes the foundation and institution (the 'natality') of a new order.

The distinction between liberation and freedom is at the heart of Arendt's much discussed and disputed distinction between American success and French (or Russian or Chinese or anti-colonial) 'deformation' when it comes to revolutionary trajectories. In the end, this boils down to foregrounding the tragic reversals that beset any attempt at *social* and *material* liberation. Terror is here the by-product of that liberation which strives to 'liberat[e] the people at large from wretchedness in order to make them free to *be* free.'[8] But what allows the American revolution to immunize freedom from the intensifying violence of material liberation, from the so-called 'social question'? Though she doesn't draw the consequences of her own acknowledgment, which is itself rather dubiously and symptomatically worded, Arendt gestures towards the pedestal of domination on which the house of freedom was erected:

> The difference [with the French revolution], then, was that the American Revolution, because of the peculiar institution of slavery and because the slave belonged to a different race, could overlook the existence of the miserable

---

7 Hannah Arendt, 'Revolution and Freedom' (Adriano Correia ed.), *Cadernos de Filosofia Alemã* 21(3) (2016): 170. Typescript available online: https://bit.ly/3Z1B657 (last accessed: 17 February 2023).
8 Arendt, 'Revolution and Freedom': 177.

and with it the formidable task of liberating those who were not so much constrained by political oppression as by the sheer necessities of life . . . The American Revolution was fortunate indeed that it did not have to face this obstacle to freedom, it owed a good measure of its success to the sheer absence of desperate poverty among the freemen and the complete invisibility of the slaves in the colonies of the New World.[9]

Or, to use her terminology, freedom's American success depended on the invisibility of all those who were not *free to be free*. The 'fortunate' invisibility of the enslaved, as a precondition of freedom, is not unrelated, in ways I will shortly touch upon, to that other conception of freedom, closely linked to the (ancient) experience of slavery, from which Arendt wants to extricate her understanding of political freedom as creative acting in concert and in public ('to be seen, to be heard, to be known, and to be remembered by others'), namely *inner freedom*. And we cannot but note the invisible invisibility, so to speak, of the settler-colonial wars of expropriation against First Nations. This should compel us to reflect on how, to quote Elisabeth Anker's recent book *Ugly Freedoms*, 'violent and world-destroying acts of dispossession were practiced by the founders as freedom: the freedom of settler to take land in order to instantiate a new government, the freedom to cordon off native territory by labor, treaty manipulation, murder, and fiat in order to exercise independence'.[10]

But Arendt's depiction of American freedom is not just grounded on the invisibility, around 1776 and after, of the enslaved

9 Arendt, 'Revolution and Freedom': 175. For a powerful critique of Arendt's inability to think through race and Blackness, and its effects on her political philosophy, see Kathryn T. Gines (now Kathryn Sophia Belle), *Hannah Arendt and the Negro Question* (Bloomington: Indiana University Press, 2014). See also Hartman, *Scenes of Subjection*, pp. 299–300.

10 Elisabeth R. Anker, *Ugly Freedoms* (Durham, NC: Duke University Press, 2022), p. 3.

and of their liberation, of the dispossessed and their indigenous polities, but on a figuration of those who are 'free to be free' which implies a sovereign distance or even separation from the domains of material, necessity, and social reproduction:

> Only those who know freedom from want are in a position to appreciate fully what it means to be also free from fear, and only those who are free from both want and fear are in a position to conceive of that passion for public freedom or to develop in themselves that '*goût*', the taste for liberty, and the peculiar love of equality which liberty carries with itself.[11]

The free, after the revolution, are also free from the continued imperative of (political and especially material) liberation—though Arendt is compelled to acknowledge that

> revolution has always been concerned with both, liberation and freedom, and since liberation is indeed a condition of freedom, though freedom is by no means the necessary result of liberation, it is very difficult to say where the mere desire for liberation, to be free from oppression, ended and the desire for freedom as the political way of life began.[12]

A couple of years after Arendt's lecture on 'Revolution and Freedom', in Fall 1969, Angela Y. Davis delivered two lectures for her course at UCLA on 'Recurring Philosophical Themes in Black Literature.' The first of these was attended by over a thousand people, who rallied to Davis' cause in the wake of the UC Board of Regents' efforts to fire her, which were first repelled by the courts and then enacted, just months before Davis would end on the FBI's Most Wanted list. Now, the terms through which freedom is articulated by Davis, in an intense dialogue with Frederick

---

11 Arendt, 'Revolution and Freedom': 176.
12 Arendt, 'Revolution and Freedom': 170.

Douglass' autobiographical writings, radically counter or unsettle Arendt's demarcations along the axes of race, interiority and mobility. Core to this difference (or even 'differend') regarding freedom is the reversal of primacy between freedom and liberation. For, in Davis' abolitionist philosophy of freedom, what is at stake is 'the crucial transformation of the concept of freedom as a static, given principle into the concept of liberation, the dynamic, active struggle for freedom.'[13]

This transformation takes its starting point from the experience of freedom of the unfree, from the lived critique that Black experience and literature in the throes and aftermath of slavery articulate vis-à-vis dominant philosophical accounts of freedom, in the understanding that 'Black people have exposed, by their very existence, the inadequacies not only of the practice of freedom, but of its very theoretical formulation.'[14] From this angle, the master is not 'free to be free,' precisely to the extent that his is a possessive investment in freedom. The prospect and desire for liberation here serves to criticize the ideology of (white) freedom. The slave, according to Davis:

> understands that the master's freedom is abstract freedom to suppress other human beings. The slave understands that this is a pseudo concept of freedom . . . The slave is actually conscious of the fact that freedom is not a fact, it is not a given, but rather something to be fought for, it can exist only through a process of struggle. The slave-master, on the other hand, experiences his freedom as inalienable and thus as a fact: he is not aware that he too has been enslaved by his own system.[15]

---

13 Angela Y. Davis, *Lectures on Liberation* (New York: Committee to Free Angela Davis, 1971), p. 4.

14 Davis, *Lectures on Liberation*, p. 4.

15 Davis, *Lectures on Liberation*, p. 7.

But what the enslaved person *exposes* is not exposed *in public*, for the gaze of a class of masters who are above all overseers managing invisibility through apparatuses of hyper-visibility and surveillance. Where Arendt had leaned on Kant to argue that 'freedom is no more ascertainable to the inner sense and within the field of inner experience than it is to the senses with which we know and understand the world',[16] Davis underscores the critical role that the enslaved's *negative experience of freedom* (as opposed to the liberal *experience of negative freedom*)[17] plays, citing a remarkable passage in Douglass where he sets out a whole bodily aesthetic of (un)freedom, while also turning a notion of essential freedom ('birthright') into a powerfully subversive principle:

16 Arendt, 'What is Freedom?', p. 144.

17 The formative role of slavery in the 'vexed genealogy of freedom' is at the core of Saidiya Hartman's *Scenes of Subjection*, which advances a searing analysis not only of the way in which the very terms of liberal freedom were shaped by the antithesis of chattel slavery, but of how emancipation was lastingly contained, neutralized, and distorted (transformed into a 'nonevent') by a liberal and capitalist norm of freedom which—in tandem with racial state and para-state terror—sought to quash any horizon of liberation. As she argues: 'The entanglements of bondage and liberty shaped the liberal imagination of freedom, fueled the emergence and expansion of capitalism, and spawned proprietorial conceptions of the self'. This placed the formerly enslaved into a double bind that both repeated and intensified the predicament of the proletarian—free to work and free to starve—engendering what Hartman dubs a 'burdened individuality of freedom': 'The antagonistic production of abstract equality and Black subjugation rested upon contending and incompatible predications of the freed—as sovereign, indivisible, and self-possessed, and as fungible and individuated subjects whose capacities could be extracted, quantified, exchanged, and alienated'. *Scenes of Subjection*, pp. 203–5. Hartman is in important respects building on Orlando Patterson's contention (which exceeds the parameters of modern chattel slavery, going all the way back to ancient Greece) that 'the very idea and valuation of freedom was generated by the existence and growth of slavery'. See *Freedom, Volume 1: Freedom in the Making of Western Culture* (New York: Basic Books, 1991), p. xiv. Or, in Hartman's striking formulation: 'Slavery was both the wet nurse and the bastard offspring of liberty'. Saidiya Hartman, *Scenes of Subjection: Terror, Slavery, and Self-Making in Nineteenth-Century America* (New York: Oxford University Press, 1997), p. 139.

Liberty, as the inestimable birthright of every man, converted every object into an asserter of this right. I heard it in every sound, and saw it in every object. It was ever present to torment me with a sense of my wretchedness, the more horrible and desolate was my condition. I saw nothing without seeing it and I heard nothing without hearing it. I do not exaggerate when I say that it looked at me in every star, smiled in every calm, breathed in every wind and moved in every storm.[18]

Davis links this sensory experience of unfreedom to the 'first condition of freedom,' 'the open act of resistance—physical resistance, violent resistance'[19]—a resistance as material as the constraints that both rivet the slave to her place on the plantation but also displace and mobilize her. Slavery's racial fix is also an affixing of the body—as Douglass declared: 'Our destiny was to be fixed for life'; 'The slave was a fixture'; 'He had no choice, no goal, but was pegged down to one single spot, and must take root there or nowhere.'[20] But it is also a condition of disposability and forced mobility, as Douglass details in a harrowing passage about his displacements, dictated by, as he puts it, 'a law which I can comprehend, but cannot evade or resist'. As Davis comments: 'For the slave, the world appears as a hostile network of circumstances which continually are to his disadvantage'[21]—whether in mobility or immobility.[22]

---

18 Davis, *Lectures on Liberation*, p. 10.
19 Davis, *Lectures on Liberation*, p. 7.
20 Davis, *Lectures on Liberation*, p. 8.
21 Davis, *Lectures on Liberation*, p. 18.
22 'As a practice, moving about accumulated nothing and did not effect any reversals of power, but indefatigably held on to the unrealizable—being free—by temporarily eluding the restrains of order. Like stealing away, it was more symbolically redolent than materially transformative. These itinerant practices were elaborations of fugitivity and extensions of the general strike against slavery.' Hartman, *Scenes of Subjection*, pp. 225–26.

Arendt's resolution of freedom's homonymy, attaching the gaining of freedom to liberation and the collective exercise of liberation to freedom 'proper,' has a *prima facie* plausibility if we recall the tragic experience of how liberation from domination can fail to bring into being the constitution of freedom as a form of political life. Notwithstanding his distance from Arendt's orientation, an analogous perception seems to motivate Michel Foucault's distinction, in a late interview on the care of the self, between, on the one hand, *processes of liberation* that tackle states of domination and, on the other, *practices of freedom* (including techniques of the self), which strive to resist and transform relations of power. Whether in sexuality or against colonialism, Foucault suggests, liberation may be a necessary, but it is never a sufficient condition for freedom.[23]

As Maggie Nelson has argued in her recent *On Freedom*, there is a compelling and challenging nuance to Foucault's ethical interrogation of freedom, which can act as a resource for those who wish to resist the ease with which freedom may be unproblematically affirmed or packaged up into a slogan.[24] And yet, if we think back to Davis and Douglass, and indeed to the expanded and diverse tradition of abolitionist thought they belong to, we may see the temporal demarcation and conceptual distinction between acts of liberation and practices of freedom as a problem rather than a solution. In her generative and incisive reading of Toni Cade Bambara in *The Hawthorn Archive: Lessons from the Utopian Margins*, Avery Gordon, criticizing the yoking of freedom to patterns of historical necessity, has spoken of 'abolitionist time', understood as 'a way of being in the ongoing work of emancipation, a work whose success is not measured by legalistic pronouncements, a work which perforce must take place while you're still enslaved.'[25]

23 Michael Foucault, 'The Ethics of the Concern of the Self as a Practice of Freedom' in *Ethics: Subjectivity and Truth* (Robert Hurley et al. trans, Paul Rabinow ed.), *The Essential Works of Michel Foucault, 1954–1984*, VOL. 1 (New York: The New Press, 1997), pp. 281–301.
24 Maggie Nelson, *On Freedom: Four Songs of Care and Constraint* (Toronto: McClelland & Stewart, 2021), p. 6.

In this time, unlike in the political temporalities projected by Arendt or Foucault, the process of liberation (whether violent or not) and the practice of freedom (individual and/or collective) can't be framed in terms of a temporal or normative order of priority, such that, in the definition Gordon draws from Bambara: 'Freedom is the process, by which you develop a practice for being unavailable for servitude,' or, in a Marcusean lexicon, the forging of 'organs for the alternative'.[26]

Freedom at 4° Celsius

To the extent that our present is that of catastrophic anthropogenic climate change, it is a now heavy with the accumulating time of fossil combustion. As Andreas Malm's has put it, our warming condition means that *'We can never be in the heat of the moment, only in the heat of this ongoing past'*.[27] The novelty or natality that attaches to political freedom for the likes of Arendt seems to be put in deep jeopardy by this social and species predicament, though as Malm also reminds us, the urgent need to dismantle and replace the infrastructure of fossil capital also 'supercharges our moment with time'.[28] But is there a figure of freedom adequate to what, depending on our schema of historical agency, may be termed the Anthropocene or the Capitalocene?

In his much-debated interventions on climate change's foundational challenge to the humanities, now collected in *The Climate of History in a Planetary Age*, Dipesh Chakrabarty has cast doubt on the ability of both Enlightenment and subaltern conceptions of freedom and liberation to traverse unscathed, or perhaps even survive, the quickly mutating landscape of climate change. As he categorically asserts:

25 Gordon, *Hawthorn Archive*, p. 42.
26 Gordon, *Hawthorn Archive*, p. 49.
27 Malm, *Progress of This Storm*, p. 5.
28 Malm, *Progress of This Storm*, p. 7.

In no discussion of freedom in the period since the Enlightenment was there ever any awareness of the geological agency that human beings were acquiring at the same time as—and through processes closely linked to— their acquisition of freedom. Philosophers of freedom were mainly, and understandably, concerned with how humans would escape the injustice, oppression, inequality, or even uniformity foisted on them by other humans or human-made systems. Geological time and the chronology of human histories remained unrelated. This distance between the two calendars, as we have seen, is what climate scientists now claim has collapsed. The period I have mentioned, from 1750 to now, is also the time when human beings switched from wood and other renewable fuels to large-scale use of fossil fuel—first coal and then oil and gas. The mansion of modern freedoms stands on an ever-expanding foundation of fossil-fuel use. Most of our freedoms so far have been energy intensive.[29]

The problem that Chakrabarty raises is undoubtedly of vital importance to any contemporary political thought worthy of the name. This is true not just in terms of querying the adequacy of our political imaginaries to our changing ecological realities; it compels us to interrogate the extent to which our desires for liberation and our institutions of freedom have depended on unsustainable arrangements of power, matter, and energy.

One response to the problem captured by Chakrabarty has been to suggest a decoupling of freedom from its fossil energy bases—its decarbonizing, so to speak. In his important environmental history of the alliance between autonomy and extractivism, liberty and the intensive appropriation and exploitation of land, *Affluence and Freedom*—which is prefaced by

29 Dipesh Chakrabarty, *The Climate of History in a Planetary Age* (Chicago, IL: The University of Chicago Press, 2021), p. 32.

Chakrabarty though is not uncritical of the Indian historian and theorist's framing—Pierre Charbonnier has delineated the question with admirable lucidity, also gesturing towards the critical nexus between political-ecological crises and fascist potentials:

> The sense of political liberty, first boosted then trapped by its alliance with the mechanisms of growth and extraction, is today at a clearly identifiable historic turning point. Either it remains subservient to the old structures of the liberal pact [*binding freedom to fossil capital*], and is condemned to shrink, to surround itself with barriers to protect itself against the new contenders for development and affluence, or it is assumed that the history of this alliance must end ... Either therefore, the project of autonomy remains rooted in the dream of affluence, in which case it will sink with it in the great reactionary and authoritarian movement that we are already witnessing, or it frees itself from it by taking the form of a post-growth autonomy, i.e. of a new kind of integration-autonomy [*by contrast with autonomy-extraction*].[30]

But if, as this historical accounting testifies, the shifting nexus of autonomy and extraction is constitutively linked to racial and colonial capitalism, we may wish to pause before we rush to speak of '*our* freedoms', as Chakrabarty does, and revisit instead the struggles over freedom's homonymy, interpreting them also as potential refusals of the 'liberal alliance'. Notwithstanding tragic reversals, elite captures and eventual failures, many anti-colonial struggles were and are intelligible as conscious repudiations of the notion that freedom—not just as freedom as a principle but, following Ruth Wilson Gilmore, freedom as a *place*, or indeed as a political ecology—is inexorably yoked to an energy and capital-intensive form of possessive investment, improvement, and development.

---

30 Charbonnier, *Affluence and Freedom*, pp. 242–43.

In entangled and sometimes contradictory ways, processes of liberation from colonialism have often been traversed by practices of freedom that pushed back against the resource-realist principle that freedom had to take the form of a nation-state competing in a capitalist world-economy on the basis of state-led and market-mediated development. To take one historical example, the struggles of liberated slaves in Haiti against the agrarian militarism imposed by revolutionary elites, beginning with Toussaint Louverture himself, tells a story of minor, oppositional but not necessarily residual imaginaries and practices of freedom that cannot simply be subsumed under an extractive autonomy made synonymous with modernity.[31] In our moment, the struggles of indigenous land defenders against pipelines and logging constitute practices of freedom which are explicitly aimed at terminating extractive autonomy as the infrastructure and ideology of ongoing colonization.

What does it mean, to borrow Arendt's formulation, 'to be free to be free'? *Who* can be free to be free? And is that freedom to be understood as a *freedom from* constraint, a *freedom for* public action, as both, or perhaps as something more, and different? In his own response to the problem of freedom in the Anthropocene formulated by Chakrabarty, Ian Baucom has suggested a dialectical overcoming of our (liberal) tendency to bounce between negative and positive freedoms, the delineation of a '*freedom toward*' our warming condition which is in its turn based on the struggle to be free to recognize and act upon our profound ecological dependency and precarity. Contra Chakrabarty, this involves not the suspension but the reinvention and refunctioning of certain modern freedoms associated with the political modernisms and materialisms that many contemporary theorists happily consign to obsolescence. As Baucom puts it,

---

31 See Gonzalez, *Maroon Nation*.

> the urgent *freedom toward* of the Anthropocene . . . needs
> to take and blend into itself . . . freedom from arbitrary
> sovereign command alongside with and braided through
> the freedom to realise the possibilities of collective well-
> being, planet-wide, across the conditions of our mutual
> precarity as the carbon accumulates, and the temperatures
> mount, and as the oceans rise toward the condition of
> History 4° C.[32]

This *freedom toward*, I would argue by way of conclusion, has to
revive but also reinvent the critique of the liberal capture of freedom in the juridical, material and ideological assemblage of
the person, the market, and the state. The greatest temptation
attendant on the claim that modern freedoms have been energy
intensive, and disastrously so, lies in treating a repudiation of the
'productivist' basis of autonomy extraction as further warrant to
think of freedom primarily at the level of circulation, consumption,
or representation. What the environmental history of freedom
compellingly illustrates is that, to the contrary, keeping freedom
out of the hidden abode of production has been a critical ingredient
in the propertied regimes of fossil-based accumulation and
hegemony that are pushing us past so many tipping points. For all
their culpable collusions with the yoking of liberation to
machinism, extraction and development, the Marxist and socialist
traditions' critiques of liberal conceptions of freedom remain vital
in arguing that if freedom is to be unshackled from individualist
and acquisitive constraints, it must also concern production (and,
as revolutionary feminists have contended, *re*production).
Important arguments to this effect have been made, from Galvano
Della Volpe's post-war plea for a communist freedom based on a
socialized relationship to nature and technics, to William Clare
Roberts' more recent excavation, from the pages of *Das Kapital*, of

---

32 Baucom, *History 4° Celsius.*

a 'republicanism in the realm of production'.[33] But perhaps we can turn to an author who could never be castigated for 'growthism,' Theodor Adorno. In a lecture delivered in January 1965 in the context of an immensely rich course entitled *History and Freedom*, refuting Arendt's reflections on the tragic consequences of tying freedom to material needs, Adorno argues that:

> The concrete possibilities of making freedom a reality are to be sought . . . in the way in which we define the locus of freedom, namely, in the forces of production. By this I mean the state of human energies and the state of technology which represents an extension of human energies that have been multiplied through the growth of material production. The growth of freedom is not to be sought in the relations of production, which is the solution proffered by superficial minds. Thus when we say that freedom can be achieved today, here and now, or in a hundred years, this does not mean that everyone should be sent to better schools, or that everyone should have enough money with which to buy a fridge and to go to the cinema, something that can only increase their unfreedom rather than their freedom. The potential for freedom lies elsewhere; it consists in the fact that the state of the forces of production today would allow us in principle to free the world from want.[34]

Disentangling, on the one hand, freedom from want, from the kind of necessity that impedes the freedom to be free, and, on the other, freedom as commodified affluence, is a difficult if important

---

33 Della Volpe, *La libertà comunista*; William Clare Roberts, *Marx's Inferno: The Political Theory of Capital* (Princeton, NJ: Princeton University Press, 2017). See 'Communism' in this volume, pp. 1–52.
34 Theodor W. Adorno, *History and Freedom: Lectures 1964–5* (Rodney Livingstone trans., Rolf Tiedemann ed.) (Cambridge: Polity, 2006), p. 182.

and timely enterprise. And the contention that unfreedom is 'increasingly . . . the function of a superfluous form of domination whose attempts to maintain itself are therefore irrational'[35] still rings true. But what Adorno misses and what we need to rethink truly to move beyond a mechanical oscillation between the realm of freedom and that of necessity,[36] is the question of how freedom can emerge in the struggles that traverse the relations of production themselves—relations of exploitation, management, property, and

---

35 Adorno, *History and Freedom*, p. 183.

36 It is worth reflecting on Maggie Nelson's observation about the pitfalls of oscillating between liberation and obligation, radical independence and radical dependence, especially when it comes to bringing questions of reproduction into the frame:

> Caring and coercion often exist in a knot, with their extrication never simple, nor sometimes even possible. That doesn't mean we shouldn't work to reduce elements of coercion from it; that is the ongoing work of abolition, as well as the socialization of the maternal. But since aspects of this paradox will always be with us, doubling down on the familiar—often leftist—insistence that our salvation lies in liberating ourselves from the dark clutches of need and ascending to freedom's bright expanse is not good enough, nor is simply exalting need, care, and obligation in freedom's place. The former conjures an all-too-familiar schema in which self-sufficiency and independence are valued over reliance, service, and infirmity; the latter throws the door open to all kinds of unrealistic and dysfunctional demands made of ourselves and others, bringing us into mirthless territory ranging from codependency to shaming to servitude. [Nelson, *On Freedom*, p. 71].

Nelson's underscoring of 'our conjoined urges toward freedom and unfreedom, self-consolidation and dissolution, interiority and sociality, control and abandon' (p. 131) is also worth heeding, and perhaps extending into a consideration of imaginaries of freedom, such as the one crystallized by Georges Bataille's anti-intuitive conception of *sovereignty*, in which liberation is best understood as a practice of abandonment, dissolution, loss. Adorno himself tried to probe 'the mysteries of the concept of freedom in which the extreme exaltation of the ego goes hand in hand in a very strange way with the abyss of the self'. Adorno, *History and Freedom*, p. 216.

so on—and in the social relations of reproduction that these entail and depend upon.[37] The 'superficial' position is to think that freedom is a matter for the political, juridical and cultural spheres treated as separate from production, which is also to continue to imagine freedom as an edifice, a superstructure (*Überbau*) or as Chakrabarty has it a 'mansion . . . built on ever-expanding foundation of fossil-fuel use'. There is no freedom, now, without bringing politics to bear on that foundation, on its forces *and* its relations. There is life for freedom still, but outside and beneath the mansion. Multitudes were never invited into it, many have refused to enter it, and some have tried to dismantle it from within.

---

37 This vision of freedom in the relations of production is instead the gambit of the chapter 'Freedom Today' in C. L. R. James' posthumously published *American Civilization* (Anna Grimshaw and Keith Hart eds) (Oxford: Blackwell, 1993), pp. 106–17.

Acknowledgments

Written over a period of over 15 years, the chapters collected in this volume are indebted in myriad ways to the solidarity, example, brilliance, conspiring and intransigence of many friends, comrades, family, students, colleagues and interlocutors—all searching for the words and visions to navigate a deeply unsettled and unsettling time. I am particularly grateful to Matteo Mandarini, Benjamin Noys, Sara Farris, Beverley Skeggs, Svenja Bromberg, Evan Calder Williams, Avery F. Gordon, Steve Edwards, Gail Day, Fredric Jameson, Ruth Wilson Gilmore, Craig Gilmore, Toni Negri, Alain Badiou, Ray Brassier, Asad Haider, Salar Mohandesi, Jason E. Smith, Joshua Clover, Jasper Bernes, Ozren Pupovac, Stathis Kouvelakis, Christopher Connery, Rebecca Karl, Peter Hallward, Sebastian Budgen, my comrades past and present in the editorial board of *Historical Materialism*, the Goldsmiths UCU branch, Adrienne E. Pagac and the The Havens Wright Center for Social Justice, and to all the editors of the journals, special issues and books in which earlier versions of these chapters were originally published. I am grateful to Diven Nagpal for the meticulous editing, to Sunandini Banerjee for her wonderful cover design, and to Naveen Kishore and everyone at Seagull for making this book and the Seagull Essays list possible. To Brenna and Esha for the love, companionship, inspiration & laughter, and to the Charles Street Commune for the radical commensality.

Sources

ONE: Communism

'Communism' in *Handbook of Marxism* (Beverley Skeggs, Sara Farris, Alberto Toscano and Svenja Bromberg eds) (London: SAGE, 2022); 'Destructive Creation, or, The Communism of the Senses' in *Make Everything New: A Project on Communism* (Grant Watson ed.) (London: Bookworks, 2006).

TWO: Radicalism

'Ad Hominem: Antinomies of Radical Philosophy', *Filosofski Vestnik* 29(2) (2008): 137–53.

THREE: Reform

'Reforming the Unreformable' in *What Are We Struggling For?* (Federico Campagna ed.) (London: Pluto, 2012).

FOUR: The Left

Co-written with Matteo Mandarini, 'The Left Out of History', *Etica & Politica / Ethics & Politics* 22(2) (2020): 591–99.

FIVE: Prometheanism

'The Prejudice Against Prometheus', *STIR*, 15 August 2011 (available online: https://bit.ly/3VVjeqs; last accessed: 9 January 2023).

SIX: The People

'A Just People, or Just the People? Althusser, Foucault and Juridical Ideology', *Consecutio Rerum. Rivista critica della postmodernità* 5(8) (2020): 163–83.

SEVEN: Resistance

'Resistance and Revolt in Pre-Political Times', *Pli: The Warwick Journal of Philosophy* 30 (2019): 1–22.

EIGHT: Dual Power

'Dual Power Revisited: From Civil War to Biopolitical Islam', *Soft Targets* 2(1) (2007): 160–65; 'After October, Before February: Figures of Dual Power' in Fredric Jameson, *An American Utopia: Dual Power and the Universal Army* (Slavoj Zizek ed.) (London: Verso, 2016).

NINE: Transition

'Transition et tragédie', *Période*, 10 April 2014 (available online: https://bit.ly/3GqVzZo; last accessed: 9 January 2023); 'Transition Deprogrammed', *South Atlantic Quarterly* 113(4) (2014): 761–76.

TEN: Leadership

'Black Sansculottes and Ambitious Marionettes: Cedric J. Robinson, C. L. R. James and the Critique of Political Leadership', *Viewpoint*, 1 February 2017 (available online: https://bit.ly/3W0S1CO; last accessed: 9 January 2023).

ELEVEN: Freedom

'Freedom, Now', lecture delivered at The Havens Wright Center for Social Justice, UW-Madison, 13 October 2022.

Bibliography

ADORNO, Theodor W. 'The Handle, the Pot and Early Experience' in *Notes to Literature*, VOL. 2 (R. Tiedemann ed., S. Weber Nicholsen trans.). New York: Columbia University Press, 1992.

———. *History and Freedom: Lectures 1964–5* (Rodney Livingstone trans., Rolf Tiedemann ed.). Cambridge: Polity, 2006.

———. *Negative Dialectics* (E. B. Ashton trans.). London: Routledge, 1990.

———. 'Vers une musique informelle' in *Quasi una Fantasia: Essays on Modern Music*. London: Verso, 1998.

———, Walter Benjamin, Ernst Bloch, Bertolt Brecht, and Georg Lukács. *Aesthetics and Politics*. London: New Left Books, 1977.

ALTHUSSER, Louis. *Cours sur Rousseau: 1972* (Y. Vargas ed.). Montreuil: Les Temps des Cerises, 2015.

———. 'Écrits sur l'art' in *Écrits philosophiques et politiques*, VOL. 2. Paris: Librairie générale française, 2001, pp. 553–620.

———. 'Le marxisme comme théorie "finie" ' (1978) in *Solitude de Machiavel* (Y. Sintomer ed.). Paris: PUF, 1998.

———. 'Il marxismo come teoria "finita" ' in Louis Althusser et al., *Discutere lo stato: Posizioni a confronto su una tesi di Louis Althusser*. Bari: De Donato, 1978.

———. *Les Vaches noires: Interview imaginaire (le malaise du XXIIe Congrès); Ce qui ne va pas, camarades!*, (G. M. Goshgarian ed.). Paris: Presses universitaires de France, 2016.

———. 'Livre sur l'impérialisme (1973) (extraits)' in *Écrits sur l'histoire (1963-1983)* (G. M. Goshgarian ed.). Paris: Presses universitaires de France, 2018.

———. 'Marxism and Humanism' in *For Marx* (Ben Brewster trans.). London: Verso, 1996.

———. 'Marxism as a Finite Theory' (Asad Haider trans.). *Viewpoint Magazine*, 14 December 2017. Available online: https://bit.ly/40GzbVl (last accessed: 4 February 2023).

———. *Politics and History: Montesquieu, Rousseau, Hegel and Marx* (B. Brewster trans.). London: New Left Books, 1972.

———. *Politique et Histoire, de Machiavel à Marx: Cours à l'École normale supérieure 1955-1972* (F. Matheron ed.). Paris: Éditions du Seuil, 2006.

———. *Sur la reproduction.* Paris: PUF, 1995.

———, Étienne Balibar, Roger Establet, Pierre Macherey and Jacques Rancière. *Lire le Capital.* Paris: PUF, 1996[1965].

ANKER, Elisabeth R. *Ugly Freedoms.* Durham, NC: Duke University Press, 2022.

ARATO, Andrew, and Paul Breines. *The Young Lukács and the Origins of Western Marxism.* London: Pluto Press, 1979.

ARENDT, Hannah. *On Revolution.* New York: Penguin, 1965.

———. 'Revolution and Freedom' (Adriano Correia ed.), *Cadernos de Filosofia Alemã* 21(3) (2016).

———. 'What is Freedom?' in *Between Past and Future: Six Exercises in Political Thought.* New York: The Viking Press, 1961.

ARICO, José. *Marx and Latin America* (David Broder trans.). Leiden: Brill, 2012.

BADIOU, Alain. *The Communist Hypothesis* (David Macey and Steve Corcoran trans). London: Verso, 2010.

———. *Images du temps présent (2001-2004).* Paris: Fayard, 2014.

———, and François Balmès. *De l'Idéologie.* Paris: Maspero, 1976.

———, et al. *What is a People?* New York: Columbia University Press, 2016.

BAKUNIN, Mikhail. 'Le communisme' (J.-C. Angaut trans.) in Jean-Christophe Angaut, *Bakounine jeune hégélien: La philosophie et son dehors.* Lyon: ENS Éditions, 2007.

BALDWIN, Kate A. *Beyond the Color Line and the Iron Curtain: Reading Encounters between Black and Red, 1922-1963.* Durham, NC: Duke University Press, 2002.

BALIBAR, Étienne. 'Althusser et "le communisme"'. *La Pensée* 382 (2015): 9-20.

———. 'The Basic Concepts of Historical Materialism' (1965) in Louis Althusser et al., *Reading Capital* (Ben Brewster and David Fernbach trans). London: New Left Books, 1970.

———. 'The End of Politics or Politics without End? Marx and the Aporia of "Communist Politics" ' in *The Philosophy of Marx*, revised EDN (Chris Turner and Gregory Elliott trans). London: Verso, 2017.

———. 'État, parti, transition'. *Dialectiques* 27 (Spring 1979): 81–92.

———. 'Les apories de la "transition" et les contradictions de Marx'. *Sociologie et sociétés* 22(1) (1990): 83–91.

———. *Les frontières de la démocratie*. Paris: La Découverte, 1998.

———. 'Mao: critique interne du stalinisme?' in 'Sociétés occidentales / Idée du socialisme', special issue, *Actuel Marx* 3 (1988): 145–54.

———. 'The Messianic Moment in Marx' in *Citizen Subject: Foundations for a Philosophical Anthropology* (Steven Miller trans.). New York: Fordham University Press, 2017.

———. 'The Non-Contemporaneity of Althusser' in E. Ann Kaplan and Michael Sprinker (eds), *The Althusserian Legacy*. New York: Verso, 1993.

———. *On the Dictatorship of the Proletariat* (G. Lock trans.). London: New Left Books, 1977.

———. *The Philosophy of Marx*. London: Verso, 1995.

———. 'Reproductions' (David Broder trans.). *Rethinking Marxism* 34(2) (2022): 142–61.

———. 'Self-Criticism: Answer to Questions from "Theoretical Practice" '. *Theoretical Practice* 7–8 (1973): 56–72.

BASSO, Luca. *Inventare il nuovo: Storia e politica in Jean-Paul Sartre*. Verona: Ombre Corte, 2016.

BASSO, Pietro. 'Introduction: Yesterday's Battles and Today's World' in Amadeo Bordiga, *The Science and Passion of Communism* (Giacomo Donis and Patrick Camiller trans, Pietro Basso ed.). Leiden and Boston: Brill, 2020.

BAUCOM, Ian. *History 4° Celsius: Search for a Method in the Age of the Anthropocene*. Durham, NC: Duke University Press, 2020.

BAUMAN, Zygmunt. 'Times of Interregnum'. *Ethics & Global Politics* 5(1) (2012): 49–56.

BELL, David A. 'The Contagious Revolution'. *The New York Review of Books*, 19 December 2019.

BELLE, Kathryn Sophia [*formerly*, Kathryn T. Gines]. *Hannah Arendt and the Negro Question*. Bloomington: Indiana University Press, 2014.

BENSAÏD, Daniel. *La politique comme art stratégique*. Paris: Syllepse, 2010.

―――. ' "Leaps, Leaps, Leaps": Lenin and Politics'. *International Socialism* 95 (2002).

―――. 'On the return of the politico-strategic question' (August 2006). *International Viewpoint Online* 386 (February 2007). Available online: https://bit.ly/3YV8KJM (last accessed: 17 February 2023).

BERKI, R. N. *Insight and Vision: The Problem of Communism in Marx's Thought*. London and Melbourne: J. M. Dent & Sons, 1983.

BERNES, Jasper. 'Logistics, Counterlogistics and the Communist Prospect'. *Endnotes* 3 (2013). Available online: https://bit.ly/3wgfup4 (last accessed: 19 January 2023).

BETTELHEIM, Charles. *Les luttes de classes en URSS: 1ère période, 1917–1923*. Paris: Seuil/Maspero, 1974.

BHANDAR, Brenna, and Rafeef Ziadah. *Revolutionary Feminisms: Conversations on Collective Action and Radical Thought*. London: Verso, 2020.

BIRNBAUM, Antonia. 'Between Sharing and Antagonism: The Invention of Communism in the Early Marx'. *Radical Philosophy* 166 (2011): 21–28.

BLACKBURN, Robin. 'A Visionary Pragmatist'. *Counterpunch*, 22 December 2005. Available online: https://bit.ly/3Hy8KZ4 (last accessed: 4 February 2023).

BLANQUI, Louis Auguste. 'Communism, the Future of Society' (1869) in Philippe Le Goff and Peter Hallward (eds), *The Blanqui Reader: Political Writings, 1830–1880*. London: Verso, 2018.

BLOCH, Ernst. 'A Jubilee for Renegades'. *New German Critique* 4 (1975): 17–25.

―――. 'Karl Marx and Humanity: Stuff of Hope' in *The Principle of Hope*, VOL. 3 (Neville Plaice, Stephen Plaice and Paul Knight trans). Oxford: Basil Blackwell, 1986.

―――. 'Karl Marx, Death, and the Apocalypse: Or, the Ways in This World by Which the Inward Can Become Outward and the Outward Like the Inward' in *Spirit of Utopia* (Anthony A. Nassar trans.). Stanford, CA: Stanford University Press, 2000.

―――. *Thomas Münzer als Theologe der Revolution*, 2nd EDN. Leipzig: Reclam, 1989[1962].

―――. *Thomas Münzer: Théologien de la revolution* (Maurice de Gandillac trans.). Paris: Julliard, 1964.

BLOOM, Joshua, and Waldo E. Martin. *Black Against Empire: The History and Politics of the Black Panther Party.* Berkeley, CA: University of California Press, 2014.

BLUMENBERG, Hans. *Work on Myth* (Robert M. Wallace trans.). Cambridge, MA: The MIT Press, 1985.

BOSTEELS, Bruno. *Marx and Freud in Latin America: Politics, Psychoanalysis, and Religion in Times of Terror.* London: Verso, 2012.

BOURDIEU, Pierre. 'The Essence of Neoliberalism'. *Le Monde diplomatique,* December 1998. Available online: https://bit.ly/2RBEyVR (last accessed: 5 February 2023).

———. 'Neo-liberalism, the Utopia (Becoming a Reality) of Unlimited Exploitation' in *Acts of Resistance: Against the New Myths of Our Time.* London: Polity, 1998, pp. 94–105.

BRAS, Gérard. *Les voies du peuple: Éléments d'une histoire conceptuelle.* Paris: Amsterdam, 2018.

BREWSTER, Ben. 'Armed Insurrection and Dual Power'. *New Left Review* 66 (1971): 59–68.

BUCHANAN, James M. 'Politics Without Romance' in *The Logical Foundations of Constitutional Liberty.* Indianapolis: Liberty Fund, 1999.

BUCK-MORSS, Susan. 'Aesthetics and Anaesthetics: Walter Benjamin's Artwork Essay Reconsidered'. *October* 62 (1992): 3–41.

BUKHARIN, Nikolai Ivanovich. 'Economics of the Transition Period' in *Selected Writings on the State and the Transition to Socialism* (Richard B. Day ed.). Armonk, NY: M. E. Sharpe, 1982.

CACCIARI, Massimo et al. *Il concetto di sinistra.* Bompiani: Milano 1982.

CAFFENTZIS, George, et al. *The Work/Energy Crisis and the Apocalypse, Midnight Notes* 3(1) (1980).

CAMATTE, Jacques (ed.). *Bordiga et la passion du communisme.* Paris: Spartacus, 1974.

———. *Capital and Community: The Results of the Immediate Process of Production and the Economic Work of Marx* (David Brown trans.). London: Unpopular Books, 1988.

CARBY, Hazel. *Race Men.* Cambridge, MA: Harvard University Press, 2000.

CASSIN, Barbara (ed.). *Dictionary of Untranslatables: A Philosophical Lexicon.* Princeton, NJ: Princeton University Press, 2014.

CÉSAIRE, Aimé. 'Letter to Maurice Thorez' (Chike Jeffers trans.). *Social Text* 103 (2010[1956]).

CESARALE, Giorgio. *A Sinistra: Il pensiero critico dopo il 1989*. Bari: Laterza, 2019.

CHAKRABARTY, Dipesh. *The Climate of History in a Planetary Age*. Chicago, IL: The University of Chicago Press, 2021.

CHARBONNIER, Pierre. *Affluence and Freedom: An Environmental History of Political Ideas* (Andrew Brown trans.). Cambridge: Polity, 2021.

CHERNOMAS, Robert, and Ian Hudson. *The Profit Doctrine: Economists of the Neoliberal Era*. London: Pluto, 2017.

CICCARIELLO-MAHER, George. 'Dual Power in the Venezuelan Revolution'. *Monthly Review* 59(4) (2007). Available online: https://bit.ly/3Iv072X (last accessed: 17 February 2023).

CIMATTI, Felice. *Naturalmente comunisti: Politica, linguaggio ed economia*. Milan: Bruno Mondadori, 2011.

CLARE ROBERTS, William. *Marx's Inferno: The Political Theory of Capital*. Princeton, NJ: Princeton University Press, 2017.

CLARK, T. J. *Farewell to an Idea: Episodes in a History of Modernism*. New Haven, CT: Yale University Press, 2001.

COULTHARD, Glen Sean. *Red Skin, White Masks: Rejecting the Colonial Politics of Recognition*. Minneapolis, MN: University of Minnesota Press, 2014.

D'HONDT, Jacques. 'Le meurtre de l'histoire' in *Hölderlin* (Jean-François Courtine ed.). Paris: L'Herne, 1989, pp. 219–38.

DARDOT, Pierre, and Christian Laval. *Common: On Revolution in the 21st Century*. London: Bloomsbury Academic, 2019.

———. *La nouvelle raison du monde: Essai sur la société néolibérale*. Paris: La Découverte, 2009.

———. *The New Way of the World: On Neoliberal Society* (Gregory Elliott trans.). London: Verso, 2014.

DAUVÉ, Gilles and François Martin. *Eclipse and Re-Emergence of the Communist Movement*. Oakland, CA: PM Press, 2015.

DAVIES, Carole Boyce. *Left of Karl Marx: The Political Life of Black Communist Claudia Jones*. Durham, NC: Duke University Press, 2007.

DAVIES, William. *The Limits of Neoliberalism*. London: Sage, 2014.

DAVIS, Angela Y. *Lectures on Liberation*. New York: Committee to Free Angela Davis, 1971.

DAVIS, Mike. *Late Victorian Holocausts: El Niño Famines and the Making of the Third World*. London: Verso, 2001.

————. 'Thanatos Triumphant'. *Sidecar*, 7 March 2022. Available online: https://bit.ly/3QARzde (last accessed: 12 January 2023).

DEBORD, Guy. *'Cette mauvaise réputation . . . '*. Paris: Gallimard, 1993.

————. *Comments on the Society of the Spectacle* (Malcolm Imrie trans.). London: Verso, 1990.

DELLA VOLPE, Galvano. *La libertà comunista* (Michele Prospero ed.). Rome: Bordeaux, 2018[1946].

DEWS, Peter. 'The Nouvelle Philosophie and Foucault'. *Economy and Society* 8(2) (1979): 127–71.

DYER-WITHEFORD, Nick, Atle Mikkola Kjøsen, and James Steinhoff. *Inhuman Power: Artificial Intelligence and the Future of Capitalism*. London: Pluto, 2019.

EDWARDS, Erica R. *Charisma and the Fiction of Black Leadership*. Minneapolis, MN: University of Minnesota Press, 2012.

FELDMAN, Alex J. 'Foucault's concept of illegalism'. *European Journal of Philosophy* 28(2) (2020): 445–62.

FICK, Carolyn. *The Making of Haiti: The Saint Domingue Revolution from Below*. Knoxville, TN: University of Tennessee Press, 1990.

FISHER, Mark. *Ghosts of My Life: Writings on Depression, Hauntology and Lost Futures*. Winchester: Zero Books, 2014.

FLINDERS, Matthew, and Jim Buller. 'Depolitisation: Principles, Tactics and Tools'. *British Politics* 1 (2006): 293–318.

FLORES, John. 'Proletarian Meditations: Georg Lukács' Politics of Knowledge'. *Diacritics* 2(3) (1972).

FOUCAULT, Michel. *Abnormal: Lectures at the Collège de France 1974–1975* (Valerio Marchetti and Antonella Salomoni eds, Graham Burchell trans.). London: Verso, 2003.

————. 'The Ethics of the Concern of the Self as a Practice of Freedom' in *Ethics: Subjectivity and Truth* (Robert Hurley et al. trans, Paul Rabinow ed.). *The Essential Works of Michel Foucault, 1954–1984*, VOL. 1. New York: The New Press, 1997, pp. 281–301.

———. 'Iran: The Spirit of a World Without Spirit' in *Politics, Philosophy, Culture: Interviews 1977–1984* (Lawrence D. Kritzman ed., Alan Sheridan et al. trans.). London: Routledge, 1988[1979].

———. 'Powers and Strategies' (1977) in *Power/Knowledge: Selected Interviews and Other Writings 1972–1977* (Colin Gordon ed.). New York: Pantheon Books, 1980.

———. 'Précisions sur le pouvoir: Réponses à certaines critiques' (published in *aut-aut*, 1978), *Dits et écrits II, 1976–1988*. Paris: Gallimard, 2001.

———. 'Préface' (1973) in *Dits et écrits I, 1954–1975*. Paris: Gallimard, 2001.

———, and Gilles Deleuze. 'Intellectuals and Power: A Conversation between Michel Foucault and Gilles Deleuze' in Michel Foucault, *Language, Counter-Memory, Practice: Selected Essays and Interviews* (Donald F. Bouchard ed.). Ithaca: Cornell University Press, 1977[1972].

GARNSEY, Peter. *Thinking About Property: From Antiquity to the Age of Revolution*. Cambridge: Cambridge University Press, 2007.

GARO, Isabelle. *Communisme et stratégie*. Paris: Éditions Amsterdam, 2019.

GAUDICHAUD, Franck (ed.). *¡Venceremos! Analyses et documents sur le pouvoir populaire au Chili (1970–1973)*. Paris: Syllepse, 2013.

GENOVESE, Eugene. *Roll Jordan Roll: The World the Slaves Made*. New York: Vintage, 1976.

GENTILI, Dario. *Crisi come arte di governo*. Bologna: Quodlibet 2018.

GILMORE, Ruth Wilson. *Abolition Geography: Essays Towards Liberation* (Brenna Bhandar and Alberto Toscano eds). London: Verso, 2002.

———. 'Ruth Wilson Gilmore Makes the Case for Abolition'. *The Intercept*, 10 June 2020. Available online: https://bit.ly/3ZLgxuG (last accessed: 19 January 2023).

GLICK, Jeremy Matthew. *The Black Radical Tragic: Performance, Aesthetics, and the Unfinished Haitian Revolution*. New York: NYU Press, 2016.

GLUCKSMANN, André. 'Fascismes: L'ancien et le nouveau'. *Les Temps modernes* 310 (1972): 266–334.

GONZALEZ, Johnhenry. *Maroon Nation: A History of Revolutionary Haiti*. New Haven, CT: Yale University Press, 2019.

GORDON, Avery F. *The Hawthorn Archive: Letters from the Utopian Margins*. New York: Fordham University Press, 2018.

GORZ, André. *Strategy for Labor: A Radical Proposal*. Boston: Beacon Press, 1967.

GRAEBER, David. 'On the moral grounds of economic relations: A Maussian approach'. *Journal of Classical Sociology* 14(1) (2014): 65–77.

GRAMSCI, Antonio. 'The Revolution against "Capital" ' in *Selections from Political Writings 1910–1920* (Quintin Hoare ed.). London: Lawrence and Wishart, 1977.

GRANDJONC, Jacques. *Communisme/Kommunismus/Communism: Origine et développement international de la terminologie communautaire pré-marxiste des utopistes aux néo-babouvistes 1785–1842, Volume 1: Historique; Volume 2: Pièces justificatives*. Trier: Karl-Marx-Haus, 1989.

GRANDJONC, Jacques. 'Quelques dates à propos des termes *communiste* et *communisme*'. *Mots* 7 (1983): 143–48.

GRIFFIN, Roger. 'Between metapolitics and *apoliteia*: The Nouvelle Droite's strategy for conserving the fascist vision in the "interregnum" '. *Modern & Contemporary France* 8(1) (2000): 35–53.

GROYS, Boris. *The Total Art of Stalinism: Avant-Garde, Aesthetic Dictatorship, and Beyond* (Charles Rougle trans.). Princeton, NJ: Princeton University Press, 1992.

GUASTINI, Riccardo. 'Materiali per una teoria del doppio potere' in *I due poteri: Stato borghese e stato operaio nell'analisi marxista*. Bologna: Il mulino, 1978.

GUHA, Rànajit. *Elementary Aspects of Peasant Insurgency in Colonial India*. Durham, NC: Duke University Press, 1999.

HALL, Stuart. *The Hard Road to Renewal: Thatcherism and the Crisis of the Left*. London: Verso, 1988.

HARCOURT, Bernard. 'Course Context' in Michel Foucault, *The Punitive Society: Lectures at the Collège de France 1972–1973* (Bernard Harcourt and Alessandro Fontana eds, Graham Burchell trans.). New York: Palgrave Macmillan, 2015.

HARDT, Michael, and Antonio Negri. *Multitude: War and Democracy in the Age of Empire*. New York: Penguin, 2004.

HARIK, Judith Palmer. *Hezbollah: The Changing Face of Terrorism*. London: IB Tauris, 2005.

HARTMAN, Saidiya. *Scenes of Subjection: Terror Slavery, and Self-Making in Nineteenth-Century America*, REV. EDN. New York: W. W. Norton & Co., 2022[1997].

HAYEK, Friedrich. 'Whither Democracy?' in *New Studies in Philosophy, Politics, Economics, and the History of Ideas*. London: Routledge, 1990.

HAZAN, Eric, and Kamo. *Prèmieres mesures révolutionnaires*. Paris: La Fabrique, 2013.

HEIDEGGER, Martin. *Nietzsche, Volume 1: The Will to Power as Art*. New York: Harper Collins, 1979.

———. *The Question Concerning Technology and Other Essays*. New York: Harper and Row, 1977.

HERRES, Jürgen. 'Rhineland Radicals and the '48ers' in Terrell Carver and James Farr (eds), *The Cambridge Companion to The Communist Manifesto*. Cambridge: Cambridge University Press, 2015.

HICKMAN, Jared. *Black Prometheus: Race and Radicalism in the Age of Atlantic Slavery*. Oxford: Oxford University Press, 2016.

HUI, Wang. 'Depoliticized Politics, from East to West' (Christopher Connery trans.). *New Left Review* 41 (2006): 29–45.

IGLESIAS TURRIÓN, Pablo. *Disputar la democracia. Política para tiempos de crisis*. Madrid: Akal, 2014.

JAMES, C. L. R. *American Civilization* (Anna Grimshaw and Keith Hart eds). Oxford: Blackwell, 1993.

———. *The Black Jacobins: Toussaint L'Ouverture and the San Domingo Revolution*, 2nd REV. EDN. New York: Vintage, 1969[1963].

———. 'Black Power' in *Spheres of Existence: Selected Writings*. London: Allison and Busby, 1980, pp. 221–36.

———. 'The Black Scholar Interviews: C. L. R. James'. *The Black Scholar* 2(1) (1970).

———. 'George Jackson'. *Radical America* 5(6) (1971): 51–54.

———. 'The Historical Development of the Negroes in American Society' (1943) in Scott McLemee (ed.), *C. L. R. James on the 'Negro Question'*. Jackson, MS: University Press of Mississippi, 1996.

———. 'Lectures on *The Black Jacobins*'. *Small Axe* 8 (2000).

———. 'Lenin and the Problem' (1964), appendix to *Nkrumah and the Ghana Revolution* (Leslie James ed.). Durham, NC: Duke University Press, 2022[1977].

———. *The Life of Captain Cipriani: An Account of British Government in the West Indies, with the pamphlet The Case for West-Indian Self Government*, (Bridget Bererton intro.). Durham, NC: Duke University Press, 2014[1932].

———. 'Marcus Garvey' (1940) in Scott McLemee (ed.), *C. L. R. James on the 'Negro Question'*. Jackson, MS: University Press of Mississippi, 1996, pp. 114–16.

————. 'Politics in a Tragic Key'. *Radical Philosophy* 180 (2013): 25–34.

————. 'Towards the Seventh: The Pan-African Congress' (1976) in *At the Rendezvous of Victory*. London: Allison & Busby, 1984.

JAMESON, Fredric. *An American Utopia: Dual Power and the Universal Army* (Slavoj Žižek ed.). London: Verso, 2016.

————. 'Lenin and Revisionism' in Sebastian Budgen, Stathis Kouvelakis and Slavoj Žižek (eds), *Lenin Reloaded: Toward a Politics of Truth*. Durham: Duke University Press, 2007.

————. 'Lenin as a Political Thinker' in *Valences of the Dialectic*. London: Verso, 2009.

————. *Marxism and Form*. Princeton, NJ: Princeton University Press, 1971.

JESI, Furio. *Spartakus: The Symbology of Revolt* (A. Cavalletti ed., A. Toscano trans.). London: Seagull Books, 2014.

JOHNSON, J. R. 'The Two Sides of Abraham Lincoln'. *The Militant*, 14 February 1949.

JONES, Daniel Stedman. 'From Private Preference to Public Philosophy' in *The Economics of Politics*. IEA Readings 18. Lancing: The Institute of Economic Affairs, 1978.

————. *Masters of the Universe: Hayek, Friedman, and the Birth of Neoliberal Politics*. Princeton, NJ: Princeton University Press, 2012.

KORSCH, Karl. 'What is Socialization? A Program of Practical Socialism' (Frankie Denton and Douglas Kellner trans). *New German Critique* 6 (1975): 60–81.

LA ROCCA, Tommaso. *Es Ist Zeit: Apocalisse e Storia—studio su Thomas Müntzer (1490–1525)*. Bologna: Cappelli, 1988.

LACOUE-LABARTHE, Philippe. introduction to Martin Heidegger, *La pauvreté (Die Armut)* (Philippe Lacoue-Labarthe and Ana Samardzija trans). Strasbourg: Presses Universitaires de Strasbourg, 2004.

LEFEBVRE, Henri. 'L'Avis du sociologue: état ou non-état' in *Colloque universitaire pour la commémoration du centenaire de la Commune de 1871*. Paris: Editions Ouvrières, 1972, pp. 173–90.

LEFEBVRE, Henri. *The Production of Space* (Donald Nicholson-Smith trans.). Oxford: Blackwell, 1991.

LENIN, Vladimir. 'The Dual Power' (9 April 1917) (Isaacs Bernard trans.) in *Lenin Collected Works*, VOL. 24. Moscow: Progress Publishers, 1964, pp. 38–41. Available online: https://bit.ly/2FHtjTL (last accessed: 17 February 2023).

———. 'Has Dual Power Disappeared?' (May/June 1917) (Isaacs Bernard trans.) in *Lenin Collected Works*, VOL. 24. Moscow: Progress Publishers, 1964, pp. 445–48. Available online: https://bit.ly/3xsshoW (last accessed: 17 February 2023).

———. 'The Tasks of the Proletariat in Our Revolution' [Draft Platform for the Proletarian Party] (September 1917) (Isaacs Bernard trans.) in *Lenin Collected Works*, VOL. 24. Moscow: Progress Publishers, 1964, pp. 55–92. Available online: https://bit.ly/3YuCc9z (last accessed: 17 February 2023).

LEOPARDI, Giacomo. *Zibaldone di pensieri*. Milan: Mondadori, 1983.

LINDEN, Marcel van der. *Western Marxism and the Soviet Union: A Survey of Critical Theories and Debates Since 1917* (Jurriaan Bendien trans.). Leiden: Brill, 2007.

LINERA, Álvaro García. 'Bloque de poder y punto de bifurcación' in *La potencia plebeya*. La Habana: Fondo Editorial Casa de las Americas, 2011.

LINHART, Robert. *Lénine, les paysans et Taylor*. Paris: Seuil, 2010[1976].

LOSURDO, Domenico. *Autocensura e compromesso nel pensiero politico di Kant*. Naples: Bibliopolis, 1983.

LÖWY, Michael. *Georg Lukács: From Romanticism to Bolshevism* (Patrick Camiller trans.). London: New Left Books, 1979.

———. 'Interview with Ernst Bloch'. *New German Critique* 9 (1976).

———. *Redemption and Utopia: Jewish Libertarian Thought in Central Europe: A Study in Elective Affinity* (Hope Heaney trans.). London: Athlone Press, 1992.

LUKÁCS, Georg. 'Reification and the Consciousness of the Proletariat' in *History and Class Consciousness* (Rodney Livingstone trans.). Cambridge, MA: The MIT Press, 1971.

———. *The Theory of the Novel*. London: Merlin, 1978.

———, Ernst Bloch and Enrico Berlinguer. 'Carteggio su Angela Davis' in Lelio La Porta (ed.), *Critica marxista* 5 (1988): 105–21.

LUPTON, Catherine. *Chris Marker: Memories of the Future*. London: Reaktion, 2005.

MACEY, David. 'The Militant Philosopher' in *The Lives of Michel Foucault*. London: Verso, 2019.

MAGRI, Lucio. *Alla ricerca di un altro comunismo: Saggi sulla sinistra italiana* (Luciana Castellina, Famiano Crucianelli and Aldo Garzia eds). Milan: Il Saggiatore, 2012.

MALM, Andreas. *Corona, Climate, Chronic Emergency: War Communism in the Twenty-First Century*. London: Verso, 2020.

———. *The Progress of This Storm: Nature and Society in a Warming World*. London: Verso, 2017.

MANDARINI, Matteo and Alberto Toscano. 'Planning for Conflict'. *South Atlantic Quarterly* 119(1) (2020): 11–30.

MANN, Geoff. *In the Long Run We Are All Dead: Keynesianism, Political Economy and Revolution*. London: Verso, 2017.

MARCUSE, Herbert. *The Aesthetic Dimension: Toward a Critique of Marxist Aesthetics*. Boston: Beacon Press, 1978.

———. *Reason and Revolution: Hegel and the Rise of Social Theory*, 2nd EDN. London: Routledge, 2000[1941/1970].

MARX, Karl. 'A Contribution to the Critique of Hegel's *Philosophy of Right*: An Introduction' in *Critique of Hegel's 'Philosophy of Right'* (Annete Jolin and Joseph O'Malley trans, Joseph O'Malley ed.). Cambridge: Cambridge University Press, 1970.

———. *Early Writings* (Rodney Livingstone and Gregor Benton trans, Lucio Colletti intro.). London: Penguin, 1992.

———, and Friedrich Engels. *Collected Works*, VOL. 24. London: Lawrence & Wishart, 1989.

———, and Friedrich Engels. *Collected Works*, VOL. 45. London: Lawrence & Wishart, 1991.

———, and Friedrich Engels. *The German Ideology*. Amherst: Prometheus Books, 1998.

MASCOLO, Dionys. *Le Communisme: Révolution et communication ou la dialectique des valeurs et des besoins*. Paris: Lignes, 2018[1953].

MAYNARD, Robyn, and Leanne Betasamosake Simpson. *Rehearsals for Living*. Toronto: Alfred A. Knopf, 2022.

MERCADO, René Zavaleta. *El poder dual en América Latina: Estudio de los casos de Bolivia y Chile*. México: Siglo XXI, 1974.

MEYER, Ahlrich. Review of *Communisme/Kommunismus/Communism* by Jacques Grandjonc. *International Review of Social History* 38(1) (1993).

MICHELSON, Annette. Introduction to Dziga Vertov, *Kino-Eye: The Writings of Dziga Vertov* (Kevin O'Brien trans., Annette Michelson ed.). Berkeley, CA: University of California Press, 1984.

MYERS, Joshua. *Cedric Robinson: The Time of the Black Radical Tradition.* London: Pluto Press, 2021.

NANCY, Jean-Luc. *Politique et au-delà: Entretien avec Philip Armstrong et Jason E. Smith.* Paris: Galilée, 2011.

NEGRI, Antonio. *Factory of Strategy: Thirty-Three Lessons on Lenin* (Arianna Bove trans.). New York: Columbia University Press, 2014.

————. *Il comunismo e la guerra.* Milan: Feltrinelli, 1980.

————. *Macchina tempo: Rompicapi liberazione costituzione.* Milan: Feltrinelli, 1982.

————. *Marx Beyond Marx: Lessons on the 'Grundrisse'.* New York: Autonomedia, 1991.

NELSON, Alondra. *Body and Soul: The Black Panther Party and the Fight Against Medical Discrimination.* Minneapolis, MN: University of Minnesota Press, 2013.

NELSON, Maggie. *On Freedom: Four Songs of Care and Constraint.* Toronto: McClelland & Stewart, 2021.

NGUYEN, Duy Lap. 'On the suspension of law and the total transformation of labour'. *Thesis Eleven* 13(1) (2015): 96–116.

OLSAVSKY, Jesse. 'The Abolitionist Tradition in the Making of W. E. B. Du Bois's Marxism and Anti-Imperialism'. *Socialism and Democracy* 32(3) (2018): 14–35.

OSBORNE, Peter. 'Radicalism and Philosophy'. *Radical Philosophy* 103 (2000): 6–11.

PANITCH, Leo. 'Rebuilding Banking'. *Red Pepper*, January 2009. Available online: https://bit.ly/3YikhTe (last accessed: 5 February 2023).

PATTERSON, Orlando. *Freedom, Volume 1: Freedom in the Making of Western Culture.* New York: Basic Books, 1991.

PAVONE, Claudio. *A Civil War: A History of the Italian Resistance* (Stanislao Pugliese ed., Peter Levy trans.). London: Verso, 2014.

PETTI, Alessandro. *Arcipelaghi e enclave: Architettura dell'ordinamento spaziale contemporaneo.* Milan: Mondadori, 2007.

POULANTZAS, Nicos, and Henri Weber. 'The State and the Transition to Socialism' in *The Poulantzas Reader: Marxism, Law and the State* (James Martin ed.). London: Verso, 2008.

POWER, Michael. *The Audit Society: Rituals of Verification*. Oxford: Oxford University Press, 1997.

PREOBRAZHENSKY, E. A. *From N. E. P. to Socialism: A Glance into the Future of Russia and Europe*. New York: New Park, 1973.

RABINBACH, Anson. 'Unclaimed Heritage: Bloch's *Heritage of Our Times* and the Theory of Fascism'. *New German Critique* 11 (1977).

RANCIÈRE, Jacques. *Dissensus: On Politics and Aesthetics* (Steven Corcoran trans. and ed.). London: Continuum, 2010.

ROBERTS, Neil. *Freedom as Marronage*. Chicago, IL: The University of Chicago Press, 2015.

ROBERTS, William Clare. *Marx's Inferno: The Political Theory of Capital*. Princeton, NJ: Princeton University Press, 2017.

ROBINSON, Cedric J. *Black Marxism: The Making of the Black Radical Tradition*. London: ZED Books, 1983.

———. *Black Movements in America*. London: Routledge, 1997.

———. 'C. L. R. James and the World-System'. *Race & Class* 32(2) (1992).

———. 'Malcolm Little as Charismatic Leader' in *On Racial Capitalism, Black Internationalism, and Cultures of Resistance* (H. L. T. Quan ed.). London: Pluto Press, 2019, pp. 267–94.

———. *The Terms of Order: Political Science and the Myth of Leadership* (Erica R. Edwards fore.). Chapel Hill: The University of North Carolina Press, 2016[1980].

RODNEY, Walter. *The Russian Revolution: A View from the Third World* (Robin D. G. Kelley and Jessie Benjamin eds). London: Verso, 2018.

ROEDIGER, David. 'Where Communism was Black' in *Towards the Abolition of Whiteness*. London: Verso, 1994.

ROSEMONT, Franklin. 'Karl Marx and the Iroquois'. *Arsenal/Surrealist Subversion* 4 (1989): 201–13.

SARTRE, Jean-Paul. 'France: Masses, Spontaneity, Party' in *Between Existentialism and Marxism* (J. Matthews trans.). London: Verso, 2008[1969].

———. 'Masses, Spontaneity, Party'. *Socialist Register* 7 (1970).

'Sartre inédit', special issue, *Études sartriennes* 12 (2008).

SCOTT, David. *Conscripts of Modernity: The Tragedy of Colonial Enlightenment*. Durham, NC: Duke University Press, 2004.

————. *Omens of Adversity: Tragedy, Time, Memory, Justice*. Durham, NC: Duke University Press, 2014.

SCOTT, James C. 'Everyday Forms of Resistance'. *Copenhagen Papers in East and Southeast Asian Studies* 4 (1989): 33–62.

SÈVE, Lucien. 'Traduire *Aufhebung* chez Marx: Fausse querelle et vrais enjeux'. *Actuel Marx* 64 (2018): 112–27.

SHANIN, Teodor (ed.). *Late Marx and the Russian Road*. New York: Monthly Review Press, 1983.

SHILLIAM, Robbie. 'Decolonizing the Manifesto: Communism and the Slave Analogy' in Terrell Carver and James Farr (eds), *The Cambridge Companion to The Communist Manifesto*. Cambridge: Cambridge University Press, 2015.

SIMPSON, Audra. 'The Ruse of Consent and the Anatomy of "Refusal": Cases from Indigenous North America and Australia'. *Postcolonial Studies* 20(1) (2017): 18–33.

SINHA, Manisha. *The Slave's Cause: A History of Abolition*. New Haven, CT: Yale University Press, 2016.

Situationist International. *The Real Split in the International* (John McHale trans.). London: Pluto, 2003.

SKEGGS, Beverley, Sara R. Farris, Alberto Toscano, and Svenja Bromberg (eds). *The SAGE Handbook of Marxism*, 3 VOLS. Los Angeles: SAGE Reference, 2022.

SMITH, Jason E. 'The Day After the Insurrection: On *First Revolutionary Measures*'. *Radical Philosophy* 189 (2015): 37–44.

SMULEWICZ-ZUCKER, Gregory R. 'Linking Racism and Reification in the Thought of Georg Lukács' in Gregory R. Smulewicz-Zucker (ed.), *Confronting Reification: Revitalizing Georg Lukács's Thought in Late Capitalism*. Leiden: Brill, 2020.

SOTIRIS, Panagiotis. 'Neither an Instrument nor a Fortress: Poulantzas' Theory of the State and his Dialogue with Gramsci'. *Historical Materialism* 22(2) (2014): 135–57.

————. *A Philosophy for Communism: Rethinking Althusser*. Leiden: Brill, 2020.

SPENGLER, Oswald. *The Hour of Decision, Part One: Germany and World-Historical Revolution* (Charles Francis Atkinson trans.). London: George Allen and Unwin Ltd, 1934.

STALLABRASS, Julian. *Art Incorporated*. Oxford: Oxford University Press, 2004.

STITES, Richard. *Revolutionary Dreams: Utopian Vision and Experimental Life in the Russian Revolution*. Oxford: Oxford University Press, 1991.

STOVALL, Tyler. *White Freedom: The Racial History of an Idea*. Princeton, NJ: Princeton University Press, 2021.

SWEEZY, Paul M., and Charles Bettelheim. *On the Transition to Socialism*. New York: Monthly Review, 1971.

TÁÍWÒ, Olúfẹ́mi O. *Elite Capture: How the Powerful Took Over Identity Politics (And Everything Else)*. Chicago: Haymarket Books, 2022.

THEOPHANIDIS, Philippe. 'Interregnum as a Legal and Political Concept: A Brief Contextual Survey'. *Synthesis: An Anglophone Journal of Comparative Literary Studies* 9 (2016): 109–24.

THÉORIE COMMUNISTE. 'Communization in the Present Tense' in Benjamin Noys (ed.), *Communization and Its Discontents: Contestation, Critique, and Contemporary Struggles*. Wivenhoe: Minor Compositions, 2012.

THEURET, Patrick. ' "Aufhebung", Karl Marx et la revolution'. *Faire Vivre le PCF!*, 8 May 2019. Available online: https://bit.ly/3Hinaha (last accessed 19 January 2023).

———. *L'esprit de la revolution: Aufhebung; Marx, Hegel et l'abolition*. Montreuil: Le Temps des Cerises, 2016.

THOMPSON, Noel. 'Hollowing Out the State: Public Choice Theory and the Critique of Keynesian Social Democracy'. *Contemporary British History* 22(3) (2008): 355–82.

TOMBA, Massimiliano. *Insurgent Universality: An Alternative Legacy of Modernity*. Oxford: Oxford University Press, 2019.

TOSCANO, Alberto. 'Always Already Only Now: Negri and the Biopolitical' in Timothy S. Murphy and Abdul-Karim Mustapha (eds), *The Philosophy of Antonio Negri, Volume 2: Lessons on Constitutive Power*. London: Pluto Press, 2007.

———. 'Communism as Separation' in *Think Again: Alain Badiou and the Future of Philosophy* (Peter Hallward ed.). London: Continuum, 2004.

———. 'The Detour of Abstraction'. *Diacritics* 43(2) (2015): 68–90.

———. ' "Everything can be made better, except man": On Frédéric Lordon's Communist Realism'. *Radical Philosophy* 2(12) (2022): 19–34.

———. 'Factory, Territory, Metropolis, Empire'. *Angelaki: Theoretical Journal of the Humanities* 9(2) (2004): 197–216.

———. 'Fascists, Freedom and the Anti-State State'. *Historical Materialism* 29(4) (2021): 3–21.

———. 'In Praise of Prometheus'. *Critical Horizons* 10(2) (2009): 241–56.

———. 'The Intolerable-Inquiry: The Documents of the Groupe d'information sur les prisons'. *Viewpoint Magazine*, 25 September 2013. Available online: https://bit.ly/3I8lY0h (last accessed: 5 February 2023).

———. *Late Fascism: Race, Capitalism and the Politics of Crisis*. London: Verso, 2023.

———. 'Liberation Technology: Marcuse's Communist Individualism'. *Situations* 3(1) (2009): 5–22.

———. 'Limits to Periodization'. *Viewpoint*, 6 September 2016. Available online: https://bit.ly/3X6V3Ha (last accessed: 13 January 2013).

———. 'Lineaments of the Logistical State'. *Viewpoint* 4 (September 2014). Available online: https://bit.ly/3wXtnc8 (last accessed: 5 February 2023).

———. 'Materialism Without Matter: Abstraction, Absence and Social Form'. *Textual Practice* 28(7) (2014): 1221–40.

———. 'Now and Never' in Benjamin Noys (ed.), *Communization and Its Discontents: Contestation, Critique, and Contemporary Struggles*. Wivenhoe: Minor Compositions, 2012.

———. 'Partisan Thought'. *Historical Materialism* 17(3) (2009): 175–91.

———. 'Politics in a Tragic Key'. *Radical Philosophy* 180 (2013): 25–34.

———. 'The Politics of Abstraction: Communism and Philosophy' in Slavoj Žižek and Costas Douzinas (eds), *The Idea of Communism*. London: Verso, 2010.

———. 'Portrait of the Leader as a Young Theorist'. *Jacobin*, 19 December 2015. Available online: https://bit.ly/411J000 (last accessed: 17 February 2023).

———. 'The Promethean Gap: Modernism, Machines and the Obsolescence of Man'. *Modernism/modernity* 23(3) (2016): 593–609.

———. 'Resistance and Revolt in Pre-Political Times'. *Pli: The Warwick Journal of Philosophy* 30 (2019): 1–22.

———. 'Tragedy' in John Frow (ed.), *Oxford Encyclopaedia of Literary Theory*. Oxford: Oxford University Press, 2021.

———. 'What is Capitalist Power? Reflections on *Truth and Juridical Forms*' in Martina Tazzioli, Sophie Fuggle and Yari Lanci (eds), *Foucault and the History of Our Present*. Basingstoke: Palgrave Macmillan, 2014.

————. 'With Lenin, Against Hegel? *Materialism and Empirio-Criticism* and the Mutations of Western Marxism'. *Historical Materialism*, 28 April 2018. Available online: https://bit.ly/3RARMh9 (last accessed: 4 February 2023).

————, and Jeff Kinkle. *Cartographies of the Absolute*. Winchester: Zero Books, 2015.

TRONTI, Mario. 'Rileggendo "La libertà comunista" ' in Guido Liguori (ed.), *Galvano Della Volpe: Un altro marxismo*. Rome: Fahrenheit 451, 2000.

————. 'Sinistra'. *Laboratorio politico* 3 (1981): 132–47.

————. *Workers and Capital* (David Broder trans.). London: Verso, 2019.

VÉRAY, Laurent. *Loin du Vietnam*. Paris: Editions Paris expérimental, 2004.

VERCELLONE, Carlo. 'From Formal Subsumption to General Intellect: Elements for a Marxist Reading of the Thesis of Cognitive Capitalism'. *Historical Materialism* 15(1) (2007).

VERTOV, Dziga. 'Kinoks: A Revolution (From an Appeal at the Beginning of 1922)' in *Kino-Eye: The Writings of Dziga Vertov* (Kevin O'Brien trans., Annette Michelson ed.). Berkeley, CA: University of California Press, 1984.

VIRNO, Paolo. *A Grammar of the Multitude: For an Analysis of Contemporary Forms of Life* (Isabella Bertoletti, James Cascaito and Andrea Casson trans). Cambridge, MA: The MIT Press, 2001.

WALLERSTEIN, Immanuel. 'New Revolts Against the System'. *New Left Review* 18 (2002).

————. 'Structural Crisis'. *New Left Review* 62 (2010).

WATKINS, Peter. 'Notes on the Media Crisis'. *Comparative Cinema*. Available at: https://bit.ly/40whl6v (last accessed: 23 March 2023).

WILLIAMS, Raymond. 'Communism' in *Keywords*. New York: Oxford University Press, 1985.

————. *Modern Tragedy* (Pamela McCallum ed.). Toronto: Broadview Press 2006.

Zapatista Army of National Liberation. 'Second Declaration of the Lacandon Jungle'. June 1994. Available online: https://bit.ly/3xvriVc (last accessed: 17 February 2023).

Index of Names